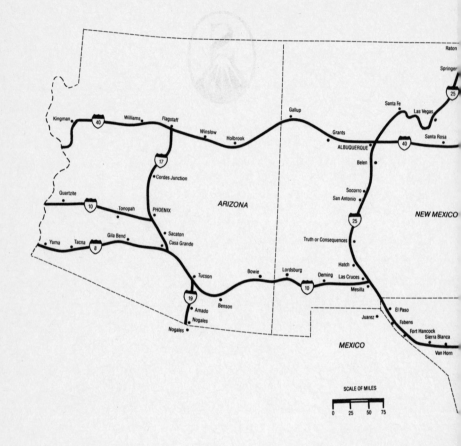

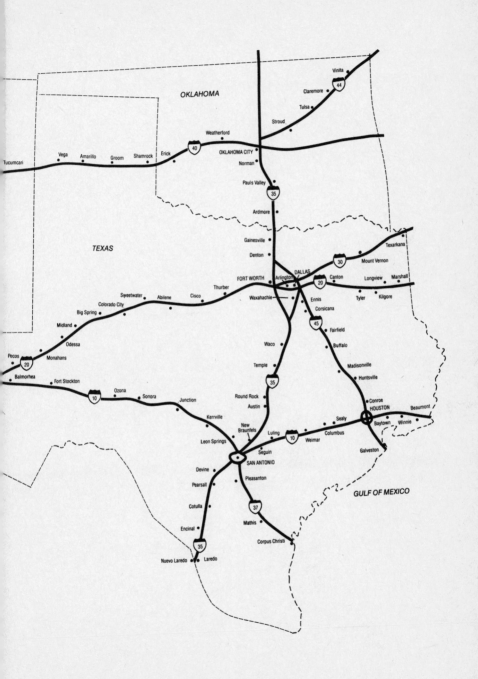

THE INTERSTATE
GOURMET

Texas and the Southwest

Barbara Rodriguez
and Tom Miller

Edited by Neal Weiner and David Schwartz

SUMMIT BOOKS

NEW YORK

The reader should be aware that the restaurant business is unpredictable. Restaurants change their menus, prices, and hours; some even change their names or addresses. While we have made every effort to update this book over the past year, we would be most grateful to hear about any changes you have encountered in your travels so that we may keep future editions up to date.

Copyright © 1986 by The Interstate Gourmet, Inc.
All rights reserved
including the right of reproduction
in whole or in part in any form
Published by SUMMIT BOOKS
A Division of Simon & Schuster, Inc.
Simon & Schuster Building
1230 Avenue of the Americas
New York, New York 10020

SUMMIT BOOKS and colophon are trademarks of Simon & Schuster, Inc.
Designed by Eve Kirch
Map by Mary Lou Brozena
Drawings by Kristin Funkhauser
Manufactured in the United States of America

Library of Congress Cataloging in Publication Data
Rodriguez, Barbara.
    The interstate gourmet—Southwest.
    Includes index.
    1. Restaurants, lunch rooms, etc.—Texas—Directories.   3. Restaurants,
lunch rooms, etc.—Southwest, New—Directories.   3. Restaurants, lunch
rooms, etc.—Oklahoma—Directories.   I. Miller, Tom   II. Weiner, Neal O.
III. Schwartz, David.   IV. Title.
TX907.R54   1986   647'.9576   86-4431
ISBN: 0-671-52334-1

ACKNOWLEDGMENTS

Heartfelt thanks to John and June, James and Karen, Scuzzy and Meg, Tuna, Cathy, Mary, Courtney and Brian, Ann, Bob and Liz, Jack and Becky, Deb and Lou, Ruthmary, Celine and David, John Jr., Gil, Natrelle and Dan—who ate, advised, consoled, financed, forgave, or tucked us in along the way. Additional thanks to Jean-Pierre Picolo, Mary Lynn Mignogna, John Davenport, Dawn Rosenquist, Bill McDonald, Linda Hudson, and Susan Farb Morris. But most of all, love and appreciation to Michael, who drove.

—B.R.

For their help, recommendations, spare couches, and Pepto-Bismol, the following people deserve gratitude: Steven Rice, Paula Ballen, Sandy Tolan, Rose Houk, Stephen Trimble, Jeff and Cherri Brown, Carol Ann Bassett, Terry and Suzi Moore, and Valerina Quintana.

—T.M.

CONTENTS

Contents

INTRODUCTION

When it comes time to eat, the long-distance motorist has a problem: driving and dining have never mixed easily on the American road. Long before either of us moved up to the front seat, we were aware of this situation, but it took many years and dozens of dyspeptic journeys before we decided to do something about it.

What we did was to take our appetites—and our notebooks—on tour. Exit by exit, highway by highway, we sought out the best meals that roadside America had to offer, and we refused to take bad food for an answer. Our goal: to make it possible to drive from New York to Miami, from San Diego to Seattle, Chicago to Atlanta, Houston to Phoenix, or any of a hundred other routes without stopping even once at a soulless turnpike service area or plasticized fast-food emporium for a barely tolerable dinner that looks like a clone of the last 23 you just had. In other words, we set out to solve the driving and dining dilemma.

The results of our gastronomic forays along the major freeways of New England, the Mid-Atlantic, Southeast, Midwest, and Pacific Coast states can be found in previously published editions of *The Interstate Gourmet* series. Within their geographic bounds, each of these books does the same thing: it guides the reader/rider to restaurants, cafes, inns, pubs, hotel dining rooms, bakeries, barbecues, and anyplace else worth stopping at. Unlike the impersonal chain restaurants and fast-food emporiums that cater to hapless travelers who are processed almost as if *they* were the burgers, the restaurants we sniffed out serve a predominately local clientele. For a few fortunate travelers in the know, they provide appealing food, agreeable prices, and—perhaps most important—a refreshing break from the interstate grind.

And, because the interstate highway system, for all its benefits, has tended to homogenize America, we especially sought restaurants where you won't have to consult a roadmap to find out what state you're in. Inside the franchised fast-fooderies that lurk just beyond the great green exit signs, Maine looks just like Montana, San Antonio like San Francisco. If you follow the well-eaten path, you'll face the same deep-fried fillet of (unnamed) fish whether you're on the shore of Lake Michigan or Lake Okeechobee. North, South, East, or West—it all looks and tastes the same in the deliberate quest for predictable mediocrity. When we undertook writing these highway dining guides, we made it our intention to squelch not only the mediocre, but also the predictable. Roadside dining should be more than just a meal: it can also be part of the adventure of travel, a window on local life, and an introduction to a region's distinctive cuisine.

In the past few years, our gastronomic travels have enabled us to mine many of America's culinary gems, but when it came time to eat our way across Texas and the Southwest, we opted for a different strategy. It seemed that the broad distances and specialized cuisines of the Southwest would benefit from assessment by people who were at home in the region. So, instead of seeking enchiladas, we sought experts.

Barbara Rodriguez and Tom Miller are food critics and professional writers, but just as important, they are southwesterners who are intimately familiar with, and clearly enamored of, the region in which they live, write, and eat. Having devoted themselves to exploring the region's cities and hinterlands over the past decade or so, Barbara and Tom are superb culinary guides: not only do they lead you to Mexican flavors so authentic that you almost wonder if it's safe to drink the water, but they explain how your meal should taste depending on whether it is a product of Tex-Mex, Arizona-Sonoran, or New Mexican cuisine. And for those who would just as soon never face another enchilada regardless of its authenticity, Barbara and Tom prove that there is much more to dining in this part of the country than what comes under the sombrero-wide rubric of "Mexican food."

In some of the most surprising places (but all within easy

access of the freeway), the authors have ferreted out a diversity of gastronomic ethnicities from German to Cajun, Indian to Italian, Greek to Thai. They've located master chefs trained in Paris just down the road from self-trained barbecue masters who produce hickory-smoked "Q" at its elbow-dripping, no-frills best. Their eclectic tastes and sensibilities generate plaudits equally for the grandmotherly buffet piled high with pork chops in homemade mushroom gravy and the country-chic purveyor of the New American Cuisine. From their years of experience (not all of it enviable), they recommend the truly reliable cafes for burgers, T-bones, buttermilk pancakes, and saucer-sized cinnamon rolls, so that *you* can avoid the imposters.

It is an unlikely crowd, this cross-cultural pastiche of roadside restaurants between the tumbleweeds, and, in fact, the eateries were chosen with just two criteria in mind: Barbara and Tom had to like them, and they all had to be just a short hop from the freeway. But that's a wide net to cast (despite the impression that fast food is the only roadside survivor), and the authors' cornucopic catch of enticing restaurants is what makes this book such a pleasure to peruse. We can hardly wait to hit the road.

Neal Weiner, Brattleboro, VT
David Schwartz, Wallingford, CT

Arizona

CHRETIN'S MEXICAN FOODS, *Exit 1, Yuma*

It has been said that Yuma has 89 restaurants but not a place to eat. That's a fair assessment—with the exception of Chretin's, which started out in the 1920s as an open-air dance hall and has grown to landmark proportions. (Now the original dance hall is but one of several dining rooms.) Chretin's appeal draws on the two best elements of any restaurant—food and atmosphere.

As noted in its menu, Chretin's (Krih-TEENS) food "is prepared as mild as possible" but served with a side of green taco sauce or extra hot salsa. This allows for hesitant snowbirds, who flock to Yuma as soon as midwestern thermometers plunge below 40°, to warm up to the burritos ($2.75 to $2.95), the tamale dinner (2 beef tamales topped with chile sauce, with beans and rice, $3.50), or the carne asada (broiled steak covered with chile strips, with side of guacamole, beans, rice, and a flour tortilla, $7.50). The chile relleno plate, served with beans, rice, and tortilla for $4.95, maintains its popularity year after year.

Nearby Marine and Army bases and the major league spring training season combine to make Chretin's a 3-ring circus. When the San Diego Padres host other cactus league teams, fans and players can often be found here; when visiting military brass check up on their underlings, they usually drop in, too. Winter visitors provide a constant backdrop to the circus. A few evenings before our visit, California Angels owner Gene Autry took his team to Chretin's and ended up singing for a table of visiting generals. Servicemen regularly compete to see who can eat the most nachos ($2.50 per dozen). Wall placards announce the winners; the current champ, a Marine, swallowed 136 nachos in 85 minutes. The women's record is 56 in one sitting, and the group record—56 servicemen—has reached an astounding 3,040 nachos. The macho nacho spirit has extended to chugging green taco sauce and the juice from cans of jalapeño peppers.

More conventionally, Chretin's food has so endeared itself to the Marines that it's routine for them to pick up a huge order to go just before taking off for foreign posts. Owner Joe Chretin was once flown over to the Orient to cater a big Marine bash. Mere civilians dine here often as well, with equally intense but less demonstrative loyalty.

Although hundreds of meals are served daily, Chretin's is as good today as when it was a small Mom and Pop place decades ago.

HOURS   Mon.–Sat. 11 am–11 pm. Closed Sun., Thanksgiving, and Christmas.

SPECS   485 15th Ave.; (602) 782-1291; MC/V; full bar.

DIRECTIONS   Take Exit 1, Giss Pkwy., which becomes 3rd St. as it crosses 4th Ave. Follow to Ave. A (which numerically would be 11th Ave.), go left 2 blocks to 5th St., and right one long block past the Carver School. Chretin's parking lot is on your right.

LUTES CASINO, *Exit 1, Yuma*

Among other things, Lutes Casino is a place to eat. Located downtown in a failed and largely abandoned urban renewal project, it should have been torn down years ago. If the 25-foot-high walls had ever worn paint, it has all peeled off by now. Just the same, Lutes is *the* place to go for dominoes, pool, video games, a beer, or the Lutes Special: a split hot dog on a cheeseburger sandwich, with lettuce, tomato, and a rolled taco! This display of Americana costs $2.

The same domino players take the same seats every day, and generally eschew outsiders. ("They're a grumpy lot," owner Bob Lutes admits.) But their exclusivity doesn't discourage the healthy lunch crowd, which mixes downtown merchants and office workers, Western Arizona College students in cutoffs, and affable drifters.

Protruding from the ceiling is a booted wooden leg; Lutes says he needed it to fill up a hole there, and the leg, left as part of a wacky artists' "Leave It at Lutes" festival, fitted perfectly. He supplied the boot. The men's room door resembles that of a phone booth, complete with large window. "That's so you can make sure your pool partner isn't moving your ball while you're away from the table," explained Lutes, who is also part owner of a nearby wedding chapel.

Lutes Casino started out as a grocery store around the turn of the century, became a billiard hall, housed wide-open gambling, and eventually developed the eclectic personality it maintains today. The only vestige of its high-rolling days is a corner booth, where state lottery tickets are sold by a bearded vendor.

Definitely not for everyone, but anyone looking for local color —or the famous Lutes Special—will not go wanting.

HOURS 9:30 am–7:35 pm daily (later in the summer). Closed Christmas Day.

SPECS 221 Main St.; (602) 782-2192; no cards; bar.

DIRECTIONS Take Exit 2, Giss Pkwy. (which becomes 3rd St. as it crosses 4th Ave.). In half a mile, turn right onto Maiden Lane (just after Gila St.). Rear entrance to Lutes Casino is a block and a half down; use public parking lot on right.

BASQUE ETCHEA, *Exit 42, Tacna*

When Fidel Jorajuria was sixteen years old, his uncle in Wyoming sent for him. Fidel, who lived in the Basque city of Sumbilla, Spain, came to the States and worked with his uncle and other sheep herders in the Rocky Mountain west. Occasionally he returned to Spain. Finally, he settled here permanently and worked in the sheep industry. But not long after he and his wife, Frances, whose parents are also from the Basque region, settled in this tiny ranching community near the Mexican border, they decided to open up a restaurant that would satisfy local cafe taste buds but feature Basque-style cooking. Basque Etchea (house, in Catalan) is a true find, even more so after miles and miles of desert highway.

We visited the restaurant on a Tuesday afternoon, when the featured special was roast marinated leg of lamb ($5.25, with fried potatoes and thick toast). The portion was large, the lamb tender and lightly spiced, and the service friendly. The secret, said Fidel, is to add wine to the lamb while it's roasting. Other luncheon specials include beef stew (with vegetables and spices, $3), beef ranchero (roast beef cooked with tomato sauce, simmered with stewed tomatoes, bell peppers, and onion, $4), and on Sundays, roast chicken Basquaise (served family style with a red pimento and green pepper sauce, $5.75). Dinners include roast beef à la bearnaise ($6.75, simmered in spices and wine) and roast leg of lamb. All lunch and dinner entrées, which are cooked by Fidel and Frances's children, include a tureen of homemade soup such as garbanzo, cabbage, or lentil (also available à la carte for $1.50).

Basque Etchea's popularity was evident even on a slow weekday afternoon. Within an hour, the manager of a visiting high school baseball team dropped in to arrange for his players to get hamburgers and fries following the game against Antelope High, a neighboring cattleman called to have Fidel cater a barbecue for three hundred guests on his ranch, and the local electric company called to say the power would be off for six hours early the next Monday.

HOURS Tues.–Sat. 11 am–10 pm; Sun. noon–10 pm. Closed Mon. and all major holidays and for 1 week in midsummer.

SPECS   Ave. 40-E; (602) 785-4027; MC/V; full bar.

DIRECTIONS   From Exit 42, turn right if westbound, left if eastbound. Basque Etchea is the low white building with a red tile roof on the right a block after the railroad tracks.

THE SPACE AGE COFFEE SHOP, *Exit 115, Gila Bend*

You may have heard of Gila Bend on the evening news—it's one of those towns regularly cited as the hottest spot in the nation. Civic pride got the better of the locals in the early seventies when it was discovered that they'd jack up the temperature after learning what nearby towns were reporting.

Exaggerated or not, it's plenty hot in Gila Bend, and muchneeded respite can be found in the Space Age, a cafe that never closes. The Spaceburger ($3.65) is a hamburger with all the trimmings, bacon, and cheese. Breakfasts include french toast ($2.25) and pancakes ($3). Five dollars gets you boneless breast of chicken, breaded and deep fried. Spaghetti and meatballs costs $4.50. This food was good, solid, rib-sticking stuff.

HOURS   7 days, 24 hours.

SPECS   401 E. Pima; (602) 683-2273; major cards; no bar.

DIRECTIONS   Take Exit 115 into town; Space Age, with a flying saucer logo, is on your right after 1.7 miles, just before the Best Western motel. To return to I-8 going westbound, go left from parking lot onto Pima and bear right onto freeway 3 miles outside town. To return eastbound, from Space Age parking lot go right for 0.9 mile and bear right. Pick up freeway after 2.3 miles.

THE CHATTERBOX, *Exit 174, Casa Grande*

We admit we selected this place for its name, hoping to find a place like Dorothy's Chatterbox Cafe of the fictitious Lake Wobegon, Minnesota, "the little town that time forgot and the decades cannot improve." (If you don't know what we're talking about, tune your FM dial to National Public Radio some Saturday evening.)

And indeed, this Chatterbox has the same small-town atmosphere as Dorothy's: the waitress forgot to take our order until we reminded her after our second cup of coffee. A box next to the cash register held $1 entries in a contest to guess the date, time, sex, and weight of a baby expected by the owner (half of the money collected to go to the winner, the balance to the baby). The talk at nearby tables centered on the cotton crop ("looks like a good'n"), pickup trucks ("Ernie got hisself a new one"), and the heat (*"hace bastante calor, ¿qué no?"*).

Once our order was taken, it didn't take long for the breakfast special ($3.25) to fill up the table—sausage and eggs, hash browns, and biscuits with gravy. The two biscuits, heavy and doughy, were so big, and the gravy so thick, that together they took up a whole large plate by themselves. Not great, but not bad either. In all, it was enough food to last the day and then some. Lunches included cheeseburger under chile and diced onion ($3.65). Dinner specials change daily; regular offerings include steaks and chickens.

HOURS　　5 am–10 pm daily. Closed Christmas.

SPECS　　1118 East Main; (602) 836-8132; MC/V; full bar.

DIRECTIONS　　From Exit 174 (Terkell Rd.), turn right if westbound, left if eastbound, for 2.7 miles before turning left onto Routes 84/93. Chatterbox is on right after a half mile.

Arizona
New Mexico
Texas

Arizona

STRATTON'S FAMILY RESTAURANT,
Exit 17, Quartzsite

Each February tens of thousands of rockhounds congregate in Quartzsite for a mammoth gem and mineral show. Every RV between the Rockies and the Pacific seems to be in town for the week. In the heat of the summer, however, the town is a thirsty desert rat—a poor man's Palm Springs, some call it.

Stratton's is among the few breathing restaurants left, and even it shuts down for July. In the other eleven months, expect a friendly local hangout, where stew with corn muffins costs $2.95, chicken fried steak runs $4.75, and fish & chips go for $3.95 on Fridays. Nothing magnificent, but salvation when it's most needed.

If you show up during July or after hours, try the Stagecoach next door.

HOURS Summer: 11 am–7 pm daily. Winter: 6:30 am–9 pm daily. Closed month of July.

SPECS Business Loop 10; (602) 927-5657; no cards or booze.

DIRECTIONS Take Exit 17 into Quartzsite. Stratton's is on left after a half mile, just before the Stagecoach.

WALTER & BETTY'S TONOPAH BAR & GRILL,
Exit 94, Tonopah

"I like roadside cafes," country music songwriter and singer Tom T. Hall said in a 1984 interview. "The ones with 'Home-Cooked Food/Help Wanted' signs out front. I could live at those places. I don't like junk food and I'm not dressed fancy for the good restaurants."

Tom T. would feel right at home at Walter & Betty's—a simple menu, no junk food, and Walter confided he was looking for a new cook. The breakfast special ($2.85), served all day, includes diced ham and scrambled eggs with biscuits and honey, and a choice of home fries or sliced tomato. Sirloin tips on noodles with soup ($3.95) fills up afternoon and evening diners. Specials such as beef stew and fish change daily, but the Thursday special—barbecued ribs—is mercifully available only in the winter. During the summer, the air in Tonopah is stickier than Walter's barbecue sauce.

HOURS   7 days, 24 hours.

SPECS   41098 W. Indian School Rd.; (602) 386-3997; no cards; full bar.

DIRECTIONS   From Exit 94, turn left if westbound, right if eastbound at stop sign; in 0.3 mile, on left, Walter & Betty's is behind the sign that says "Coffee Shop."

FINA COCINA, *Exit 196, Phoenix*

We love success stories like this: neighborhood hole-in-the-wall becomes so popular people come from all over town just for carry-out orders, owners find more centralized location, move and expand menu. Will everyone live happily ever after? We don't know, because Fina Cocina was just opening its spiffy downtown spot when we dropped in.

Co-owner Norman Fierros, a Phoenix native who has cooked continental and oriental styles in Los Angeles, has implemented what he calls *nueva mexicana*. What's that? "I apply techniques of French and Chinese cooking to Mexican food," Fierros explained. "From the French, for example, we'll cook meats in their own juices. Borrowing from the Chinese, we'll stir-fry a lot of our dishes."

Not only is the restaurant new, but the décor is practically New Wave. Bright, hard surfaces and a bold red-and-white color scheme are striking, but not so severe as to detract from the display of wall art provided by local Chicano arts groups. Cooking can be viewed from the dining area, and your basic items—refried beans and chile with rice and salad ($3.50), for example—are available in a cafeteria-style line. Most items, such as machaca con huevos ($2.65) or calabacitas con queso ($1) are prepared to order.

HOURS Mon.–Sat. 7 am–9 pm; Sun. 7 am–5 pm. Closed major holidays.

SPECS 19 E. Adams St.; (602) 258-5315; no cards; beer and wine.

DIRECTIONS Eastbound: Take Exit 196 (7th Ave./Central Ave.), go straight at the traffic light, and turn left after 0.6 mile onto Central. ■ Stay on Central through the short railroad tunnel after 1.1 miles, and turn right onto Adams. Fina Cocina is in the middle of the block on the right, across from the Phoenix Hilton Hotel.

Westbound: Take Exit 196 to Central Ave., turn right, and follow eastbound directions as above, from ■.

Return to I-10: From Adams, turn right onto 1st St. to Washington at the next corner. Right on Washington and left at 1st Ave. Stay with 1st

Ave. about 1½ miles as it swings left and joins Central. Get in left lane and turn left onto freeway access road.

1895 HOUSE, *Exit 195B, Phoenix*

This place, named for the year of its construction, is a prime example of the downtown restoration going on in so many western cities. The condition of the 1895 House is even better, we've been told, than it was in its early years as a cathouse. Meals are served in a front patio or on two floors inside. Although it gives the genteel air of a women's tea parlor, the 1895 House is thoroughly up to date in its offerings. For $4.95, you can lunch on Greek moussaka, seafood and avocado salad, chicken stew, or tuna Waldorf (apples, walnuts, celery, raisins, with tuna on top). Mildly seasoned, the seafood curry ($5.25) pleased us most. A variety of sandwiches ($3.95) are also served, as well as a daily soup—cream of banana squash the afternoon we dropped in.

More formal (and more expensive) dinners include a choice of appetizers (including Japanese seafood dumplings) and dessert. Among the entrees are chicken breast in champagne sauce, monkfish fillet with lobster sauce, and New Orleans barbecue shrimp, all in the $14–$16 range.

Lunch or dinner, on a budget or a splurge, save room in your stomach and your wallet for the pecan cheesecake, one of the most seductive versions of the classic dessert we've ever had the privilege to savor.

HOURS Lunch: Mon.–Fri. 11:30 am–2 pm. Dinner: Mon.–Sat. 5–9 pm (except in summer, when there is no dinner on Mondays). Closed Sun. Open most major holidays.

SPECS 362 N. 2nd Ave.; (602) 254-0338: MC/V/AE; full bar.

DIRECTIONS **Westbound:** From Exit 195B go straight on freeway frontage road at the light; turn right onto Central Ave. after 0.6 mile, and continue until Van Buren, 1.6 miles later. Left on Van Buren, then right onto 2nd Ave. The 1895 House is on the left in the middle of the first block.

Eastbound: At the I-17 interchange, get onto I-17 northbound, take un-numbered Van Buren St./Jefferson St. exit, and turn right onto Van Buren (left, if coming from I-17 southbound). In 1.9 miles, turn left onto 2nd Ave. The 1895 House is on the left in the middle of the block.

Return to I-10 eastbound: From the 1895 House parking lot, turn right on 2nd Ave., then left at the corner onto Van Buren, and right at the next corner onto 1st Ave. Stay with 1st Ave. for 1.7 miles as it swings left and joins Central Ave. Get in left lane and turn left onto the freeway access road.

Return to I-10 westbound (and I-17 northbound): Go back to Van Buren the way you came, turn right, and continue straight out to I-17. Head south on I-17 to Buckeye Rd. and turn right after exit. (I-10 from this point west is scheduled for completion by the end of 1986, at which time all of this will be a lot simpler, but until then it's necessary to use Buckeye Rd.)

MRS. WHITE'S GOLDEN RULE, *Exit 195B, Phoenix*

Every day, the menu at Mrs. White's is posted on the wall within full view of the Formica booths, tables, and counter seats. Regular dishes include smothered chicken, baby beef livers, fried chicken, and the ubiquitous chicken fried steak ($3–$4 range). Each comes, of course, with two of three vegetables, and—could a soul house be without it?—an order of cornbread.

In a one-woman operation like Mrs. White's, quality tends to fluctuate. Our first visit yielded one of the best cafe meals we'd had in months; the next time we were disappointed by the 45-minute wait and the fat in the sauce. Having been in operation since 1970 or so, Mrs. White has built up a strong and loyal following among downtown government workers, construction crews, and others, as well as those looking for a friendly change of pace. And Mrs. White is adamant—no smoking and no alcohol. Not for nothin' does she call it the Golden Rule.

HOURS Mon.–Fri. 7:30 am–7:30 pm. Closed weekends and all major holidays.

SPECS 808 E. Jefferson; (602) 262-9256; no credit cards; no liquor.

DIRECTIONS   Eastbound: From Exit 195B (7th St./Central Ave.), turn left at the first traffic light (7th St.). ■ On 7th, cross Mohave, Buckeye, Lincoln, go over the overpass, and turn right on Jefferson. Stay in far left lane; Mrs. White's is a half block down. Look for goldenrod-colored cinderblocks and potted plastic flowers in the windows. (It's 1.3 miles from the exit.) Return to interstate eastbound by continuing down Jefferson to 16th St. and turning right on 16th, then left at Buckeye; just past 20th St., turn right to freeway; stay in left lane.

Westbound: From 7th St. exit, turn right to head north on 7th St. and then follow eastbound directions from ■. Return to interstate westbound by the same route as if returning to eastbound (above).

GILA INDIAN CENTER, *Exit 175, Sacaton*

Indian cafes in the West are usually quite a distance from interstates, but this one, about one minute from the highway, practically has its own exit.

Opened in 1971 by the Gila River Indian Tribe, made up of Pima and Maricopa Indians, the cafe offers standard roadside Mexican food (tamales, tacos, or enchiladas, $1.25; burros, $2.50; chile with rice and beans, $4.25). The Indian contribution to the menu is the popover, a variation of fried bread. The dough is made from flour, vegetable shortening, salt, and baking powder, patted into a medium pizza size, and quick fried. "The pan is so hot it's almost at the flashpoint," explained Jon Long, the center's director. "That way it doesn't soak up any grease."

Popovers are golden brown, crunchy yet soft, and are best eaten hot. They come plain (with honey and powdered sugar on the side), with beans or chile, or as a taco stuffed with lettuce, tomato, ground beef, and cheese. The Pima taco appeases vegetarians—it's the same as the popover taco, with whole pinto beans substituted for the beef. Prices for these popover variations range from $1.75 (plain) to $4.25 (with chile and beans).

Adjoining the cafe is a gift shop and museum, also run by the tribe. During the second weekend of every March, the Gila River Indians stage a gathering of the tribe, with the public invited to watch dancers and others perform.

HOURS   9 am–5 pm daily. Closed all major holidays.

SPECS   Sacaton; (602) 963-3981; MC/V/AE; no liquor.

DIRECTIONS   Eastbound: From Exit 175, turn right to Indian Center.

Westbound: From Exit 175, turn right at the stop sign and right again after 0.3 mile. The cafe is in the Gila River Arts & Crafts Center after another 0.6 mile.

THE CHATTERBOX,
"I-8 San Diego" Exit, Casa Grande

See page 23 for description of this cafe, where you can pick up on the talk of the town from your waitress, the neighboring table, or the walls.

DIRECTIONS   Take I-8 West (toward Yuma and San Diego); leave I-8 at Exit 174 (Terkell Rd.), turn right, and go 2.7 miles before turning left onto Routes 84/93. Chatterbox is on right after half a mile.

EL CHARRO, *Exit 257A, Tucson*

Lookin' for a friendly argument? Just tell Ray Flores that Tex-Mex food tastes good, or that New Mexico style cooking pleases you, or that you've had good Mexican food in Los Angeles. Ray, who with his wife, Carlotta, owns El Charro, will take it from there. About Tex-Mex: "I think it's godawful. It lacks flavor, and it all has the same harsh taste. Surely their beans are not flavorful." Regarding food prepared in New Mexico, which he agrees grows the best chile peppers: "They use chile in *everything*, chile that's so hot you can't taste the food." As for Southern California: "There are millions of Mexicans in Los Angeles, and I don't think a one of them is eating decent food."

¡Ay, caramba!

But Ray doesn't have to denigrate other cooking to promote El Charro. It's excellent on its own. Start with the chips and salsa. Hardly worth mentioning elsewhere, here the chips are noticeably warm and crisp, and salsa is spiked with the Mexican chiltepín pepper, giving it a sharp, but not burning, bite. Our stuffed avocado plate ($7 with tortilla, soup, rice, and beans) looked like a child's finger painting—yellow cheese swirling through brown beans beside orange Spanish rice and shredded lettuce. The avocado itself, stuffed with ground beef, seasoned with chorizo, and doused with red salsa, was unlike any dish we'd ever tried in the places Ray abhors. Though we weren't ready to swear off Mexican food from other regions, El Charro was starting to make believers out of us.

A dollar cheaper are dinners featuring seafood enchiladas, country-style spare ribs, and white boneless cod. An occasional special not found on the menu is chicken with peanut sauce. While quite reasonable considering the quality, prices here are slightly higher than your run-of-the-road Mexican restaurant, but diners younger than 10 or older than 62 get breaks on some dishes. Sunday brunch is a bargain for all: $3.50 brings chilaquilas, an egg over easy, and frijoles, among other dishes.

El Charro, which Carlotta's aunt Monica Flin started in 1922, is situated between downtown and El Presidio, a city neighborhood now undergoing gentrification. How Monica's father, Jules, dug through the caliche to make a basement puzzles current builders, but the walls, from a stone quarry at the base of "A" Mountain on the city's west side, keep the ground floor dining room and gift shop cool in the sweltering summer heat. Upstairs walls, in a nicely arranged clutter, display paintings, blankets, ponchos, shawls, and decades of Mexican calendars dominated by muscular Aztecs fighting for God, country, and sexy-looking señoritas.

HOURS   11 am–9 pm daily. Closed major holidays.

SPECS   311 N. Court Ave.; (602) 622-5465; MC/V/AE; beer and wine.

DIRECTIONS   From Exit 257A, turn right if westbound, left if eastbound, onto St. Mary's Rd., and go straight through the traffic light at Granada. In 0.4 mile, bear right at the sign reading "Central Business District" and then take an immediate right onto Court St. El Charro is in the second block on the right, the second building from the corner, with a front porch patio.

CAFE OLÉ, *Exit 258, Tucson*

This light and airy place has Scottish and Nicaraguan owners who blend their homelands into the background music, the wall posters, and the menu. Within walking distance of downtown offices and art galleries, the spread of patrons ranges from feds with ominous bulges under their jackets to secretaries to card-carrying members of the N.V.M.S. (no visible means of support) crowd. It's a place to plot unthinkable schemes with strangers or relax and read the newspaper with friends. (By the time Cafe Olé opens, the morning's *New York Times* and *Wall Street Journal* have arrived at the Crescent Smoke Shop around the corner; ask directions from the cashier.) Table service starts at 11 am; before that, place your order at the counter.

Teas and coffees from Lousiana, the Caribbean, Europe, Central America, and elsewhere get the meal going; luscious-looking pastries and cakes placate your sweet tooth; luncheon plates with cheese ($2.65–$3.75) or sliced meats ($3.30–$3.85) fill you up; quiche specials ($4.75) and soups like black bean with cumin and sour cream, or curried potato, earn compliments. The kitchen closes about 9 pm, but the joint stays alive until closing with performers playing flamenco, jazz, blues, and other musical flavors.

Scones in the Sonoran desert? Why not, thought co-owner Muriel, a native Gaelic speaker from the Isle of Skye in the Scottish Hebrides. Scones are a traditional hand-made tea biscuit Muriel makes from honey, baking powder, flour, vanilla, buttermilk, and cinnamon. "I've experimented a bit with the flavoring, so sometimes I use molasses, butterscotch, or walnut," she explained. But she gets even more adventuresome than that. "I make a piña colada scone with pineapple and coconut. Once I put together green chile scones as a joke, but they turned out to be both delicious and popular, so I still make them now and then." Has Muriel told her mother about the different flavors? "Oh, *no*," she exclaimed. "It'd make my ancestors roll over." The scones (95 cents) come with butter or cream cheese. As we prepared to leave, one of the scone-maker's Gaelic students came in for a lesson. *Slainte mhath!*

HOURS   Mon.–Thu. 7:30 am–midnight; Fri. & Sat. 7:30 am–1 am. Closed Sun. and major holidays.

SPECS   121 E. Broadway; (602) 628-1841; no cards; beer and wine.

DIRECTIONS   From Exit 258 (Congress St./Broadway), turn left if eastbound, right if westbound, and go 0.8 mile to Cafe Olé on your left, half a block after the light at 6th Ave. (look for the green awning).(Note statue of Mexican revolutionary cutthroat Pancho Villa on left after 0.4 mile.) Return to interstate by turning left onto Fifth Ave. at corner, then left again on Congress St. straight out to freeway.

CORA'S CAFE, *Exit 261, Tucson*

Ah, a Mexican restaurant, you say. Framed posters of Guadalajara, steaming tortillas in an embroidered basket, imported beer, a heavily made-up hostess in a peasant blouse and long flowing skirt, strolling mariachis. It can be done that way, and very nicely, too. But eliminate all the overhead and *cosas que no valen nada* and you still need to fix good Mexican food.

Cora's Cafe takes another approach. It is the quintessential stripped-down Mexican restaurant: unpretentious clientele, plain décor, waiters and waitresses who remember your last order, and classic Sonoran-style Mexican food. The restaurant is justly well known for its soups. Albóndigas (meatballs), cazuela (beef jerky), queso (cheese), and pozole (beans and hominy) are all popular, but the cafe's reputation around Tucson is built on its cocido, a beef-based broth containing corn on the cob, carrots, celery, potato, zucchini, string beans, peas, cilantro, garbanzo beans, cabbage, chile verde, green onions, tomato, pepper, and roast beef chunks. That's not soup, that's a grocery store in a bowl! All soups come in two sizes ($2–$3) and include a flour tortilla so thin you can read the Treaty of Guadalupe Hidalgo through it.

The rest of the menu has well-prepared standard Mexican dishes, plus a 99-cent breakfast special of two hotcakes and an egg. And who can stay solemn too long in a place with a sign on the wall that says: "OUR MEXICAN FOOD IS SO AUTHENTIC WE URGE YOU NOT TO DRINK THE WATER."

HOURS Mon.–Fri. 7 am–3 pm; Sat. & Sun. 8 am–1 pm (breakfasts only). Closed major holidays.

SPECS 24 W. Irvington Rd.; (602) 294-2146; MC/V; no booze.

DIRECTIONS **Eastbound:** Bear right from Exit 261 onto 6th Ave. ■ Take 6th for 1.7 miles through a series of lights to Irvington Rd. Turn right; Cora's is the second building on your right.

Westbound: Take unnumbered 6th Ave. exit, turn left at the light onto 6th Ave., and then as above, from ■ .

THE HI-WAY CHEF AT THE TRIPLE "T" TRUCK
STOP, *Exit 268, Tucson*

"Just look for the places where all the big trucks are parked and good food's a sure bet." That's one of the biggest lies you'll ever hear, ranking right up there with "The check is in the mail." The fact is, truckers' taste buds are no better than those of accountants or electricians. Still, the Triple "T," one of the largest truckstops in the West, has some special characteristics. Lots of auto travelers eat here, too, and since opening back in 1960 the Triple "T" has developed quite a local following as well.

The Triple "T" is best known for that roadside favorite, deep-dish, hot apple pie topped with vanilla ice cream ($2.10). The pie —you can get cherry, too—is drowned beneath six inches of soft vanilla ice cream. Both ice cream and pie are made on the premises. Every day, the Triple "T" fills 1,500 orders for its revered deep-dish dessert, which means it takes in an astounding one million dollars a year on a single dessert!

Aside from its million-dollar dessert, the rest of the Triple "T" fare is good, if unimaginative, at budget prices—a special of chicken potato soup, Reuben burger, and blueberry tart costs only $3.95; a giant malted waffle runs $2.30, German sausage with eggs, hash browns, toast or biscuits and gravy costs $4.05. Another nice touch is the wall telephone at each booth from which you can make collect or credit card calls explaining to your boss or spouse why you'll be a few days late. While we were enjoying the novelty of a phone at the table, the waitress came with a full pot of coffee, looked at our empty cups, and asked, "Would you like another cup of whoopee?"

Well, any place where a waitress asks if we want more whoopee is all right with us.

HOURS   7 days, 24 hours.

SPECS   5451 E. Benson Hwy.; (602) 574-0961; all major cards; no liquor.

DIRECTIONS   Eastbound: From Exit 268, turn left onto Craycroft and pass under freeway to the restaurant on your left.

Westbound: From Exit 268, cross Craycroft at the bottom of the off-ramp, and the Triple "T" is on your right.

THE HORSE SHOE CAFE, *Exits 303 & 306, Benson*

In 1970, The Dusty Chaps, a long-haired country and western band, spilled into Marie's Truck Stop in Benson on their way to a gig. The gaggle of out-of-town hippie musicians spurred a tableful of locals to start singing the first verse to Merle Haggard's patriotic classic, "Okie From Muskogee." Imagine their shock, then, when the hippies responded from their table by singing the second verse to the song. By the time the chorus rolled around everyone, including the waitress, had joined in, and it was free refills all around. Benson can be that sort of town.

These days when they want something to eat in Benson, people stop at the Horse Shoe Cafe, known for its (alas, now burned out) neon horseshoe on the ceiling. The Horse Shoe is *the* reliable cafe in these parts for traveling salesmen's burgers ($2.70 with mashed potatoes), ranchers' T-bones ($7.55 with extras), neighborhood breakfasts (chorizo—spicy Mexican sausage—and eggs, with biscuits and hash browns, $2.85), and after-school malts ($1.05). The staff was frank enough to admit that the soup specials usually come from a can and that most of their pies do not come from the oven of the sweet little old lady down the street, but rather frozen from a distributor. Two points for honesty, and another two for a fine C&W jukebox selection (Don Williams, Charly McClain, Earl Thomas Conley) and classic cowboy art paintings of horses on the walls. "They're signed Tony Parker," our waitress said, "but they were done so long ago no one remembers who he was." Where have you gone, Tony Parker?

Marie's, incidentally, changed names a few years after the "Okie" sing-along to "The Upper Crust Cafe," and some years later, the building collapsed. The Marie's sign, however, remains as the town's outstanding landmark—high in the air, a faded orange semi sitting on steel girders, topped with pigeons lined up like, well, pigeons.

HOURS   Mon. 6:30 am–2 pm; Tues.-Thu. 6:30–8:30 pm; Fri. & Sat. 6:30 am–9 pm; Sun. 7 am.–8:30 pm.

SPECS   121 4th St.; (602) 586-3303; V/MC; full bar.

DIRECTIONS   Eastbound: Exit 303 will put you on 4th St.; follow it 1.5 miles to Horse Shoe, on the right just after the light. To continue east, bear left underneath the railroad tracks at the fork, go straight to Pomerene Rd., jog left, then right onto the freeway.

Westbound: Take Exit 306/Pomerene Rd., turn left, then right, and proceed 1½ miles straight into town over the San Pedro River and under the railroad tracks, and you'll end up on 4th St. The Horse Shoe is on your left just before Benson's sole traffic light. To continue west, go straight on 4th St. all the way through town.

THE THING?, *Exit 322, east of Benson*

All those obtrusive blue and yellow billboards lead to a very strange gift shop and "museum" called "The Thing?" (Yes, the question mark is part of the name.) The gifts—mugs, pennants, moccasins, dolls, pottery, cactus plants, T-shirts, sand paintings, rugs, and so on—fill a small warehouse-sized room. Out back, a series of metallic barns house an oddball assortment of exhibits: antique vehicles (an ancient tractor, a 1921 pickup truck, a 1937 Rolls-Royce, an 1849 covered wagon, and a fringed surrey), life-sized wood-carved replicas of torture devices (including the rack, whipping, and a decapitator), and assorted other items (a 1654 Matchlock rifle, an old Morse telegraph sender, the makings of a copper moonshine still). "The Thing?" itself appears to be a papier-mâché imitation mummy. As we said, very strange. The "museum" costs 75 cents admission; a quarter less if under 18, and free for kids under 6 years old.

On our way from the exhibits to the door we glanced at the snack bar menu and noticed that SHAKES & MALTS included vanilla, chocolate, strawberry, and prickly pear. Not knowing what to expect from the last, we ordered one. "It's made from the fruit of the prickly pear cactus," the snack bar lady said. "We boil it down to make jelly, but we also use the syrup to mix with ice cream for shakes." And we're glad they do. A prickly pear milkshake (95 cents) hits the spot—it's got a lively, refreshing taste, somewhat citrus-like, but not tangy.

HOURS   7 am–6:30 pm daily. Closed Christmas.

SPECS   Johnson Rd. east of Benson; (602) 586-2581; V/MC/AE; no liquor.

DIRECTIONS   Westbound, turn left after taking Exit 322. Eastbound, turn right.

BOWIE TRUCK STOP, *Exits 366 and 362, Bowie*

This is the best—and, apparently, only—cafe in town. It came recommended to us for its roast beef smothered under cheese and green chile ($2.95), but a recent change in owners and cooks led us to make another selection. We looked on the menu for *tres cebollas* (three onions), the town's original name, but didn't find it. The day's special was 2 chicken enchiladas, a taco, rice, and beans for a reasonable $3.50. The Senior Citizens (*50* and over!) Discount breakfast—egg, bacon, hash browns, and toast—costs $1.49, as does the Senior Cowboy Discount breakfast: bacon, egg, and pancake.

Trailways and Greyhound both stop here, so several times a day a dozen or more travelers and their driver swoop into the place for a quick bite, then just as suddenly disappear. The best feature of the Bowie Truck Stop, however, is its view of the Home on the Range Motel across the street. After a satisfactory navy bean and ham soup (90 cents, $1, or $1.50, depending on size) we walked over to the motel to inspect its imaginative art work: inlaid mosaics of randomly selected bathroom tiles shaped in Native American motifs dot the outside walls. They looked terrific in the early afternoon sun.

When we returned to the cafe, we jotted down the waitress's answers to some of our questions about the restaurant. "Let's see now," we said, looking at our checklist. "What are your hours?"

"Oh," she replied with a shy grin. "I get off at two." Well, she was undoubtedly the best thing to come out of the kitchen during our brief visit, and Tom considered staying that extra half hour.

HOURS   7 days, 24 hours (except Christmas).

SPECS   Business Loop 10; (602) 847-2455; MC/V; full bar (5 pm–1 am).

DIRECTIONS   **Eastbound:** Follow Exit 362 over the Interstate onto Business Loop 10 into town; restaurant is on your left. Continue in the same direction 2.9 miles to rejoin I-10 eastbound.

Westbound: Take Exit 366 into town onto Business Loop 10 for 2.9 miles. The restaurant is a low white building on the right, kitty corner from the

Home on the Range Motel. Continue westbound by following Business Loop 10 straight out to the freeway.

New Mexico

CHINA DOLL RESTAURANT, *Exit 20, Lordsburg*

A Chinese restaurant in the Chihuahuan Desert? Why not, we thought, so we gambled that it'd be our discovery of the week. It fell short of that, but Loy Loo's Cantonese fare made for a rewarding stop anyway. A roomy place with Chinese scroll prints on the wall, the China Doll served up a Chinese vegetable dish with beef and steamed rice ($3.25) that would have passed in a far larger city. The house special, "China Doll fried rice," along with chop suey and chow mein, all include shrimp, chicken, and pork ($4–$5 range). American dishes are served, too.

The nicest part of the China Doll is the unobstructed view to the north of the Pyramid Mountains rolling across the desert. It was a perfectly reasonable—and thoroughly unexpected—place to stop for lunch or dinner. We did, however, regret the lack of fortune cookies at meal's end.

HOURS   Sun.–Thurs. 10 am–9 pm; Fri. & Sat. 10 am–10 pm; closed Wed. Open half-day Christmas.

SPECS   728 W. Motel Dr.; (505) 542- 8026; V/MC; no bar.

DIRECTIONS   Bear right onto West Motel Dr. after taking Exit 20; the restaurant is on your right in a mile.

CACTUS CAFE, *Exit 82A, Deming*

This is the town billboards tout as having "pure water and fast ducks!" Pure water we could understand, but fast ducks? It turns out residents stage annual duck races in the early autumn, with entries from politicians, social and civic clubs, businesses, and crazed individuals. It's lots of foolish fun, we're told. Feeding all the spectators must be a problem, but while many restaurants in Deming look as though they should be sent to a nursing home, the Cactus Cafe gets better each time. On our most recent visit we were delighted that the place had expanded and taken on an air of permanence.

The same reliable food we remembered from previous visits came out of the kitchen—chiles rellenos (large stuffed green chile peppers) served with a vigorous Spanish sauce and refried beans ($4.10); or, for the same price, 2 large sopapillas stuffed with refried beans, red or green chile sauce, and Spanish rice. The nachos ($3.10) are the spicy real thing, not a packaged imitation. A plateful serves as an appetizer for four (or a meal for one). We also enjoyed a dessert of homemade rice pudding. Our booth afforded a clear view of traffic rumbling by on the Interstate highway.

HOURS 7 am–9 pm daily; 7 am–2:30 pm Christmas Eve; closed Christmas Day.

SPECS 218 W. Cedar; (505) 546-2458; V/MC/AE; beer & wine (except Sundays).

DIRECTIONS Westbound: Take Exit 82-A and turn left at the bottom of the ramp to the traffic light; go right two blocks on Pine, then right again one block. Restaurant is on the right corner.

Eastbound: Take Exit 82-A, and the Cactus will be on your right almost immediately.

TANDOOR, *Exits 140 and 142, Las Cruces*

See page 107 for description of this Indian (East, not Pueblo) rarity.

DIRECTIONS Westbound: Take Exit 142 (Main St./NM State Univ.) and go straight at the light onto Valley Dr. Bear right onto Main St. at next light; very shortly after you pass the light at Idaho Ave., Tandoor's sign will be high in the air on the right. It's 1.2 miles from the freeway. To return to I-10 West, turn right on Main, make a U-turn between median islands at the first opportunity, and turn right at the first light. Stay on Avenida de Mesilla 0.7 mile to I-10.

Eastbound: From Exit 140, turn left, which puts you on Avenida de Mesilla; cross railroad tracks after 1 mile, and turn left onto Main St. Tandoor appears on your right after one block. To return to I-10, turn right on Main, make a U-turn between median islands at the first opportunity, go straight to Valley Dr., then under and up on the freeway.

ABOUT MESILLA

Allow extra time to wander over to Mesilla Plaza, kitty-corner to La Posta. The center of town has retained, to a remarkable extent, the atmosphere of a Spanish settlement while opening itself up to curious tourists. Coronado, the 16th-century Spanish explorer, passed through the area, beginning a steady parade of Europeans whose influence gradually replaced the Indians' as the dominant force in the region. Mesilla and the surrounding countryside have, at various times, been part of New Spain, the Mexican state of Chihuahua, the New Mexico Territory, the Military District of Arizona, the Confederacy (for thirteen months during the Civil War), and, since 1912, the state of New Mexico itself. Geronimo and the Mescalero Apaches found Mesilla an inviting target in the 1880s.

A marker in the plaza commemorates the Gadsden Purchase, in which the final strip of the Southwestern United States was bought from Mexico. The corner giftshop was used as the courthouse where William Bonney (you know him better as Billy the Kid) was found guilty of murder and sentenced to death. Gift shops, galleries, and restaurants line the plaza.

The Mesilla Book Center carries an extensive selection of hard-to-find books on history and contemporary life in the Southwest. On Mexican Independence Day (September 16) and again during the ten evenings leading up to Christmas, Mesilla becomes as Mexican a town as it was before 1853, with celebrations and processions centering at the plaza. As we walked about, an Indian craftswoman from one of the pueblos up north lumbered from store to store clutching a felt display tray of turquoise jewelry. A man rode his horse into town; he wasn't a hokey Chamber of Commerce come-on but simply a nearby resident there to carry out some business.

LA POSTA, *Exit 140, Mesilla (Las Cruces)*

Three basic types of Mexican cooking characterize Texas and the Southwest: Tex-Mex, New Mexico style, and Sonoran style (found in Arizona). The standout ingredient for New Mexico style Mexican food is the chile pepper, which grows best here in the Mesilla Valley. (Even Texans, for all their braggadocio, acknowledge that the best chile comes from New Mexico.) Although some chile, it's true, warrants a call to the fire department, when prepared right, the flavor can also be mild. In the heart of the Mesilla Valley, where strings of chile peppers, called *ristras*, hang from almost every front porch, you'll find some of the best New Mexican cooking. For us, a trip to La Posta is a reminder that regional cooking can still be carried out without compromise, and in a comfortable atmosphere, too.

We chose the "Specialty of La Posta" ($7.95) from their menu of thirty or so selections. The meal began with warm corn chips (a starter to dip in a pleasingly pungent green salsa), guacamole salad, chile con queso, and corn tortillas. These were only appetizers! The serious eating included a red enchilada, tamale, chile relleno, frijoles, chile con carne, and a rolled taco. But we weren't finished. The price of dinner also included dessert—an empanada (apricot, cherry, or mince), ice cream, or sherbet.

La Posta's red enchiladas ($3.85 on their own) warrant further discussion. Made in the traditional New Mexico Indian method, they consist of onion and grated sharp cheddar cheese layers sandwiched between soft corn tortillas and soaked in red chile sauce. Then the whole shebang is topped with a sunny-side-up egg. Tostadas compuestas, another favorite, is original with La Posta—it's a deep-fried corn tortilla in the shape of a cup, holding chile con carne and refried beans and garnished with lettuce, tomato, and grated cheese (1 to 3 cups, $2.10–$4.80).

We ate our ridiculously filling meal in what's called The Lava Room, one of a half dozen or so rooms that date back to the days of the Butterfield Trail when Anglo settlers established a mail route through land newly acquired from Mexico. The Lava Room once held stables for stagecoach horses; other dining rooms housed a blacksmith shop, a bunkhouse, a saddlery, and a schoolroom. The entrance, an open-air patio years ago, is lined with bougainvillea, and has a floor-to-ceiling bird cage holding exotic tropical parrots; nearby, piranha swim in an aquarium. Jewelry, ceramics, and other gifts are sold in shops just off the entrance hallway. The three-feet-thick adobe walls, and the *vigas* —wooden ceiling beams—date back to the original construction more than a century ago. Two generations of the Nuñez family have run La Posta, which celebrates its golden anniversary in 1989.

HOURS　　11 am–9 pm; closed Mon., Thanksgiving, and Christmas.

SPECS　　Mesilla Plaza; (505) 524-3524; major cards; beer and wine.

DIRECTIONS　　From Exit 140, turn right if eastbound, left if west-bound, onto Route 28. In 1.1 miles, turn right onto Calle Paran at "Historic Mesilla Plaza" sign; La Posta is one block down on the left, adjoining the plaza. Return to Interstate by turning right at the plaza, right again at the corner, and left back onto Route 28.

ABOUT JUÁREZ, MEXICO

There can be no doubt that some of the best food to be had within a hundred miles of El Paso is to be found in Juárez, a short international bridge away. If you have the time to venture into El Paso's sister city, you mustn't miss a meal at **Julio's Café Corona** (16 de Septiembre at Avenida de las Américas), a traditional watering hole among border hoppers. Specialties at Julio's include whole broiled black bass (swimming in chiles, tomatoes, and onions) and massive combination plates laden with all the traditional Mexican favorites. But most of all, this is the place to experience a well-balanced mole, that spicy, slightly sweet sauce of chiles, chocolate, nuts, and spices. Wash it all down with a margarita or two and you won't even notice that the waiters move in slow motion. (Open every day, 10 am–1 am.)

Texas

JJ's, *Exit 11, El Paso*

More than one source recommended JJ's to us, but not one mentioned the fact that the restaurant is housed in a rehabilitated Sonic Drive-In (plenty of parking space). We thought it a little odd to neglect to mention such a fact until we got inside and realized that there is so much going on with this funky little cafe that it's easy to forget the details of its former life.

There are no tables here, just some 20 stools scattered around a horseshoe-shaped counter. A single server takes your order for deep-fried, rolled tacos (flautas), avocado burritos, charcoal-broiled burgers, or fried cheese. He then disappears into the kitchen, reappears to fetch your drink, and dashes around the inside of the horseshoe like a caged animal. All around the room it's stare and stare alike with the other patrons, from the tattooed bandidos and Izod-shirted golf pros to freckle-faced, pre-teen girls and Spanish-speaking laborers.

The food is simple, authentically Mexican, cheap, and delicious. Whether you're here for breakfast (some of the best huevos rancheros and scrambled eggs with chorizo that we've eaten anywhere) or lunch, you must sample the gorditas, a house specialty (85 cents). Gordita means "little fat one," a name that could refer either to the puffy, fried corn cakes stuffed with beans, meats, lettuce, and tomato or to the aficionados who can't stop eating them. We like them three or four at a time, splashed with green chile sauce and washed down with coffee. There's no better way to start the day, warm up for lunch, revitalize an afternoon, or encourage sweet dreams.

JJ's menu is simple and unpretentious, but it does include

some not-so-standard burritos filled with barbecue beef ($1.49) or chicken mole. Service and atmosphere are slightly eccentric, but all in all we liked it just fine. In fact, we almost didn't tell you that it used to be a Sonic Drive-In.

HOURS   Sun.–Thurs. 7 am–10 pm; Fri.–Sat. 7 am–11 pm.

SPECS   5326 Doniphan; (915) 581-7267; no cards; no beer.

DIRECTIONS   Eastbound: Take Exit 11 to light and turn right on Mesa/US Hwy. 80. ■ Drive ½ mile to Doniphan. Turn right on Doniphan to JJ's a couple of blocks down on the right, past the Shur-Sav.

Westbound: Take Exit 11 and turn left. Go under I-10 on Mesa/US Hwy. 80, then as above from ■ .

SILENT PARTNERS
JAXON'S TERRITORIAL HOUSE, *Exit 16, El Paso*

There are two restaurants in El Paso that we were anxious to try, but both happened to be closed during our visit. Of the two, Jaxon's is one of El Paso's classic Mexican restaurants but one also reputed to grill the best steaks in town. Silent Partners was also recommended to us by the shopkeep at Goody Two Shoes (a tony boutique in Peppertree Square) as an elegant hot spot for vegetables (broccoli in Hollandaise), homemade soups, quiche, and even chicken cordon bleu. The description of the food alone had us drooling. Our sources seemed reputable enough, so if you're hungry for steak or tired of potatoes as the vegetable of the day, go adventuring at Jaxon's or Silent Partners.

HOURS   Silent Partners: Mon.–Sat. noon–10 pm. Closed Sun.
Jaxon's: 11 am–10 pm daily.

SPECS   Silent Partners: 5407 N. Mesa; (915) 833-2804
Jaxon's: 4799 N. Mesa; (915) 544-1188

DIRECTIONS   Westbound: Take Exit 16 to Executive Center Dr. and turn right. ■ Drive ½ mile to Mesa and turn left. Jaxon's is ½ mile down, on your left. Silent Partners is another mile down, also on the left.

Eastbound: Take Exit 16 and turn left to I-10 on Executive Center Dr., then as above from ■ .

LA HACIENDA, *Exits 16 and 18B, El Paso*

A sense of well-seasoned grandeur and Mexican graciousness make La Hacienda one of our all-time favorite restaurants. Everything about it will lead you to believe you have forded the Rio Grande rather than merely driven right to its American brink. First of all there are the prices—nothing here (tacos to steaks) costs much over 5 bucks, and the Mexican entrees are all less than 3. Then there's the service—an estimated 4.5 waiters per customer. Finally, the ambience clinches the illusion—foot-thick walls, arched doorways, waiters in *guayaberas*, and barmen in black tie harken not only to another country but also to another era.

Lunch at La Hacienda is a truly grand experience. We ordered the house specialty of cadillo (a goulash of ground beef, onions, chiles, tomatoes) and a second plate lunch of chicken *a la Mexicana*. Within minutes, waiters formed a procession, each bearing little mismatched bowls of food—sliced peaches, rings of pineapple, mushroom soup, shredded cabbage and lettuce in a creamy garlic dressing, followed by a basket of bolillos (Mexican French rolls) and crackers, and a mini-cauldron of salsa cruda—all included in the $2.95 price! Inspired to gluttony, we ordered a round of asadero, a soft white cheese, to melt in our soup. We nibbled contentedly until the arrival of the plastic plates filled with modest, tasty portions of chicken and pepper strips, cheesy refried beans, and rice (still the wimpy white rice in tomato sauce that is so popular in New Mexico). With the cadillo came a side of French-style green beans and Mexican spaghetti (like Chinese glass noodles in a light tomato sauce). We were simply overwhelmed by the quality, the quantity, and even the atmosphere.

To set the mood for dinner, order a pitcher of margaritas and work up an appetite by wandering through the maze of dining rooms. Be sure to stick your nose into the kitchen. You can't miss it—it's about the size of a city block and its wonderful smells are the best appetizer in the house.

One of the four current owners of La Hacienda stopped by our table to see if we found the hot sauce too picante. On the contrary, we found the Tex-Mex pico de gallo (cilantro, chile, onion, and tomato) just hot enough. He told us that the original house salsa was so hot it bubbled. When he insisted the cook cool it off with tomatoes, she smiled, shook her head, and followed his orders. The owner may have won the battle, but he lost the war. The current sauce costs him three times the price of the straight chile version, and it is so popular, the kitchen must make up two batches a day (he still taste-tests it for heat) to meet the demand.

Built in 1849, the low-slung adobe building with sycamore and willow-limb roof was a model for the surrounding settlement of El Molino, a community long ago absorbed by El Paso. The downtown snafu makes La Hacienda a pain in the neck to find, even though it's just a tortilla toss from the interstate. If you get lost, ask anyone for directions; if they don't know La Hacienda, you can be sure they're out-of-towners.

HOURS   Tues.–Sun. 10 am–10 pm. Closed Mon.

SPECS   1720 W. Paisano; (915) 546-9197; no cards; beer, wine, and margaritas.

DIRECTIONS   Westbound: Take Exit 18B and continue west across Porfirio Díaz to second stop, which is Yandell. Turn left onto Yandell (as it curves down you will see the roof and sign of La Hacienda below, to your left). As you get to the bottom of the hill, Paisano is running parallel to Yandell, to your left. Turn left at the first opportunity (at the gas station) and immediately double back on Paisano, which looks like an access road. La Hacienda is two blocks down, on the right. If in doubt, ask the gas station attendant. He's used to the question.

Eastbound: Take Exit 16 and turn right onto Executive Center. Continue along Executive Center to Paisano and turn left. Stay right on Paisano and jog even farther right onto what looks like an access road at the gas station at the foot of the overpass ramp. The access road is actually Paisano, while the ramp is Hwy. 85 curving up to downtown. La Hacienda is two blocks down, on the right.

CATTLEMAN'S STEAKHOUSE, *Exit 45, Fabens*

When El Pasoans drive forty miles to dine in the desert, there has got to be a good reason. When you arrive, if the Old West theme makes you want to ride on out of Fabens, rest assured that the steaks are said to be equal to the view (especially glorious at sunset). Dinners are served with rice pilaf, corn on the cob, home-cut steak fries, and sautéed mushrooms. Cheesecake, Bavarian chocolate cake, and hot apple pie à la mode defy you to believe you're in the middle of nowhere. We pass all this along second-hand, because Cattleman's is open only after 5 on weekdays. We did make the drive out, however, and we can vouch for the view.

HOURS   Tues.–Fri. 5 pm–10 pm; Sat. 4:30 pm–10 pm; Sun. 12:30 pm–9 pm.

SPECS   County Rd. 793; (915) 544-3200; AE/DC/MC/V; bar.

DIRECTIONS   **Eastbound:** Take Exit 45 to yield sign and turn left onto FM Rd. 793. Drive 4¾ miles to the restaurant, the only building in sight.

Westbound: Take Exit 45 to FM Rd. 793 and turn right, then as above.

MANDY'S, *Exit 72, Fort Hancock*

This 100-year-old tract house was spiffed up and moved to its current location long before Mandy hung her name over the front door. In fact, numerous owners both pre- and post-Mandy have tried to make a go of Fort Hancock's only restaurant. The current owners are in their fifth year and popular enough that regular customers call ahead to reserve a place.

There are more tables in this tiny two-room cottage than ants on a picnic blanket, but squirm your way to the back dining room to check out the original portion of the house. Carved wooden bows still grace the windows, and the light fixtures and beaded board walls are also original.

The current menu at Mandy's is an even mix of burgers, plate lunches, and Mexican food, all of which seems rather pricey ($7 for a baked ham lunch). Mexican entrees are more moderate, but it doesn't take a mathematician to figure out that by ordering 2 tacos, 2 enchiladas, and tamale à la carte, you save $2.40 over the price of the $6 combination dinner—unless the rice and beans that come with the platter are worth the 2-buck difference.

All that said, restaurants are few and far between along this stretch of I-10, and we had no complaint with Mandy's $2 hamburger, served with potato and tortilla chips, and a dish of oniony green chile.

HOURS   Open 7 days, 6 am–9 pm.

SPECS   I-10 at Fort Hancock; (915) 769-3970; no credit cards; no bar.

DIRECTIONS   **Eastbound:** Take Exit 72 and veer right on Spur 148. Mandy's is on the right, just past the end of the ramp, between the hotel and gas station.

Westbound: Take Exit 72. Turn left to cross over I-10 to Mandy's, on the right, just after you cross.

THE CHUCK WAGON, *Exit 105, Sierra Blanca*

We heard lots of good reports about the Chuck Wagon before we drove up here one blazing hot spring day. But rumors of buttered carrots and homemade rolls aside, something about the place just struck us wrong. Maybe it was the fill-in-the-blank menu that listed the day's special as "smothered steak with home-fried potatoes and a choice of potatoes ($3.25)." Or it might have been the three waitresses who reminded us of Macbeth's witches. Then there were the two hulking, blank-eyed women who ordered burgers, left to wait in the car, reappeared to fetch

the food and left again to eat in the parking lot (it was about 90°
outside). Whatever it was, we balked at the thought of testing
Chuck Wagon's chow.

But pie seemed safe enough, and we'd heard it praised all
along I-10. So we boldly ordered slices of apple and pecan (there
were pineapple and cherry, too). While we aren't convinced that
the pecan was homemade (the crust was too perfect) we thought
both pieces quite good. The apple was especially delicious: double crusted, and not too sweet, it showed all the signs of true
homebaking.

As we ate, our humpty-dumpty waitress stared at us relent-
lessly, until at last a lady in a pale-blue sweat suit arrived and
demanded her attention.

"Is the floor moving, or have I got the highway in my legs?"
the newcomer asked. When she asked what a chicken-fried steak
was, we considered warning her, but instead quite heartlessly
decided to let her do our job for us. Waiting around for her food
to arrive, we tried to enjoy the view, but the picture windows are
too high for anyone under six feet to make use of while seated.
The food came, the waitress left, and finally we queried the lady
with the highway in her legs about her smothered steak, to which
she replied by blowing out her cheeks, shutting her eyes, and
shaking her head. Enough said.

HOURS Open 7 days, 24 hours.

SPECS Exit 105, I-10; (915) 369- 2982; no credit cards; no bar.

DIRECTIONS **Eastbound:** Take Exit 105, turn left and go over I-10
to the Chuck Wagon, on the right.

Westbound: Take Exit 105 and turn right to the Chuck Wagon.

THE HATTERY, *Exit 140-A, Van Horn*

Met with the tragic news that the four-star classic cafe, the Big
Bend, had closed since our last visit, and knowing that our other
favorite, the Iron Rail (beef stroganoff, chicken Jerusalem, honey-
and-melon margaritas), is open only for dinner, we were stuck
for a noontime alternative. Stuck, that is, until a well-fed local

took note of our dilemma and directed us to The Hattery, opened for business a mere four weeks before.

Installed in a built-to-order brick building with tile floors, a stone fireplace, and a blooming selection of real and silken flowers, The Hattery would be right at home in any metropolitan suburb. But then, during hunting season Van Horn is populated with the residents of such places who flock to the area in hopes of bagging a pronghorn antelope or a mule deer. Some pretty tony establishments have sprung up to cater to such high-rolling crowds. Despite some service problems related to its youth, The Hattery seems like a good choice for lunch.

Settling in beneath a whirring ceiling fan, we ordered a couple of the day's $3.95 specials: chile rellenos and chicken-fried steak. Both platters proved extremely generous (three mild, cheese-stuffed chiles and a plate-lapping steak). The rellenos were a little on the salty side but forgiveably so, and the steak was fork tender, fried to a turn, and wallowing in creamy peppered gravy.

We liked the hat collection (you're encouraged to contribute), especially the veiled pillboxes, but we were most impressed to be served a garnish plate—strawberries and parsley—the first for miles. Equally appreciated was the selection of cranberry, grape, apple, tomato, and orange juices, served in tall glasses over crushed ice (95 cents). When the waitress offered us Boston cream pie for dessert, we almost forgot we were in West Texas.

HOURS   Open 7 days, 6 am–10 pm.

SPECS   I-10 at Hwy. 90; (915) 283-2418; no credit cards; no bar.

DIRECTIONS   **Eastbound:** Take Exit 140-A and turn right onto Hwy. 90. The Hattery is on the left.

Westbound: From Exit 140-A, turn left and cross under I-10 to The Hattery, on the left.

CHICKEN CHARLIE'S, *Balmorhea Exit, Balmorhea*

Everyone who lives within a hundred miles of Balmorhea knows Chicken Charlie's, one of the few good restaurants in an area so bereft of first-rate chow that people think nothing of driving two hours for dinner.

We've eaten breakfast, lunch, and dinner at Charlie's and it nearly broke our hearts when word rolled round that the restaurant had burned. But as we were going to press, the Chicken was rising from its ashes, ready to greet customers with a whole new stack of Big Chief pads scribbled with the menu: steaks, burgers, chicken, frogs' legs, lobster tails, biscuits, and a whole slew of desserts baked fresh by local ranchers' wives.

You won't have any trouble finding Chicken Charlie's. It is one of a handful of businesses along the main drag of a widespot town that's home to less than 1,000 people.

SARAH'S, *Exit 259, Fort Stockton*

Sarah's used to be a well-guarded local secret, but sometime during the 57-year life of this homespun Mexican restaurant someone let the cat out of the bag. These days *everyone* knows about Sarah's, writes about Sarah's, raves about Sarah's. Not so easily impressed, we tried other restaurants in town, and we're here to tell you it's true. Sarah's is the best restaurant in Fort Stockton.

Not that Sarah's is flawless. We found the chips (made on the premises) and hot sauce to be a cut above the average, but thought the flat (as opposed to rolled) chicken enchilada downright awful. What was supposed to be a green chile sauce looked like melted white cheese and tasted like a very bland flour gravy. Try as we might, we never did find anything in the dish that resembled chicken or green chiles. It's hard to believe that Mother Sarah passed this recipe down to daughter Cleo.

On the other hand, the chalupas—fresh beans spread on a crisp tortilla and heaped with guacamole—were worthy of the restaurant's reputation, as was the table hot sauce, although it's a bit tomato-mild for our taste.

Still, you can't help but like the red on red on red at Sarah's (chairs, curtains, flowers, uniforms, glasses), and the service is young, giggly, and friendly. Even better, first-timers (ladies only) leave with a souvenir, a miniature Mexican pot. Rumor had it that male visitors receive a complimentary quesadilla (a soft tortilla filled with cheese), but ours was nowhere in sight. Maybe it was just an off day.

HOURS   Lunch: Mon.–Sat. 11:30 am–2 pm. Dinner: Mon.–Sat. 5 pm–9 pm.

SPECS   106 Nelson; (915) 336-7124; no credit cards; no bar.

DIRECTIONS   Westbound: From Exit 259 turn left and go over I-10 on Main St. ■ Drive 1½ miles to 5th and turn right. Turn left at the next corner, onto Nelson. Sarah's is on the right, between 5th and 6th.

Eastbound: Take Exit 259 and turn right on Main St., then as above from ■.

EL CHATO, *Exit 365, Ozona*

Ozona, according to the sign posted at the city limits, is the biggest little city in the world. We're not sure what that means, but we do know it is the only town in a county the size of Delaware and filled with a surprising number of stout trees and sprawling mansions.

In addition, this town of some 3,500 souls supports a good number of restaurants. Of the several taquerías (taco huts) and cafes doing business hereabouts, El Chato is one of the newest and spiffiest. Cattlemen (the local catch-all term for oilmen, ranchers, and anyone with a big hat and a bigger car) hang out at the Ozona Steakhouse, but we couldn't rustle up a waitress there.

Something about the interior of El Chato is off-kilter. Maybe it's the staircase that gets wider at the top, but the restaurant looks like it was assembled from a kit that had no instructions. Still, we found the white stucco walls and massive Spanish crests somehow familiar and appealing.

We were lucky enough to discover El Chato on a Wednesday, the night when virtually everything on the menu is on special for less than $3. At those prices we couldn't pass up the fajita plate: strips of steak charbroiled with tomatoes and onions, and served in a skillet with refried beans, rice, guacamole, and pico de gallo (a crude onion, tomato, and chile salsa). We weren't disappointed in a single bite—the meat was tender and flavorful, the beans and rice were fresh, and the guacamole had us believing we were somewhere close to an avocado tree. A pleasantly thick, not-so-hot sauce and a bottomless basket of chips rounded out the meal. But as good as the food was, nowhere have we tasted a better margarita; spiked with lime *and* lemon and an honest ratio of tequila, this marg made our night, our week, and our book of memorable bests.

HOURS   Open 7 days, 11 am–10 pm.

SPECS   Box 37, I-10; (915) 392-3622; no credit cards; full bar.

DIRECTIONS   **Eastbound:** Take Exit 365 to the end of the ramp and immediately turn right to double back west on the frontage road. El Chato is on the left, a block down.

Westbound: Take Exit 365 ¾ of a mile to the second light and turn left to cross under I-10. As soon as you cross under, immediately turn right onto Maple (the frontage road) and continue west along the frontage road as above.

THE COMMERCIAL, *Exit 400, Sonora*

Sometime in the 1920s Mrs. Lopez's "sainted" father invented santos, a simple but delicious dish the Commercial has become famous for. Santos are tortillas fried to a puff and stuffed with beans, cheese, and tomatoes ($3.25). Simple, but delicious. If you're really hungry, follow the "saints" with fajitas, huevos rancheros, or a jalapeño cheeseburger.

Grilled with onion and served with beans, rice, guacamole, and a salsa of onions, peppers, and tomatoes, fajitas are served by the ounce. Buy the 8-ounce platter ($6.75) and share it; you'll have to order extra tortillas, but you'll want to mop up every bite.

The tortilla chips are fried on the premises, and can only be rivaled by Sarah's (Fort Stockton). The mural of the fighting cocks is without rival, at least along this stretch of interstate. The weathered boards of the Commercial's exterior look as if a good breath of wind would leave them in a heap, but inside the restaurant is as slickly modern as a McDonald's. At least the santos haven't changed.

HOURS   Lunch: Mon.–Sat. 11 am–2:30 pm. Dinner: Mon–Sat. 5 pm–9 pm.

SPECS   154 S. Plum; (915) 387-9928; no credit cards; beer.

DIRECTIONS   **Eastbound:** Take Exit 400 and turn right on Hwy. 277 to light and then left onto Crockett. Continue 1 mile to Plum (one block past the light) and turn right. The Commercial is on the right, at the corner.

Westbound: Take Exit 400 and turn left under I-10 on TX Hwy. 277, then as above.

HOTEL LAS LOMAS, *Exits 456 and 457, Junction*

Outlaws used to crisscross the countryside surrounding the junction of the North and South Llano rivers in order to rob the San Antonio–Fort Concho stageline. Peering up at the limestone hills, it's easy to imagine they're still hiding along the rough ridges surrounding this quiet, tidy river valley town.

We rolled into the heart of it all, past our favorite junk shop, A Little of This and A Lot of That, and stopped in at Issak's, the local cafe (good grits). Where, we asked the golden-eyed waitress, do you go when you really want a special meal? Those eyes squinched closed a bit in contemplation, then glowed. We followed her directions.

Unfortunately, the interior of Las Lomas is not as intriguing as the building's 1926 Mediterranean architecture. All bell curves and stucco niches out front, the historic hotel long ago lost its guts to veneer paneling and wall-to-wall carpet. Not that the renovation is horrifying. Las Lomas today is a comfortable apartment building (there's a rumor of a Bed and Breakfast Inn someday) with a past that can only be guessed.

As for the restaurant, well, Gay Renfroe's cooking is every bit as glorious as the old hotel's façade. Accomplished in the preparation of everything from quiche to Chinese food, Renfroe handbreads her shrimp, bakes her own desserts, and stuffs her own chiles rellenos ($1.50). As if that weren't enough, she creates dished of her own. Pericos, beef and guacamole nachos ($4.25), are delicately spiced and delicious. The shrimp were so fresh, we suspected she caught them herself, but looking at the banana nut bread that had just come out of the oven and the freshly stocked salad bar, we knew she'd been too busy to get to the coast that day.

If you're headed west, take heed: Las Lomas is the best all around restaurant between Kerrville and El Paso. Eat hearty. Fill up your canteen. Rest a minute. From here on out it's just you, the tumbleweeds, and 350 miles of enchiladas.

HOURS   Open 7 days. Lunch: 11:30 am–2:00 pm. Dinner: 5 pm–10 pm.

SPECS   609 College; (512) 446-3127; V/MC; Private Club.

DIRECTIONS   Eastbound: Take Exit 456 and turn right onto US Hwy. 83/290 and continue toward town. After 1 mile turn right onto Rock Springs. Continue 2 blocks and then turn left onto College. Las Lomas is on your right, across from the post office.

Westbound: Take Exit 457 and turn left to cross over I-10 to a stop sign. Turn right at the stop onto Business 83 and cross the river into town. Turn left on Rock Springs Hwy. and left again on College. Las Lomas is on the right, opposite the post office.

THE YELLOW RIBBON, *Exit 508, Kerrville*

You haven't seen anything until you've seen blackened red snapper prepared in the close quarters of a Victorian-era kitchen.

If you can keep the kitchen staff from calling the fire department, you still have to convince the neighbors watching the smoke billow out the back door that you've got everything under control. Such are the worries of C.C. and Naomi Huffhines, the owners of The Yellow Ribbon, Kerrville's most elegant restaurant. As much as they would like to expand their kitchen, the Huffhines feel strongly about preserving the lines of the circa 1890 home out of which they operate their 12-table restaurant, upstairs antique shop, and office.

A new kitchen in the backyard is a possibility, but in any case, the snapper is well worth any risk of smoke inhalation, and the selection of other fresh fish (not all of which are seared) is varied but uniformly delicious. House specialties include southern dishes such as deep-fried catfish ($5.95), an oyster and artichoke casserole, and veal sautéed in lemon juice and topped with butter and a medley of vegetables and parmesan cheese ($9.95). All entrees are served with the fresh vegetable of the day, soup or salad (served with the addicting house cheese wafers), and homemade bran rolls.

The day of our visit we were too full for more than a mouthful of the day's special King Ranch Casserole but found it so delicious we ended up making a serious dent in our serving. A famous Texas dish with no documented connection to the King Ranch, this cheesy chicken and tortilla casserole is one of those formless, filling dishes you always find at church suppers and everyone always wants the recipe. When a dish of eggs florentine passed by our table (poached eggs on spinach in Mornay sauce) we could only bemoan our lack of appetite.

The merciless waitress, however, encouraged by Mrs. Huffhines, forced us to taste the famed Lemon Alaska Pie (ice cream and lemon sauce layered in a pecan crust and topped with baked meringue) and we pronounce it worth every calorie.

An eccentric clutter of Victoriana, massive ball and clawfoot furniture, and incongruous Mexican folk art decorate the four downstairs dining rooms. An upstairs parlor serves as a bar and waiting room, and is adjacent to the gift shop filled with the Huffhines' overflow of antiques, geegaws, and whizbangs. The Yellow Ribbon is a very popular restaurant, so if you run into a wait, order a brandy milk punch, unfurl your fan, and wander about to your heart's content.

HOURS   Open 7 days, 11:30 am–2 pm, 5:30 pm–9:30 pm.

SPECS   Tivy at Jefferson; (512) 896-6416; AE/DC/MC/V; full bar.

DIRECTIONS   Eastbound: Take Exit 508 to stop sign and turn right onto TX Hwy. 16 (Sidney Baker). ■ Continue 2½ miles to Jefferson and turn left. The Yellow ribbon is 5½ blocks down, on the right-hand corner of Tivy and Jefferson.

Westbound: Take Exit 508 and cross under I-10. Turn left onto TX Hwy. 16, then as above from ■.

STALLION ON THE ROOF, *Exit 551, Leon Springs*

Driving the old stagecoach road to the Stallion on the Roof at night, it is easy to imagine you are winding through the wood-lands in anxious search for some sign of civilization (during the day, the seeping edges of San Antonio are more than obvious). Around a dark bend in the road, three miles from an empty, sterile stretch of interstate, this country-gourmet cafe appears bright and welcoming beneath the pawing hooves of its name-sake.

Casual elegance, an accessible menu, and an accommodating kitchen are the draw in a restaurant that invites huntsmen to bring their game to the chef, who's happy to spit your boar or roast your pheasant. Not in the mood for lobster bisque? Ask for something else; special requests are welcome. If you are on a diet you need only ask for a special preparation. Not that the fare isn't varied enough to please all palates—mesquite-grilled ham-burgers and steaks provide a hearty balance to a crepe and ome-lette lunch menu, while dinner features lamb chops with fresh green mint sauce, coq au vin, sweetbreads with port wine and mushrooms, and quail or duck in orange or green sauce. A spate of regional American specialties complement the gourmet dishes: chicken and dumplings, veal liver, and chicken-fried steak. For those intent upon self-indulgence from the the the start, appetizers include baked brie with almond ($3.75), imported foie gras with truffles ($15), and Beluga caviar.

Rather than tell you about the delights of the dessert table, you are invited to peruse the offerings; should mere invitation be insufficient, you are plied with a meringue or two until your resolve weakens sufficiently. Having gorged ourselves on a huge fillet of red snapper in lemon butter and a flawless dish of quail in grape-apple sauce, we guiltlessly made an after-dinner foray, returning with a marquise au chocolat so rich it made our throats ache. Service is gracious, well-informed, and often unabashedly seductive.

Whether your table sits beneath the basket-hung ceiling of the Grill Room or in the trellised Green Room (a white-tiled garden porch), you'll be surrounded by orchids and mums, immense pepper grinders, the smells of good cooking, and the cheerful clatter of forks.

HOURS   Wed.–Mon. 11:30 am–10:30 pm. Closed Tues.

SPECS   Boerne Stagecoach Rd. at Scenic Loop; (512) 698-2386; AE/DC/MC/V; full bar, extensive wine list.

DIRECTIONS   **Northbound:** Take Exit 551 and follow ramp 0.4 mile to Boerne Stagecoach Rd. and turn left. Continue 3 miles to restaurant, on the left.

Southbound: Take Exit 551 to Boerne Stagecoach Rd. and turn right. Go 3 miles to restaurant, on the left.

ABOUT SAN ANTONIO

See our overview of San Antonio restaurants on pages 144–146. **La Fogata** (below) is the easiest to reach from I-10.

LA FOGATA, *Exit 565C, San Antonio*

You can't go to San Antonio and *not* eat Mexican food, and for our pesos, La Fogata serves the best in the city. When we first started coming here there was always a wait for the eight tables and six counter stools. There's still a wait, but you can't distinguish the former Dairy Queen for the awnings and fountains, umbrellas and patios that surround it. The new surroundings are elegant and comfortable; still, we like to beg a seat in the heart of it all where we can reminisce about the days before the maitre d' wore a tuxedo.

Long before Bert Greene declared this one of the best restaurants in America, we were lining up here for the frijoles borracho (beer and bean soup that puts all other versions to shame) and the fork-tender carne adobada (pork tips marinated with red peppers). Now, we still line up, but it gets increasingly difficult to make a choice among the 44 entrees.

This trip we landed our favorite tile-topped table, the one with the view of the house collection of beauty queen photos. Directly across from us was the door through which employees stream like bees leaving the hive (the prep kitchen is across the alley in a separate building). Feeling nostalgic, we had to start with the bean soup ($1.25) just to see if it was as good as we remembered. It was better. Next, we determined to try the tacos chivero, a fried tortilla shell stuffed with goat cheese, beans, guacamole, and jalapeños ($1.99).

Our serious eating began with the enchiladas de mole, chicken enchiladas smothered in a highly complex sauce of 30-plus ingredients including chile, nuts, and a variety of peppers, in addition to the requisite chocolate. We have eaten this dish all over Mexico, including Puebla, where it was invented, and we declare La Fogata's mole right up there among the very best. (Three enchiladas with rice and beans cost $5.75.)

As we waited between courses (this is not fast food), we put away several baskets of fluffy, light, handmade tortillas and at least one bowl of a perfectly blended hot sauce.

Finally, we ordered dessert. La Fogata's empanadas (turnovers) are made fresh when you order. It takes some time but they emerge golden brown and steaming hot (order ahead on a really busy night). Of all the fillings (mango, membrillo, guayaba), we're addicted to the guayaba. Yes, we know the fruit is canned, and yes, it's too sweet, but the pairing of this pink, fleshy tropical fruit with cream cheese is beyond our ability to resist ($1.50).

Next trip we're gonna try the poco loco (chicken thighs broiled in butter and garlic) and homemade Mexican hot chocolate.

HOURS Tues.–Thurs. 7:30 am–10 pm; Fri. & Sat. until 11 pm; Sun. 8 am–9 pm.

SPECS 2427 Vance Jackson; (512) 341-9930; V/MC/AE/DC; full bar.

DIRECTIONS Take Exit 565C to Vance Jackson and turn right if westbound (i.e., toward El Paso), left if eastbound (i.e., toward Houston). La Fogata is a mile down, on the left.

GREENERY STATION, *Exit 610, Seguin*

We learned about Greenery Station from a local gas station attendant (he crawled out from under a car to recommend it), and while such sources are usually totally unreliable, this guy convinced us we just had to give the place a try. Not a restaurant you'd ever discover on your own, the caboose-flanked Greenery Station turned out to be something of a sleeper.

We weren't impressed with the interior decoration but ordered anyway. The first thing to surprise us was the basket of breads—gingerbread, blueberry, and wheat muffins—a totally unexpected treat (served, alas, with margarine). Next, our fried chicken livers arrived lightly breaded, fried to a turn, piled on a slice of Texas toast, and accompanied by bowls of home-canned green beans with bits of ham and white gravy (a little thin)—satisfying and downright cheap at $3.25. An old-fashioned hamburger turned out to be just that: beefy, juicy, cooked to order, and surrounded by at least two potatoes recently filleted into big fat steak fries ($2.95).

There's absolutely nothing wrong with the food or the prices here, and after we'd forced ourselves to sample the homemade peach pie (a difficult choice among the blueberry, cherry, and apple), we forgave the countryfied decor. Only one quibble: in the hometown of the World's Largest Pecan (adjacent to the courthouse), there wasn't a single slice of pecan pie to be had.

HOURS   Open 7 days 6:30 am–10 pm.

SPECS   606 Bypass 123; (512) 379-3242; MC/V; full bar.

DIRECTIONS   **Eastbound:** Take Exit 610 and turn right onto TX Hwy. 123. Continue 2.5 miles to Greenery Station, on the right just past the four-way stop. To return to I-10, you have to turn right out of the Greenery Station parking lot and drive one block south before you can make a U-turn and retrace your route back down 123.

Westbound: Take Exit 610 and continue along the access road to TX Hwy. 123 and turn left. Go 2½ miles to the restaurant, on the right.

LULING CITY MARKET, *Exit 632/TX Hwy. 80, Luling*

Backroom barbecue is a long-standing Texas tradition. Cut through the market to the pit at the back of the store, and line up for a butcher paper parcel of pit-smoked meat at its inelegant best. Lean and tender brisket, link sausage, and pork ribs (our favorite) are sold by the pound, with a complimentary side of white bread or crackers. Purists ask for nothing more, content to lean up against the wall and gobble; others eat in the front room where the fixings of potato salad, slaw, beans, and beer are sold. If you like your barbecue saucy, help yourself to the bottle on the table.

If you like the idea of a barbecue lunch, but the thought of eating in a market cools your appetite, carry your lunch out to Luling's handsome and shady city park on the west side of TX Hwy. 80, halfway back to the interstate. And don't neglect to stop should you spot a truck farmer selling watermelons along the way—Luling is the home of award-winning specimens, as anyone who's ever attended the June Watermelon Thump well knows.

HOURS   Mon.–Sat. 7 am–6 pm. Closed Sunday.

SPECS   633 E. Davis; (512) 875-9019; no credit cards; beer.

DIRECTIONS   **Westbound:** Take Exit 632 and turn right on TX Hwy. 80 and drive 2 miles into town. City Market is in the strip of shotgun storefronts just across the railroad tracks, second building over, on the left.

Eastbound: Take Exit 632 to TX Hwy. 80 and cross over I-10 left and into town, as above.

WEIMAR COUNTRY INN, *Exit 682, Weimar*

Built in 1909 as the San Jacinto Hotel, the Weimar has recently been resurrected as a country inn many times more posh than its former self. The owners claim they opened the inn only to provide themselves with a place to eat when visiting their area ranchette. Ringed by lace-curtained windows and stained glass, wallpapered in delicate prints, and furnished with English antiques, the Weimar is an oasis of country elegance filled with fresh flowers and the aromas of good cooking.

The food is spruced-up down-home cooking, as interpreted by a Houston-trained chef who once spent only his weekends at the inn, a sort of chef du jour, but is now in full-time residence. (He's even created a line of jellies and spices.) We tried his shrimp, broiled in garlic butter, and found them fresh, pink, and lip-smacking good ($10.95). All entrees include a choice of potatoes, tossed garden salad, or salad of the day. The menu's emphasis is on steaks and seafood, including a highly praised, plate-dwarfing chicken-fried steak—trucked in fresh from Houston and handbreaded in the Weimar's kitchen ($4.95).

The daily specials when we visited were Swiss steak with vegetable soup and salad ($4.95), seafood gumbo ($1.75), and a peach shortcake that made us yearn for summer (95 cents). Ask for a tour of the rooms before you leave, but beware—once you've checked them out you may be overwhelmed with an urge to check in.

HOURS   Lunch: Wed.–Sun. 11 am–2 pm. Dinner: Thurs.–Sat. 6 pm–10 pm.

SPECS   101 Jackson; (409) 725-8888; AE/MC/V; full bar.

DIRECTIONS   **Westbound:** Take Exit 682 and turn right on FM Rd. 155. ■ Drive 1 mile to Market St. (just past Rubin's Grocery). Turn left. Drive 3 blocks to Center St. and turn right. You'll see the Weimar Inn on the left, fronting the railroad tracks.

Eastbound: Take Exit 682 to FM Rd. 155, turn left, then as above from ■.

SCHOBEL'S, *Exit 696, Columbus*

You'll find the sheriff, the highway patrol, the Baptist preacher, Aunt Susie, and maybe that no-good cousin of yours here at Schobel's along with everybody else that lives within a hog call of Columbus. A restaurant just doesn't grow up to live in a monstrous pre-fab barn of a building without the loyal patronage of the local citizenry.

Schobel's epitomizes a family-style restaurant at its crowd-pleasing best. Here's their formula for success: To make the *whole* family happy you serve a wide variety of food and plenty of it (except on the diet plate). In the spirit of community service you add meeting rooms for the Lion's Club and more intimate dining rooms for anniversary celebrations. All those people and their young-uns can get pretty noisy, so you layer the ceiling in acoustical tile. As much as the locals love you, you can't overlook the tourist trade, so you tack on a gift shop. And as a patron of the arts, you offer the works of local artists for sale (some efforts more primitive than others).

As for the food, well, the Schobel's pride and joy is the daily buffet—an impressive line-up of standard roadhouse fare such as (but not limited to) tuna salad, mashed potatoes, broccoli, squash, Mexican food, steaks, and seafood. A rabbit run through the line costs $3.90, and the all-you-can-eat carnivorous spread is $6.95. Substantial, dependable, good, but not great. We liked the homemade bread best of all—and the wagon wheel lights.

HOURS Sun.–Thurs. 6 am–9 pm. Fri.–Sat. 6 am–10 pm. Weekday buffet served 11 am–2 pm, Sun. 11 am–3 pm. Breakfast buffet served Sat.

SPECS 2020 Milan; (512) 732-2385; DC/MC/V; full bar.

DIRECTIONS **Westbound:** Take Exit 696 to stop sign at US Hwy. 71/Business and turn right. You'll see Schobel's a block down, on the right.

Eastbound: Take Exit 696 to US Hwy. 71/Business and turn left to cross under I-10. Schobel's is one block, on the right.

TEA LEAF RESTAURANT, *Exit 720, Sealy*

We've browsed and grazed buffets from Kingman to Brownsville, but nowhere have we seen the likes of the bountiful table set by the Tea Leaf: platters piled high with pork chops in mushroom gravy, ranks of golden-baked chicken, serving bowls brimming with field-fresh green beans and medallions of summer squash, a three-tiered serving tray layered with old-fashioned relishes, and a tureen of homemade vegetable soup. The Tea Leaf isn't like a restaurant at all really—more a sort of grandmotherly buffet spread across a sideboard like Sunday supper. Even the dining rooms lend to the impression that you're a dinner guest rather than a paying customer—an eccentric combination of attic antiques and garage sale bric-a-brac, lace curtains, and mismatched china. But despite the tearoom atmosphere, the most faithful customers are men, big men who do serious damage to the all-you-can-eat $5.95 spread (a dollar more at night). But that's just fine with the Tea Leaf. Chuckling over three men making their third trip through the line, our waitress rushed off to replenish the depleted platters.

Those of smaller appetite may order more delicate menu items —finger sandwiches and fresh fruit salad with poppyseed dressing, china teacups filled with cheese-broccoli-noodle soup; and chicken crepes served with the vegetable of the day, hot rolls, soup, or salad ($5.95).

As much as we wanted to dive into the buffet, we hadn't the appetite to spare, so we settled on a cup of soup and a chicken salad sandwich—a "light meal" which turned out to be only slightly less hearty than the big spread. The slightly curried chicken-heavy salad was mounded so high, we thought someone must be worried that sandwich eaters don't get enough to eat.

A homespun dessert selection includes chocolate pie, oatmeal cake, and cheesecake with strawberries or chocolate topping; and the waitresses all make you feel as if it would do you good to put on a little weight. All in all, it's just like being home for supper, except you don't have to do the dishes.

HOURS   Lunch: Mon.–Sat. 11:30 am–2 pm. Dinner: Thurs.–Sat. 6 pm.–9 pm.

SPECS   304 Fowlkes; (409) 885-3759; MC/V; no bar.

DIRECTIONS   Westbound: Take Exit 720/TX Hwy. 36 and stay on the access road as it loops around to the stop. Turn left on Route 36 and ■ drive 2 miles north into town. Turn right at Main St. and the Tea Leaf is 1 block down, on the right, above the light company.

Eastbound: Take Exit 720 to TX Hwy. 36 and turn left, then as above from ■.

NINO'S, *Exit 765B, Houston*

We heard a lot of good things about Nino's before we got there but were warned that a visit during the lunch or dinner rush could mean an interminable wait. Not the types to take such a warning lightly, we overcompensated by being the first customers in the door of this two-story brick cottage 11 o'clock one morning. Italian food for breakfast? Why not? The Italian loaf— fresh, steaming hot, chewy, and lovely—shamed many a biscuit, and the rigatoni (those tubular noodles) in zucchini sauce was an elegant and memorable way to start the day ($6.95). Just the right amount of finely chopped al dente zucchini elevated an already rich and garlicky tomato sauce to heavenly heights.

The dining room is plain though not unpleasant, but the lunch and dinner menus are elaborate—from pizza and pasta to stuffed artichokes—and off-menu specialties include dishes like steak Nino, a rib-eye grilled with onions, peppers, mushrooms, and served with a side of fettuccine. Everything is honest-to-goodness homestyle Italian, which means (1) servings are copious, and (2) everything is made from scratch, including the pasta. Even the breadsticks are worth mentioning.

And, sure enough, the area bankers, lawyers, and pottery makers were streaming in as we were leaving. If you'd rather not wait for a table, or you're not in the mood for a heavy meal, head over to Vincent's Sandwich Shop, next door. Vincent serves specialty salads, soups, and sandwiches on homebaked rolls—and while we didn't sample the food, we figure it's got to be good. Vincent is family.

HOURS   (Nino's) Lunch: Mon.–Fri. 11 am–2:30 pm. Dinner: Mon.–Thurs. 5:30 pm–10 pm. Closed Sun.

SPECS   2817 Dallas; (713) 522-5120; AE/MC/V; full bar and wine list.

DIRECTIONS   Eastbound: Take Exit 765B and ■ continue east on access road to the first light and turn right onto Durham. Continue on Durham 2 miles to the light past Memorial and turn left onto W. Dallas. Nino's is ¾ mile, on the right, under the La Rue traffic light.

Westbound: Take Exit 765B to Durham and cross over I-10 left, then as above from ■.

CADILLAC BAR, *Exit 765B, Houston*

A riot of activity, even during off hours, the Cadillac makes an entertaining lunch stop. And the food is pretty good, too, even if it costs a few more pesos than we're used to spending for Tex-Mex. The specialty of the house is cabrito, but as the menu tells you, a good cabrito is hard to find, and the Cadillac, unlike some restaurants on the other side of the border, believes in serving only the plumpest, most tender, milk-fed kids available. Believe us, no goat is better than an old goat. If it's available, go for the cabrito al Pastor (split and roasted, shepherd-style, $13.95).

Another house specialty is a hands-on delight that redeems mesquite from its reputation as the rancher's bane: mesquite-roasted quail, pricey at two for $10.95, but delicious. Forget the knife and fork (the bones are too small) and learn why the ultimate Mexican accolade is to say a dish is "finger-sucking." Of the more traditional Tex-Mex options, we like the fajitas ($5.25) and spicy frijoles borrachos, or "drunk beans," cooked with beer ($2.50). If you have trouble choosing between enchiladas and rellenos, the Cadillac is more than happy to combine any of the entrees onto a platter so that you can sample a variety of dishes.

Cloned from the Cadillac Bar in Nuevo Laredo, Houston's Cadillac is a somewhat more elegant but equally incongruous jumble of white-jacketed waiters, gorgeous woven rush figures, inverted chairs (hanging from walls and ceiling) and walls webbed with graffiti such as "I banged my head right here." And there's no shortage of the bathroom variety. Anytime you drop in at the Cadillac, you're likely to find some sort of happy madness. (The carafes of margaritas might have something to do with it.) But for the best of eating and people-watching, squeeze in during the weekend brunch, an all-you-can eat orgy of omelettes, rellenos, enchiladas, flautas (rolled and fried tacos), and free champagne ($9.95).

HOURS Mon.–Thurs. 11 am–10:30 pm; Fri. 11 am–midnight; Sat. noon–midnight; Sun. noon–11 pm. Weekend brunch is served Sat. and Sun. noon–3 pm.

SPECS 1802 Shepherd; (713) 862-2020; AE/MC/V; full bar, margaritas by the pitcher.

DIRECTIONS   Eastbound: Take Exit 765B and continue east on access road to first light (Durham). Turn right onto Durham (one way south). ■ Turn left at the first cross street, Nolda, and then left again onto Shepherd. The Cadillac is on the right. Follow Shepherd (one-way north) back to I-10.

Westbound: Take Exit 765B to Durham and turn left to cross over I-10. Continue on Durham to Nolda, then as above from ■.

LONGHORN TEXICAN CAFE, *Exit 788B, Baytown*

When we discovered that there wasn't a single eatery between I-10 and Baytown proper, we were inclined to head back to the interstate and on to Winnie. But a Houston Power and Light serviceman we met at a gas station convinced us that a visit to this reproduction frontier cafe-saloon was worth the extra mile. You know the kind of place: gallon iced tea glasses, grandmother's recipe for chicken-fried steak, central bar, and tin billboards advertising Bovinal ("protects cows against flies and controls ticks on sheep"). But don't get us wrong: there's nothing seedy about this country-chic cafe catering to long-legged urban cowgirls, pin-striped bankers, and the gimme cap crowd.

It used to be the plain old Longhorn Cafe, until the management added several Tex-Mex dishes weighted toward ketchup-catchers: french fries, onion rings (a freshly fried ten gallon basketful costs $1.30), meat loaf, hamburgers, and catfish. The macho nachos and stuffed jalapeños were an instant success, and the HPL man claims that Bevo's Best (bits of round steak cooked on a griddle with onions and topped with queso) keeps him coming back. Tacos aside, we thought the burgers were the best-looking we'd seen in a long while.

The day's special of red beans and rice turned out to be what we'd call Cajun-Mexican—red beans and rice topped with melted cheddar. It was pretty, gloppy, and good, and we were pleased to discover some links of a garlic-and-chile-spiked pork sausage buried beneath the beans. A side of rough textured corn muffins left us hungry for more. We had no complaints about the food, and the service (mostly blue-jeaned and pony-tailed) was especially pleasant. But the nicest touch came when a roving cowboy stopped at our table and without a word, cleared back the numerous bottles of condiments to give us more elbow room. We can only assume he worked there.

HOURS Mon.–Fri. 6 am–10 pm; Sat. 8 am–11 pm; Sun. 8 am–10 pm.

SPECS 1303 Garth; (713) 420-3579; AE/CB/DC/MC/V; full bar.

DIRECTIONS **Eastbound:** Exit 788B veers south to TX Hwy. 330/Decker. ■ Continue along Decker 4.5 miles to the light at Garth and turn left. The cafe is on the left, next to the Pizza Hut.

Westbound: Follow Exit 788B as it feeds south to TX Hwy. 330/Decker. Then as above from ■.

A1-T'S, *Exit 829, Winnie*

A1-T's has been around a lot longer than the new building it now occupies (just take a look at that mile-high sign out front to get some idea of the restaurant's real age). But wall murals and tiffany lamps aside, there's nothing too precious about a restaurant that serves fried alligator ($9.95/lb.), barbecued crabs, pork cracklins, and gumbo in bowls of serious increments: small ($3.50), medium ($4.25), and large ($7.25).

We stopped in for breakfast, but having arrived ten minutes too late for biscuits and omelettes, we followed our noses and neighbors to the just-stocked steam table, heaped high with chicken-fried steak and shrimp creole (your choice), fresh corn, mashed potatoes, and crowder peas ($4.50). And while it isn't a help-yourself, all-you-can-eat belt-buster, the line servers are plenty heavy-handed. To make sure there are no holes left in your appetite, a crusty loaf of homemade white bread meets you back at your table.

Feeling gluttonous, curious, and hopeful that some soul food might restore our flagging spirits, we ordered up a second lunch of sweet potato, cracklins (fried pork skins), and cornbread. Unfortunately the kitchen reported a shortage of taters, so we changed our order to red beans and rice with a side of boudain ($3.95). The boudain, a spicy liver and rice stuffing (a crude pâté

71

in a casing) was like nothing we'd ever eaten before. We loved it. The red beans and rice were just plain well-cooked and purposely bland to inspire liberal dashes from the bottles of Cajun Chef Hot Sauce, Cajun Chef Sport Peppers, Tabasco, and filé (ground sassafras) assembled on each table.

If Cajun cooking doesn't tickle your fancy, A1-T's also serves fresh-shucked oysters and steaks cut and cooked to order. Don't pass up the pickled eggs on your way out.

HOURS Mon. 10 am–10 pm; Tues.–Wed. 6 am–10 pm; Fri.–Sat. 6 am–11 pm; Sun. 8 am–10 pm.

SPECS Hwy. 124 Spur 5; (409) 296-9818; AE/MC/V; full bar.

DIRECTIONS **Eastbound:** Take Exit 829 to stop sign and turn right. A1-T's is set back off the highway on the left, in just under ½ mile.

Westbound: Take Exit 829 to stop sign and turn left under I-10, then as above.

THE GAZEBO, *Exit 852B, Beaumont*

Behind the leaded glass door of the Gazebo lurks a dessert table so compelling you'll never get out with your diet intact. Early American antiques, pink and green table linens, and pastel arrangements of silk flowers do their best to distract, but all around the room grande dames in brooches and debs in pearls have to struggle to pay full attention to their finger sandwiches. They speak anxiously of weddings and parties, wardrobes and college, but their hearts belong to the lemon chiffon pie.

Light lunches of soups and sandwiches, crepes and salads maintain an air of nutritional propriety. So if your mother's watching, mind your manners and begin with the shrimp remoulade, served in an avocado with fruit and a basket of garlic bread ($6.95). The homemade cheese soup is pleasantly light, not spoon-bogging, with a strong flavor of cheddar and an afterthought of onion. Nibblers will love the Taster's Salad Plate: chicken, tuna, crab, and shrimp salad served with fresh fruit ($6.95). Hamburgers and crepes are offered for those of more manly appetite, and dinner specials include top sirloin, broiled snapper, shrimp scampi, and lamb chops served with au gratin potatoes, fresh vegetables, and salad.

Once you've cleaned your plate, it's time to cruise the desserts (try not to bolt out of your chair): lemon chiffon pie beautiful enough to make you weep but light enough to absolve you from your sin (except for a devilishly rich crushed-pecan crust); a chocolate cream pie as dark as all secret desire; Amaretto cheesecake (don't be fooled by its apparent simplicity—this cake has done in many a diet); and the decadence of a pecan ball (ice cream rolled in pecans and smothered in hot fudge).

Those who resist the whipped-cream sirens should treat themselves or their loved one to one of the exquisite silk dresses at Jo Ann's Jazz, next door. A fitting reward for such a splendid show of self-control.

HOURS Lunch: Tues.–Sat. 11 am–2pm. Dinner: Fri–Sat. 6 pm– 9:30 pm. Closed Sun. and Mon.

SPECS 6445 Calder in The Carillon West; (713) 860-3594; AE/MC/V; full bar and wine list.

DIRECTIONS **Westbound:** Take Exit 852B/Calder and follow the access road to Calder (the third light). Turn right onto Calder, which is also Phelan at this point. ■ Stay on Phelan when Calder splits off. After about 1½ miles you reach the Kennedy light. Turn left at Kennedy and immediately right, back onto Calder (which zigzags across Phelan all along the route). Stay on Calder until you see The Carillon West, a blue, peach, and yellow Victorian façade.

Eastbound: Take Exit 852B and continue along access road to Calder. Turn left and cross under the interstate, then as above from ■.

CHEZ RENÉE, *Exits 853C and 855B, Beaumont*

We have to say right off the bat that we didn't have much luck the day we dined in the pink and maroon dining room of this white elephant of a mansion (although we did love the poppy print wallpaper). The day's lunch special of oven-fried chicken, corn on the cob, and cauliflower had been warmed to death (we were the last diners of the lunch hour,) and the home-

made bread had been reheated so often it was about as edible as shoe leather.

But we were still impressed with Renée, who stopped by our table to recommend we try his Cajun cooking next time. He sounded convincing enough about his kitchen abilities; maybe he should spend more time overseeing the ovens and less time glad-handing the customers. He did leave us hungry for his alligator sauce picante and frogs' legs, and the promise of crawfish coupled with the abilities of the piano player make us want to give Chez Renée a second chance.

The waitress of the century award goes to Norma-the-head-waitress (so said her badge); as the only waitress in sight, she ran herself half to death with her smile clamped in place.

If you're not inclined to take your chances on Renée's kitchen, head a block over to the Green Beanery (2121 McFaddin between 5th and 6th), a quiche and crepe restaurant that gets a lot of raves. A much-touted Italian restaurant that we didn't get to try (we were too busy getting lost) is Patrizi's (2050 IH 10 between College and Washington).

HOURS   Lunch: Tues.–Fri. 11:30 am–2 pm. Dinner: Tues.–Sat. 6 pm–11 pm.

SPECS   797 N. 5th; (713) 838-4003; AE/MC/V; full bar.

DIRECTIONS   **Eastbound:** Take Exit 853C and continue along access road east to the stop sign and turn right. Drive 7 blocks to Hazel and turn right. Chez Renée is on the right-hand corner of 5th and Hazel, 1 mile from the interstate. To return to I-10 without backtracking, follow 5th south (right) 3 blocks to Calder. Turn left on Calder and continue to Pearl. Turn left on Pearl and drive to I-10.

Westbound: Take Exit 855B to Magnolia, turn left, and cross under I-10 to Calder. Turn right onto Calder and drive 2 miles to 5th. Turn right on 5th and drive 3 blocks to Chez Renée on the left-hand corner of 5th and Hazel. To return to I-10, take Hazel to 7th and turn right. Follow 7th St. 7 blocks to I-10. Cross under and turn left on access road to continue west on I-10.

Arizona

1895 HOUSE, *Van Buren St. Exit, Phoenix*

See page 28 for description of this downtown restaurant where secretaries and judges feel equally at ease.

DIRECTIONS From Van Buren St. Exit, turn right if northbound, left if southbound. In 1.9 miles, turn left onto 2nd Ave. The 1895 House is on the left in the middle of the block.

THE GOOD EGG, *Camelback Rd. Exit, Phoenix*

This breakfast and lunch place is a bit farther from the freeway than we'd like, but neither the highway department nor the restaurant owner were willing to relocate for us, so in rush-hour traffic it may take you a little longer than ten minutes to get here. But after tasting the food, we doubt you'll regret the extra time.

Popular among The Good Egg's breakfasts are frittatas. Our favorite is Swiss Scramble, a melange of ham, mushrooms, tomato, black olive, and sour cream held together with eggs and topped with melted cheese. With a side of country potatoes and an English muffin, the Swiss Scramble weighs in at $4.90. Another dish, called The Pope, is described as a "plump Papal Polish sausage" with mustard and Swiss cheese plus eggs, potatoes, and muffin ($4.95). A variety of omelettes and pancakes (how does cashew blueberry strike you?) are also big pleasers here, and the breakfast special—2 scrambled eggs under chile and melted cheese, with a side of potatoes, and a tortilla—is terrific

($4.75). The chocolate chip walnut muffin, made with whole wheat flour and blueberry yogurt, just melted us away.

At lunchtime, salads and sandwiches are popular, the latter served with potatoes and fruit ($4.25–$5.50).

The atmosphere and design are pure yupster—framed wall prints, soft, distinct colors, an outdoor patio, cutesy menu—but the high-quality food makes it more than bearable.

HOURS   6:30 am–2:30 pm daily. Closed Christmas.

SPECS   606 E. Camelback; (602) 274-5393; MC/V; no booze.

DIRECTIONS   Northbound, take unnumbered Camelback Rd. Exit, and turn right (left, if southbound). The Good Egg, marked by a chicken wearing a top hat, is on the left after 3.1 miles, shortly after 7th St. light.

THE CAFE AT ARCOSANTI, *Exit 262, Cordes Junction*

In the 1960s an Italian-born architect named Paolo Soleri began a most ambitious and wondrous project—the construction of a city from scratch in the high desert country, a city based upon novel approaches to design, society, and environment. The concept he calls "arcology," and the city, Arcosanti. The initial stages are nearing completion, more is built every year, and the vision remains. Viewing the progress is encouraged, and tours ($4) are scheduled daily. Students of architecture, design, urban planning, and environment are especially interested.

A handful of people live and work at Arcosanti, so for them and the tourists who motor in, a dining spot was established in 1983. All the food is as whole grain and natural as it can be. A breakfast burrito ($1.50) contains potato, eggs, bell peppers, salsa, mushrooms, and onion. French toast (3 slices, $2.50) is popular, as are the fruit salad (with yogurt or cottage cheese, $3.75) and soups ($2). One flight up, a bakery supplies fresh rolls ($1.10) and desserts. In a garden and greenhouse, Arcosanti produces its own lettuce, spinach, snow peas, herbs, mushrooms, and carrots. Leftovers go in compost heaps to help the next crop

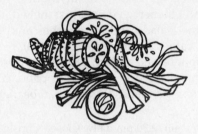

along. "We serve a large variety of vegetarian meals," explained cafe manager Ron. "People seem to expect it."

Upstairs, the visitors' center displays schematic diagrams and three-dimensional scale models of the envisioned city. Most of Arcosanti's activities are funded by the sale of Soleri's famous wind chimes, some ceramic (as low as $11), others bronze (one 3-story aluminum cast bronze alloy set costs $15,000). With a gentle breeze, your visit will be serenaded by wind chimes in their unmistakable symphonic clatter.

HOURS   8:30 am–5:30 pm daily. Closed Thanksgiving and Christmas (and the three or four days annually when the mud-caked road is absolutely impassable).

SPECS   Cordes Junction; (602) 632-7135; MC/V; beer.

DIRECTIONS   **Northbound:** take Exit 262 into the gas station and minimart village of Cordes Junction (southbound: Exit 262-A), turn left; Arcosanti is at the end of a 2½ mile winding dirt road. (Believe the sign that says "SLIPPERY WHEN WET—MUD RISK.")

LA BELLAVIA, *Route 89A, northernmost freeway exit,* *Flagstaff*

See page 185 for description of this comfortable hangout in the city beneath the San Francisco Peaks.

DIRECTIONS   Continue north when the freeway ends. In about 1 mile, turn right at the light onto W. Clay Ave. In 3 blocks, turn left onto Beaver St. In 2½ blocks, La Bellavia is on the right, with picket fencing out front (just before a laundromat).

SALSA BRAVA, *Route 89A, northernmost freeway exit, Flagstaff*

See page 183 for description of this quality Mexican fast-food joint.

DIRECTIONS Continue north when freeway ends; in 0.3 mile, turn right into Greentree Village Shopping Center. Salsa Brava is on the near end of the main row of stores.

I-19

Arizona

ABOUT INTERSTATE 19

I-19 has the odd distinction of being America's only interstate whose signs measure distance in kilometers only. That 107 between Tucson and Nogales is kilometers, not miles. Let us know if driving 107 killometers makes you hungrier than driving 67 miles.

ABOUT NOGALES, MEXICO

It'd be a shame to travel within two miles of another country and not cross into it. Jack Kerouac called the sensation of crossing into Nogales "a great feeling of entering the Pure Land." We sought out that feeling by driving to the border, locking the car on the U.S. side, and walking into Mexico. Clothing and arts & crafts items from Mexico's interior crowd every curio shop. Some handmade goods are admirable, some are tacky, but all deserve a good look. On Calle Campía—the big street leading to Avenida Obregón, the main tourist drag, blow U.S. 50¢ on a lottery ticket (drawings held twice weekly, results posted at virtually every street corner in the country) or U.S. $2 at the Nogales Turf Club, the legal off-track betting parlor featuring U.S. and Mexican dog and horse tracks. Or if you'd prefer to waste your money on a sure thing, spend $3 to have a picture taken of you and your family wearing silly oversized sombreros, sitting astride a donkey harnessed to a cart.

Eating in Nogales, Mexico, has always been a treat. One favorite is **Elvira's** (to the right a couple of blocks just after you cross over, pressed up against the international fence), from whose door you can watch the game—cat and mouse to some, life and death to others—of Mexicans climbing through and over the fence into the United States. **Cafe Olga** (Juárez 37, a half-block down from Calle Campía), a working-class diner with a lengthy, bilingual menu, is a reliable stop for good solid meals (the lengua entomada—tongue in tomato sauce—costs $3.50). For somewhat more cheerful surroundings, **La Posada** is popular for its lunch specials ($2.85) and steak tampiqueña ($4.25). (With your back to the fence, walk a few blocks down Obregón to Pierson, turn right to No. 116, on your right.) The seafood at **El Merendero** (ten minutes more down the street to Obregón 601—look on the left side for the shark above the restaurant) invariably pleases us, especially its full-flavored soups—shrimp, seafood, and turtle, among others ($1.25 to $2.85); its octopus, breaded, curried, or with oyster sauce ($3.05–$3.65); and its sea bass, served 11 different ways ($3 tops).

All these restaurants are within walking distance of the border, and all prices are given in U.S. dollars.

ZULA'S *Exit 4, Nogales*

"If you're from Nogales," a friend said, "the biggest and best treat you could ever have was a Zulaburger. Your folks would take you there as a kid, you'd go there after school football games with your date, and if you moved away, you'd sneak in a Zulaburger whenever you visited home." So when we got to Nogales, we assembled a party and headed straight for Zula's.

The youngest person at our table ordered the item in question and we discovered that a Zulaburger by any other name is a cheeseburger. A very good cheeseburger, but a cheeseburger nonetheless ($2.25). Another of our party went for Tita's Burger, ensconced in Swiss cheese, bacon, and 1,000 Island dressing—a hybrid of a Zulaburger, a Reuben sandwich, and a BLT, and also very good.

That left two of us. One had the day's special, baked lamb shank and rice pilaf ($5.95), while the other splurged on shrimp Papachuris ($10.95), named for the Greek-Mexican owner and cook. (Posters of Greece line the walls.) The well-proportioned lamb delighted us with its tenderness; in fact, it verily slid off the shank. The large pieces of shrimp, imported from Guaymas, on Sonora's west coast, were marinated in ouzo and then baked into a casserole with feta cheese; it's original with owner George P., and although the ingredients were excellent and the concept intriguing, we found that the anise-flavored ouzo and the delicate shrimp made for a less blissful marriage than we'd expected.

Other dishes include a Greek salad they make in two sizes ($3.50 and $4.95), and carne machaca—shredded beef served with green chile, onion, tomato, and a flour tortilla. Slices of hot apple and pecan pie come topped with a light cinnamon sauce that impressed us all, especially the Zulaburger consumer. "Tell 'em not to miss it for the world," he said.

HOURS   Mon–Sat. 6 am–9 pm; Sun. 6 am–8 pm. Closed Thanksgiving, Christmas, and New Year's Day.

SPECS   1267 Grand Ave.; (602) 287-2892; no credit cards; beer and wine.

DIRECTIONS   From Exit 4, turn right if northbound, left if southbound, and right in 0.9 mile at the traffic light. Drive 1.3 miles, and just before overhead railroad tracks Zula's will be on the left. If you're coming directly from the international border, go straight for 1.8 miles; Zula's will be on the right just after you pass under the railroad tracks.

THE COW PALACE, *Exit 48, Amado*

This used to be a fairly authentic local cowboy joint on the Old Nogales Highway, but since the interstate was built and a sizable retirement community plunked down just up the road, fancy new cars far outnumber dusty old pickups.

Had we arrived for breakfast, we would have tried the chocolate-covered pancakes with whipped cream ($2.25), or the charbroiled rib-eye steak with eggs, hash browns, and toast ($5.75). What we found at dinnertime was a full sandwich selection ($3–$4), but given the unseasonably chilly temperature, we opted instead for one of the Cold Weather Specials, a bowl of wrangler stew ($2.25). Tender chunks of beef made this offering far superior to your basic run-of-the-road stew, and to show our pleasure we hoisted our huge (16-ounce!) margaritas to the photograph behind the bar of John Wayne sitting in The Cow Palace. We were aware, of course, that when he was here, the Duke probably skipped the stew and dug into one of The Cow Palace's hefty steaks, clearly their biggest draw ($9–$13). But we also supposed that he would have found, as we did, that the hot apple pie with rum butter sauce dessert promised more than it delivered.

The place is especially full on weekend evenings, when diners accompany a piano and saxophone to "Home on the Range," "Deep in the Heart of Texas," "Wild Irish Rose," and other sing-alongs. On your way out, take a good look at the outrageous thirty-feet-tall cow skull framing the entrance to the otherwise undistinguished cafe across the road; it was featured in the Ellen Burstyn–Kris Kristofferson movie *Alice Doesn't Live Here Anymore*.

HOURS 8 am–9 pm daily including holidays, except Christmas Day.

SPECS 28802 S. Nogales Highway; (602) 398-2201; V/MC; full bar.

DIRECTIONS **Southbound:** From Exit 48 (Arivaca Rd.), turn right to stop sign, and right again. Cow Palace is on your left.

Northbound: From Exit 48 (Arivaca Rd.), turn left to stop sign, then right to Cow Palace on left.

CORA'S CAFE, *Exit 99, Tucson*

See page 34 for description of this working-class restaurant, where a sign on the cash register says "OUR MEXICAN FOOD IS SO AUTHENTIC WE URGE YOU NOT TO DRINK THE WATER."

DIRECTIONS From Exit 99 (Ajo Way), turn right at the light and right again after 1 mile onto 6th Ave. At the next major intersection, turn right on Irvington Road. Cora's is in the second building on your right.

EL CHARRO, *Exit 101B, Tucson*

See page 31 for description of this Tucson landmark known for its excellent food and its argumentative owner.

DIRECTIONS From Exit 101B enter I-10 West. In 1.7 miles, leave I-10 at Exit 257A, and turn right. Go straight through the traffic light at Granada. In 0.4 mile, bear right at the sign reading "CENTRAL BUSINESS DISTRICT" and then take an immediate right onto Court St. El Charro is in the second block on the right, the second building from the corner, with a front porch patio.

CAFE OLÉ, *Exit 101B, Tucson*

See page 33 for description of this leisure-time coffee house run by a Nicaraguan and Scottish couple.

DIRECTIONS From Exit 101B enter I-10 West. In about 1½ miles, leave I-10 at Exit 258 (Congress St./Broadway) and turn right. Go 0.8 mile to Cafe Olé, on your left, half a block after the light at 6th Ave. (121 E. Broadway).

Texas

AMERICAN MOTOR INN RESTAURANT, *Exit 39,*
Pecos

The local gimme cap (you know, those billed "GMC" and "Cat" caps that the good ol' boys get when they tell their tractor and truck dealers: "gimme one of them caps") and Stetson crowd likes the American Motor Inn Restaurant just fine. In fact, when we turned up here one evening there was scarcely a hatless head in sight.

A fairly generic coffee shop complete with metallic gold booths, wall-length counter, and loud-mouthed waitresses, the American keeps customers happy with mounds of mashed potatoes, slabs of steak, ladles of pan gravy, and healthy doses of home-canned green beans ($4.50). Hamburgers demand an attentive two-hand grip (even by lion-pawed roughnecks), and when you order them medium rare you get them that way.

The homemade vegetable soup was good enough, and our waitress (who wore sunglasses on top of her head in lieu of a hat) was anxious to please despite our arrival just before the CLOSED sign went in the window. Not wanting to keep her any later, we passed on the home-baked pies and cakes, and listened as the good ol' boys said their good-nights and promised to be back for homemade biscuits in the morning.

HOURS Every day, 6 am–10 pm.

SPECS 2116 W. Hwy. 80; (915) 445-5431; no credit cards; no bar.

DIRECTIONS   Westbound: Take Exit 39, turn right, and continue 1 mile to 3rd St. (U.S. Hwy. 80). ■ Left on 3rd. American Motor Inn is several blocks down, on the left.

Eastbound: Take Exit 39 as it curves around to the right. Turn right to cross under I-20 and continue 1 mile to 3rd, then as above from ■.

COLONIAL INN RESTAURANT, *Exit 80, Monahans*

Monahans has the truly West Texas distinction of being home to the world's largest oil tank, a 1,500-foot boondoggle built by Shell Oil in 1928 and used unsuccessfully until the invention of pipelines put it out of its leaky misery. Of more interest is the nearby Monahans Sandhills State Park, a desert wonderland of blowing dunes and Harvard oaks. You could picnic at the park, but if gritty sandwiches stick in your craw, skip off the interstate and into the parking lot of the Colonial Best Western.

For a motel restaurant, the Colonial Inn was pleasantly surprising. Both the coffee shop and the more formal dining room are newly decorated in pastel shades of pink and green, and the day's all-you-can-eat buffet ($4.30) was a bounteous spread featuring chicken in sweet and sour vegetables, baby carrots, corned beef, chicken-fried steak, green beans (canned), au gratin potatoes, cornbread, five or six different molded salads, a salad bar, and tapioca pudding for dessert. The food was satisfying, if not overwhelming, and for the price you can scarcely be disappointed.

Breakfast offerings include grits and some fine homemade biscuits served with real butter and honey.

You may eat in either dining room but in the coffee shop expect to find oil men as thick as flies, sharing their tables with calculators (and reams of calculations), drinking bottomless cups of coffee, and swapping tales about bottomless wells.

HOURS Every day, 6 am–10 pm.

SPECS I-20 at TX Hwy. 18; (915) 943-4345; V/MC; no bar.

DIRECTIONS **Westbound:** Take Exit 80 and turn left to cross under I-20; immediately turn right on the access road. The Colonial is on the left.

Eastbound: Take Exit 80 and stay on access road to the Colonial.

THE BARN DOOR
PECOS DEPOT, *Exit 116, Odessa*

We think we must have been at the Barn Door on the wrong day. *Everyone,* from national travel writers to *Texas Monthly* magazine, has given the nod to this 48-year-old restaurant. But at four in the afternoon the place was empty and our sandwich was tired, cold, and unimpressive. There's a bawdy red Gay Nineties Room and a mock-opulent Gold Room, and, of course, the Barn Room (we liked the primitive farm implements). But so much decor always makes us wonder how well the food competes.

From our samplings, we determined that the homemade soup is worth your full attention—macaroni and tomato, okra and rice, vegetable, cream of potato, or whatever the daily offering might be. And after five you are greeted with a block of cheese the size of a bundt cake and a whole loaf of homemade bread. Soup, cheese, and bread—a satisfying peasant tradition. If you want nothing more than cheese and bread, it will cost you two bucks, but it's complimentary with dinner.

Beyond the cheese, soup, and bread, we advise you to stick with the steaks. We tried the day's special prime rib sandwich and though the meat was rare (as requested) the bread was stale store-bought rye. The French fries were cold, mealy, and flavorless. Still, we don't see how you could go wrong with a T-bone, tenderloin, or pepper steak. There's a five-foot red-hot grill in the middle of the Barn Room, and we can imagine that when the restaurant gets busy you can hardly hear yourself think for all the sizzling. Even in the dead quiet of late afternoon, the heat of the grill reminds you it's there, waiting for action.

The adjacent Pecos Depot is primarily a bar but does serve a limited menu of soup and sandwiches.

HOURS Mon.–Thurs. 11 am–10 pm. Fri. & Sat. 11 am–11 pm. Closed Sun.

SPECS   23rd and North Grant (Hwy. 385); (915) 337-4142; all cards; full bar.

DIRECTIONS   **Westbound:** Take Exit 116/Hwy. 385, turn left onto access road, and continue to stop sign. Turn right onto Grant (Hwy. 385) and drive 2½ miles to the Barn Door, on the right.

Eastbound: Take Exit 116 and turn left on Grant (Hwy. 385) to cross under interstate. Go 2½ miles to the Barn Door, on the right.

MURRAY'S SUBURBAN, *Exit 134, Midland*

We were looking for the famed Robert's Copper Pot when we found Murray's Suburban. And while even Murray's owner Bart Hotchkiss praises Robert's relocated deli, we were so happy with what we found at Murray's that we ended our search for the Copper Pot.

When Hotchkiss moved here from Houston many years ago, he was distressed to find that Midland was lacking in delis. A man who knows a good Wiener schnitzel when he bites into one, Hotchkiss determined to set things to rights by opening a deli of his own. Murray's (there is no Murray) is a delicatessen lover's delight, as much for its unexpectedly luxurious setting as for the quality of its food.

Located in a strip shopping center filled with carpet stores and real estate offices, Murray's is nevertheless worthy of at least an hour's stopover. Play a game of darts, read a book (the shelves are spilling over with everything from Gothic romances to encyclopedias). Trivial Pursuit buffs can terrorize other diners while indulging a yen for Chinese beer and the Permian Basin's best Reuben sandwich ($3.75).

While everything Murray's serves is made fresh daily, we have to rave most about the stew. Eighteen spices (lots of marjoram and basil) and an honest proportion of beef to veggies make this a stew to challenge an Irishman's loyalty. And then there's the crab salad, more crab than salad; it had us thinking that we were at the seashore.

Soon, Hotchkiss promises, after-five specials will include a build-your-own burger and a pork schnitzel, but for the time being, you'll just have to decide between bratwurst and Polish sausage, between Turkey Mornay on an English muffin and any of a dozen sandwiches made with Murray's homemade mayonnaise on fresh-baked bread. Not to mention the 60 varieties of imported beer, and cheesecake, brownies—whatever Bart Hotchkiss might be cooking up. He's already considering opening his own bakery, just so he can get a decent croissant to go with his morning coffee.

HOURS   Mon.–Sat. 10:30 am–9:30 pm. Closed Sun.

SPECS   3211 West Wadley; (915) 697-3433; V/MC; beer and wine.

DIRECTIONS   From Exit 134 turn right if westbound, left if eastbound, onto Midkiff. In 4½ miles turn right on Wadley. Murray's is one block down, on the right. It's a bit out of the way, but worth the drive.

Note: Murray's Downtown is closer to I-20, but it serves only cold sandwiches. If that's all you want, you'll find Murray's Downtown at 111 West Wall (see the Wallstreet Bar and Grill, below, for directions to Wall). By the way, Robert's Copper Pot, the other deli in town, is now located in the Claydesta National Bank, on Wadley at North Big Spring.

WALLSTREET BAR AND GRILL, *Exit 136, Midland*

After miles of chuckwagon chow, this intimate, dimly lit restaurant was an oasis of uptown elegance. We'd missed table linens, and our salivary glands, long since paralyzed by jalapeños and hickory smoke, were moved by the sight of the lightly fried oysters on our neighbors' plates. When we saw the fresh mushrooms sautéed in butter, we knew we'd left the Crisco trail at last.

From our table at the very back of the restaurant, we enjoyed an excellent view of the action, but it was the city noises that amazed us after a week of dining in quiet cafes. The drone of investment bankers met the whispers of platinum blondes, and bounced off the guffaws of men in silvery Stetsons. The men in vested suits clattered over the fresh fish of the day (gulf red snapper), while the denim crowd slurped oysters from their shells. Above the front door, a Wall Street ticker tape (the *real* Wall Street) clacked out market trends. Amid this luncheon chorus our clam chowder arrived steaming hot, and thick with fresh clams, potatoes, and cream. Although we had intended to follow it with boiled shrimp (2 dozen for $5.50), the soup proved to be so filling that we felt gluttonous even considering a slice of almond Amaretto cheesecake—but not so gluttonous that we didn't succumb. The only flaw in an otherwise soul-regenerating experience was the oily coffee, which we blamed on the West Texas water (we guess it tastes of a wildcatter's fantasy).

As the last of the spike heels tapped out the door, we closed our eyes and listened to the whir of the ceiling fans, and sighed at the thought of the desert drive ahead.

HOURS Lunch: Mon.–Fri. 11 am–2:30 pm. Dinner: Mon.–Sun. 5–11 pm (till midnight on Fri. & Sat.). Sun. brunch: 11 am–2 pm.

SPECS 115 E. Wall; (915) 684-8686; V/MC/AE; full bar and wine list.

DIRECTIONS From Exit 136, turn right if westbound, left if eastbound, onto TX Hwy. 349 (Rankin Hwy.). This road becomes Big Spring as you drive into town. After 2 miles, turn right onto Wall. The Wallstreet Bar and Grill is 3 blocks down, on the left (across from the post office).

ALBERTO'S CRYSTAL CAFE, *Exit 177, Big Spring*

There are seven Mexican restaurants in Big Spring. "We eat a lot of that stuff," one local told us. When we asked which one was the best, we were directed to Alberto's, with only one qualification. Aficionados of chile con queso are advised to search out La Posada. Since we weren't in the mood for a chile pepper cheese dip, we decided to see if Alberto's was as good as it was popular.

Albert and Sally Rodriquez started their cafe ten years ago, in the corner of an old pharmacy. Before long, Alberto's Crystal Cafe had expanded to fill the entire building, and now it's a turquoise and orange Mexican hodgepodge, with an emphasis on bulls, matadors, and mirrors.

As for the food, Alberto's serves huge, sizzling-hot platters of pleasantly gloppy Mexican homestyle cooking. There's nothing slick about the presentation—they just load up the plates at the stove like mama used to do. We split Alberto's Macho Platter, a he-man combination of beef burrito, first-rate chile relleno, refried beans, Spanish rice, and the obligatory three green peas. ($5.95). The only thing on the platter that was below par was the taco, overflowing with ground beef, but a little on the greasy side. The crock of hot sauce was filled with crudely chopped onions, tomatoes, and serrano peppers. Hot as a *pistola*, it could cure the common cold.

HOURS Mon.–Sat. 11 am–9:30 pm. Closed Sun.

SPECS 120 E. 2nd; (915) 267-9024; no credit cards; beer and wine.

DIRECTIONS From Exit 177, turn left if westbound, right if eastbound, onto TX Hwy. 87. Continue straight into town, and in about 1 mile, turn left on 2nd. Alberto's is two blocks down, on the right, at the corner of 2nd and Runnels.

TAYLOR'S TRUCKTOWN, *Exit 217, Colorado City*

Our innkeeper did his level best to keep us out of this place. "You never know who'll be sitting next to you," he warned. Instead, he convinced us to try Mac-Michael's, a brand new, country-cute restaurant just up the access road from Trucktown. Mac-Michael's is clean, neat as a pin, and boring. A trip through the undistinguished salad bar cost $4.75, and the baked fish was light-years away from its swimming days. We should have known better than to order anything other than steak in a place like this. (Our very respectable dining neighbors were sawing into theirs with satisfied expressions.) If you want to give Mac-Michaels a chance, stick with the beef. After our thoroughly unsatisfying meal, we decided to try Trucktown to see what it might offer in the way of dinner amusement.

As expected, it was splendidly grimy, from the orange-and-black murals (coyotes, cowpokes, and prairie dogs) to the curio pieces (Bob the Dachshund and a black-velvet version of *The Last Supper* complete with clock). As for the chow, it is very popular with a crowd that proved to be far from unsavory. We were surrounded by truckers, farmers, travelers, and local grandmothers paying careful attention to their chicken-fried steaks and enchiladas. We had intended only to check out Trucktown's ambience, but when we heard that there was only one piece of sweet potato pie left, we had no choice. It proved worthy of its popularity. Besides, it was the biggest wedge of pie we've ever seen served anywhere. So, while we can't vouch for the rest of the food, the pie and local color make Trucktown worth a stop.

HOURS 7 days, 24 hours.

SPECS I-20 at TX Hwy. 208; (915) 728-5325; no credit cards; no bar.

DIRECTIONS **Eastbound:** Take Exit 217 and drive along the access road half a block to the giant red CAFE sign. (Mac-Michael's is half a mile east, at the stop sign.)

Westbound: Take Exit 217 and immediately turn left to cross under the interstate. Mac-Michael's is dead ahead and Trucktown is ½ mile west, on the access road.

LA COCINA, *Exit 244, Sweetwater*

You're going to think we've led you astray when you first pull up here. Sure, La Cocina is the size of a dollhouse and yes, it's in the barrio—but once you've tasted the homestyle Mexican food, you'll remember that all the best Mexican restaurants started this way.

Everything about La Cocina (the "kitchen") is authentic family-style Mexican. Grandmother cooks (*"no habla inglés"*), daughter shuttles between the dining room, the drive-in-window, and the CPA office next door, and granddaughter serves up the chips and hot sauce. We had a hard decision between the gorditas (deep-fried corn cakes served with a spicy meat sauce, 95 cents) and the daily special of tamales ($4/dozen). We compromised and ordered the Number 1 Plate (taco, enchilada, tamale, rice, and beans—$2.45). We hadn't had Tex-Mex this good since San Antonio; the taco meat was spicy and greaseless, the tamale thick and meaty, and the enchilada was topped with a cheesy chili sauce so delicious that we ordered extra tortillas to sop up the last mouthfuls. A complimentary sopapilla is served with the Mexican dinners; though not the airy puff of dough we had expected, it was tasty in its own way—crunchy and cinnamon crusted, like an unstuffed fried pie. If you're lucky enough to show up here in warm weather, finish your meal with a raspa (snow cone), sold in a stand out back.

The food at La Cocina is not only delicious, it's cheap; miles down the road, we kept thinking about those tamales and fantasizing about shipping them home on dry ice by the caseload.

HOURS   Mon.–Sat. 11 am–2 pm; 5 pm–9 pm. Closed Sun.

SPECS   907 W. Alabama; (915) 235-2927; no credit cards; no bar.

DIRECTIONS   From Exit 244, turn right if westbound, left if eastbound, onto TX Hwy. 70/Lamar. Follow Lamar for just under a mile, then turn left onto Alabama (second light). Drive ½ mile down Alabama, past the baseball diamond, to La Cocina, tucked back off the street in a tiny brick house with a hand-lettered sign.

TURNERHILL HOUSE OF BAR-B-QUE, *Exit 279, Abilene*

There are three things to eat when you're in West Texas: steak, Mexican food, and barbecue. In Abilene we think we found the best restaurant in each category, all within a cowchip throw of each other. Of the three—the Royal Inn, Herrera's, and Turnerhill's—Turnerhill's is the tiniest, plainest, and the one most likely to inspire you to come this way again.

Turnerhill's serves West Texas barbecue at its smokiest, juiciest, no-frills, heart-breaking best. Ribs, brisket, chicken, ham, and sausage are slow-cooked in pits over smoldering hickory. And, we do mean *smoked:* spend two minutes here and you'll smell the hickory all the way to Sweetwater. We didn't mind, since the aromas that hitchhiked out on our clothing reminded us of the finger-licking good time we'd left behind.

Turnerhill's is about as fancy as a cowpuncher's picnic—paper napkins, paper cups, everything available to go, or you can spread your meat, white bread, onions, pickles, and peppers out at the counter. Not in the mood for a picnic? Stake out a table. A sign says: "BARBECUE IS HABIT-FORMING AND GOOD FOR YOUR HEALTH." We won't swear to the latter, but we guarantee the former to be God's truth.

HOURS Mon.–Sat. 9 am–7:30 pm. Closed Sun.

SPECS 320 North 1st; (915) 624-0465; no credit cards; no bar.

DIRECTIONS **Eastbound:** Take Exit 279 and turn right onto U.S. 80 Business, and continue through town. U.S. 80 becomes South 1st in town, and North 1st parallels South 1st, but north of the railroad tracks. About 5 miles into town, turn left at Willis. ■ Cross over the tracks and turn right immediately onto North 1st. Turnerhill's is a block east, on the left, in the Briarwood Crossing Shopping Center (behind Lusky's Western Wear).

Westbound: Exit on U.S. 80 Business, just east of Abilene, and follow the highway through town (it becomes South 1st). After about 5 miles, turn right at Willis, then as above from ■.

HERRERA'S, *Exit 279, Abilene*

Convicted scamster Billy Sol Estes made at least one good move for which he has never been given proper credit. When he decided to give up the restaurant business and move on to bigger investments, he sold the Herrera family just the property they'd been looking for. They've been here ever since, adding rooms every few years, until the original one-room cafe was surrounded by four square dining rooms and a lounge. We liked the colorful cubicles, the sequined sombreros, the Mexican dresses (for sale), and the fluorescent matchbook covers. But most of all, we liked the food.

Rule Number One: Forget the hamburgers and french fries. Concentrate your appetite on the 17 Tex-Mex entrees. For those who can't decide, Dinner Number Five is a good sampler platter (enchilada, tamale, taco, rice, beans, and guacamole for $6). Fajitas (chicken and beef) are the newest addition to the menu, and they arrive sizzling hot and juicy, with a full escort of pico de gallo along with guacamole and fresh tortillas ($6.25). Equally good is the chile relleno dinner; we heard several hosannas sung about the green enchiladas. We can't imagine that any dish here would disappoint. Even the homemade chips and hot sauce were equal to our most stringent demands: warm, non-greasy, sided with a bowl of just-so picante sauce.

Burro Alley, a stucco village of galleries and boutiques surrounding Herrera's, makes for a pleasant stroll, and in warm weather the restaurant offers al fresco dining in the courtyard.

HOURS Lunch: Mon–Fri. 11 am–2 pm. Dinner: Mon.–Fri. 5–10 pm; Sat. 11 am–10 pm; Sun. buffet 11 am–2 pm; Sun. dinner 5–9 pm.

SPECS South 1st (U.S. 80) at Willis; (915) 677-0961; V/MC; full bar.

DIRECTIONS Eastbound: Take Exit 279/U.S. 80 Business (which becomes South 1st in town) and drive 5 miles straight to Herrera's, on the right at Willis.

Westbound: As U.S. 80 Business cuts directly across Abilene, it is easiest to follow it into Herrera's from the point at which it branches off of I-20 just east of town. Exit onto U.S. 80 Business and drive 5 miles to Herrera's at Willis (on the left). To rejoin I-20, continue to follow U.S. 80 West out of town to the point at which it rejoins I-20.

ROYAL INN, *Exit 279, Abilene*

Looking for all the world like a Las Vegas stage designer's notion of King George's dining hall, the Royal Inn's lobby restaurant seats 500 amidst the pseudo-splendor of flocked wallpaper, low-hung chandeliers, gilded mirrors, pillars, and statuary.

But forget the décor. There may be a fine line between elegance and tackiness out here on the frontier, but there can be no doubt that the Royal Inn's line of steaks are in the best of taste. Don't even consider eating anything else here. A perfectly grilled Kansas City Strip for two ($15.80) easily serves three, and an order of prime rib overwhelms a standard dinner plate. Doubting Thomases should preview the inch-thick cuts displayed in the refrigerated case across from the registration desk—a carnivore's delight.

HOURS   Open 7 days, 6 am–10 pm.

SPECS   Hwy. 80 West; (915) 692-3022; V/MC/A; full bar and wine.

DIRECTIONS Eastbound: Take Exit 279/U.S. 80 Business and drive 3 miles to the Royal Inn, just west of Hwy. 277.

Westbound: Exit onto U.S. 80 Business just east of Abilene and follow the highway through town. Although the Royal Inn is about 7 miles from the interstate going into town, it is only 3 miles from the interstate on the west side of town (U.S. 80 cuts right through town, while I-20 skirts it). To rejoin I-20, continue following U.S. 80 west past the Royal Inn.

TRADITIONS, *Exit 332, Cisco*

Modest little Cisco, Texas, has at least two claims to fame: Conrad Hilton bought his first hotel here, and Santa Claus pulled his first heist just down the street from the original Hilton. The future hotelier bought the downtown Mobley Hotel in 1919, an investment that grew into a worldwide chain. As for poor old Santa, he was among three fellows who got full of the old Nick, dressed up in whiskers and fur one Christmas Eve 50 years ago, and robbed the local bank. The ringleader was hanged for his lack of holiday spirit.

The Cisco Chamber of Commerce directed us to several local restaurants that sounded promising: J.J.'s Picnic Basket (508 Conrad Hilton) is said to have great soup and admirable sandwiches; and the Cisco Steak House (on the access road just east of Traditions) is a favorite of the chamber director, but she admits that her aunt is the cashier there.

Traditions, the newest restaurant in town, is a former hotel coffee shop transformed into a tidy, family-run cafe. The menu is, well, traditional, but then what would you expect? We dropped in as they were serving up the day's special of chalupas ($2.50). The refried beans were flavorful and the tortillas were crisp, but the topping of pasteurized cheese was disappointing. Everyone around us seemed more than happy with their enormous burgers and grilled-to-order steaks. We think you're well advised to give them a try. We were too full to try the homemade pies delivered fresh daily by a local woman (blue-ribbon winners, from the looks of them). One more thing: there's a salad bar in a bathtub.

HOURS Mon.–Thurs. 6 am–9 pm; Fri. & Sat. 6 am–10 pm.

SPECS 302 East I-20; (817) 442-4020; no credit cards; no bar.

DIRECTIONS Westbound: From Exit 332, turn right immediately into the Oak Motel parking lot adjacent to Traditions.

Eastbound: From Exit 332, cross under the interstate and turn right immediately onto the north access road. Traditions is on the left.

THE SMOKESTACK, *Exit 367, Thurber*

You can't miss the Smokestack, the red-brick centerpiece of the fragmentary Thurber, a town that gave its life for the labor movement. In 1885, Thurber was a company-owned coal-mining town of 10,000 souls. In 1903, it became the only all-union town in the world, but fourteen years later the coal company broke the union's contract and attempted to operate the mines with scab labor. The townspeople held firm, the mines were closed, the company moved out, and Thurber—left to survive on the strength of a single brick factory—became a ghost town. Still standing is the handsome brickworks building which today houses one of the most popular restaurants along I-20.

There's nothing particularly interesting about the interior of the Smokestack (except for photographs of Thurber in its heyday), and the food falls somewhere between dependable and rib-sticking. But it's adequate and, even better, it's cheap! The standard traveler's breakfast of eggs, hashbrowns, biscuits (huge and light), and coffee goes for less than two bucks, and the Coal Miner's Special of two center-cut porkchops, two eggs, biscuits, country gravy, hash browns, and coffee is $4.50. Smokestack luncheon specials include a "Best in the West" Texas-sized meal of chicken-fried steak (hand-battered), *real* country cream gravy, salad, potatoes, and home-baked rolls for $5.75. For a light lunch, order the garden-fresh vegetables in a butter sauce ($1.35) or a hickory-smoked chopped barbecue sandwich ($3.25). Highly recommended is the pan-fried catfish, served with salad, potatoes, and a tangy red sauce. We noted a "Cowboy Lunch" special called the Super Randy Burger, and decided it had to be named after someone locally famous, not for its effect on the diner.

The Smokestack is given a good report in every guidebook covering these parts, but our friends who live down the road say the best restaurant in the area is Will's Cafe. Will's specialty is seafood, and patrons drive from as far as Fort Worth to enjoy it. Frogs' legs, a beer-and-wine license, and a lamp operated by an ivy plant are equally famous. We didn't set foot in Will's (they were mopping the floor), but we yelled in the door to find out the hours and to get a peek at that ivy lamp. If you are in this neck of the prairie Tuesday through Saturday anytime between 4:30 and 9 pm, give Will's a try—and let us know what you think of our friends' taste. Spic-and-span Will's is in Mingus, on TX Hwy. 108, half a mile north of the Smokestack, in what appears to be a trailer home sans wheels.

HOURS   Open 7 days, 8 am–10 pm.

SPECS   I-20 at TX 108 North; (817) 672-5505; no credit cards; no bar.

DIRECTIONS   From Exit 367/TX 108, turn right if westbound, left if eastbound; almost immediately, turn right into the Smokestack's parking lot.

ABOUT FORT WORTH

Barbara grew up in Fort Worth. Here are a few of her favorites that have withstood the test of time.

Massey's (1805 8th St.) is still the best place in Texas for chicken-fried steak, even if the waitresses think nothing of carrying fly swatters (or used to).

Barbara cut her teeth on the ribs at **Angelo's,** (2533 White Settlement), and she's never found another barbecue joint to call home. Every time she runs across brisket nearly as good, it turns out that the pit master learned his trade from Angelo. Even the *New York Times* has raved about this place; we give them credit for being Texas-savvy.

Aunt Betty took Barbara to **Hong Kong** (3522 Bluebonnet Circle) about once a week from the time she was old enough to hold chopsticks. You won't find better shrimp in lobster sauce, wonton soup, or cinnamon rolls anywhere.

Carshon's (3133 Cleburne) is the best deli in the city.

Joe T. Garcia's (2201 N. Commerce) is a longtime favorite for family-style Tex-Mex. It's a slope-floored *casita* grown into a brick-and-tile empire. We realize that bigger isn't necessarily better, but Garcia's is a tradition and if you want to *do* Fort Worth, you gotta go there just once.

Mi Charrito (5693 Westcreek) was discovered many years ago by our native daughter's brothers John and Jim, and the three of them still think it serves some of the best flautas (deep-fried, rolled tacos) in the state.

For Hunan cuisine, a complete description follows.

HUNAN, *Exit 433, Fort Worth*

This is a restaurant that pays attention to detail. It isn't enough to head the menu "Hunan-style Country Cooking";

there is also a map pinpointing the featured region of China. Good show, we thought, and got ourselves oriented.

This is not your typical lacquered-red Chinese restaurant. Instead, the interior is rather like a gray flannel suit gone high-tech. Tucked and rolled high-backed vinyl booths have an imperious quality; tables are dressed in linen; and just beyond all these blues and grays, as viewed from our table, a fuchsia light glows in a back hallway. Chinese music gargles in the background.

The food is equally understated, with first one flavor, then another jockeying for attention. And in everything we tried, there seemed to be an interplay of color and texture. An egg-drop soup was as golden and thick as honey yet crunchy with noodles. The flaky crab of the Crab Velvet had been marinated in frothy egg whites and sautéed with chewy mushrooms, crisp water chestnuts, and—unexpectedly—smoky bits of ham ($10.50). The menu is as poetic as the dishes. Phoenix shrimp is described as a "twin feast of taste and color."

Luncheon specials (served from 11:30 am–3 pm) include a spicy shrimp-with-peanuts dish, served with steamed rice and soup ($4.25). We were delighted with its slightly caramelized, hot pepper sauce, the slivers of fresh ginger throughout, and, best of all, almost four dozen shrimp. (We couldn't believe it either!) Just don't let that first bite fool you into thinking this isn't the spicy-hot dish it claims to be. Give the food a good stir, then ferret out the red peppers and set them aside. They're lovely to look at, but for the sake of your lips and tongue, let it go at that.

A side dish of stir-fried vegetables was as artfully presented and admirably prepared as the other dishes. In fact, the only sour notes of the day were growled by our waiter, an unaccountably surly fellow. The year of the ox, perhaps?

HOURS　Mon.–Thurs. 11:30 am–10 pm; Fri & Sat. 11:30 am–11 pm; Sun. noon–10 pm.

SPECS　4500 Bellaire Dr. South; (817) 737-7285; V/MC/AE; full bar.

DIRECTIONS　**Westbound:** Take Exit 433 and continue along access road west to the second light (Hulen); turn right on Hulen. ■ Drive 2 miles to Hunan, at the bottom of the hill, in the shopping center on the left.

Eastbound: Take Exit 433 to Hulen Dr. and turn left to cross under I-20, then as above from ■.

ABOUT DALLAS

See our overview of Dallas restaurants on pages 158–159, and other descriptions of Dallas restaurants on pages 129–130, 131–132, and 160–163. Unfortunately, none of these fine places is easy to reach if you're traveling through town on I-20, but after reading our reviews you might decide to take off your hat and stay awhile.

TRADER'S RESTAURANT, *Exit 527, Canton*

Since the 1870s, Canton has been host to First Monday Trade Day, an event that began with the monthly round-up and sale or trade of stray and wild stock. Over the years, the horse-trading day has evolved into an entire weekend of buying, selling, and swapping everything from coondogs to Queen Anne dining tables. As you drive into town, you'll pass the 35-acre pasture where the world's largest flea market convenes the weekend preceding the first Monday of the month. And where do the flea-swappers and horse-traders eat? Why, Trader's Restaurant, of course.

Vintage cafe outside, early Formica inside, Trader's isn't fancy, but it's a dependable place to eat a no-frills, meat-and-potatoes lunch or dinner. Calf's liver, chicken-fried steak, and deep-fried chicken are the old standbys here, served up steaming hot, with fresh vegetables, baked, mashed, or fried taters, and yeasty rolls (about $3.50). For those who can't pass up home-made grits, they're served all day long, as are all the breakfast items. Three-egg omelettes with hashbrowns, grits, biscuits, and gravy ($2.60) will keep you high in the saddle for many a mile.

HOURS   Sun.–Tues. 6 am–2 pm; Wed.–Sat. 6 am–9 pm.

SPECS TX Hwy. 64 at TX Hwy. 19; (214) 567-2296; no credit cards; no bar.

DIRECTIONS From Exit 527, turn right if eastbound, left if westbound, onto TX 19. In 1½ miles, it's on the right.

THE LOFT BAR-B-QUE, *Exit 562, Tyler*

It's next to impossible to see beyond the interstate hereabouts; the surrounding hills roll up on either side of the highway like the swells of a velvet ocean. To thwart the landscape, restaurants and service stations mount mile-high billboards. The one floating high above the Loft touts the Log Kabin Restaurant. Well, the "Kabin" is still here, but under a new name. No one has bothered to change the sign.

No matter. One look at the tiny log cabin surrounded by a hazy cloud of smoke and you know you're in barbecue country. Inside, piles of juicy, finger-sucking ribs, smoky brisket, slabs of ham, and chains of link sausage make you feel as though you're in a smokehouse. Not a bad feeling on a frosty evening. Order your beef by the pound ($4.50) or by the plate. Plate lunches come with beans, slaw, bread, onion, and such. Roast pork sandwiches ($2.05) are good enough to make you slap your grandmother, and the pies—oh, Lordy, the pies—are East Texas through and through. A sweet cinnamon-apple filling is ladled onto shortbread masquerading as a crust, and a—my, oh, my—sweet potato custard ($1.00 with coffee) will make you swear off pumpkin pie forever.

HOURS Mon.-Thurs. 9 am–6 pm; Fri & Sat. 9 am–7 pm; Sun. 10 am–7 pm.

SPECS I-20 at TX Hwy. 14; (214) 593-0381; no credit cards; no bar.

DIRECTIONS **Eastbound:** Take Exit 562 to first left (TX Hwy. 14), and cross over I-20. The Loft is on the left just north of the interstate.

Westbound: Take Exit 562 and continue straight across TX Hwy. 14 to the Loft.

LA HACIENDA, *Exit 589, Kilgore*

The mansion is a staid bastion of colonial stuffiness. The manicured grounds, home to the first swimming pool in East Texas, look much as they did the day FDR came to call on the Tom Potters, builders of this estate. You cruise up the drive, park in front of one of three garages, and enter a front door. Art deco mirrors and round windows surround a winding staircase—and therewith terminates the stately 1935 Potter home.

The entire center of the building has been transformed into the most Mexican of courtyards, a sensory fiesta of splashing fountains and brightly colored wallpapers splattered with the naive motifs of Indian bark paintings. Beneath the skylights of the second floor perch Bustamante-style papier-mâché toucans, parrots, and macaws. The effect of all the merriment surrounded by the façade of the old house is absolutely astonishing. Better yet, the Mexican food served here is a delightfully incongruous marriage of traditional Tex-Mex and Louisiana seafood. Seafood burritos? A colonial hacienda? Why not? It all seems to work beautifully.

All the house specialties are recommendable, but we were especially taken with the seafood tostada—a shell-shaped tostada stuffed with crabmeat, bay shrimp, and Pacific red snapper, served with Spanish rice, seafood sauce, avocado, sour cream, and even more shrimp ($5.95). The platters of more traditional fare—enchiladas, beans, rice, tamale, and taco ($6.95)—are huge and just picante enough to make them memorable. If you love fajitas but hate to pass up the more exotic fare, try the nachos al carbon as appetizers—nachos with fajita meat ($5.25). It's all great fun, except for the fried ice cream—forget it! Have one of the 26 coffee drinks instead.

HOURS Mon.–Thurs. 11 am–2 pm and 5 pm–9:30 pm; Fri. & Sat. 11 am–10:30 pm.

SPECS TX Hwy. 259; (214) 983-1629; V/MC/AE; private club with memberships available ($6.00) (non-alcholic "mocktails" served in the dining room).

DIRECTIONS **Eastbound:** Take Exit 589 to TX Hwy. 259 and turn right; La Hacienda is 1½ miles down, on your left, across from the Ramada Inn.

Westbound: Take Exit 589 (stay in left lane of I-20 for the exit), and follow TX Hwy. 259 South for 1½ miles; it's on the left, across from the Ramada Inn.

JOHNNY CACE'S, *Exit 596, Longview*

Red vinyl, wrought iron, plate-slinging plush—Johnny Cace's is a bring-the-whole-family gourmet restaurant serving first-rate renditions of Louisiana Cajun classics. No-nonsense waitresses hustle to your beck and call. The kitchen is fast, the fish arrives cooked to flaky perfection, and the rice and gumbo come steaming but not mushy.

From the moment we sat down in this large, efficient restaurant, there was food on the table; after 3 pm, a tray of house relishes featuring lagniappe (the traditional "little gift" of a Cajun merchant) is served. We dug right into the crock of cheddar cheese, delicate fingers of okra, and bread-and-butter pickles served with a basket of herbed bread sticks.

After ordering a Royal Trio Platter (a monstrous shrimp stuffed with fresh crabmeat, perfectly prepared trout almondine, and plump and buttery scallops à la maison, $8.95) and crawfish étoufée (a thick and spicy gumbo studded with crawfish tails and petite shrimp, $8.95), we settled back to watch the oyster shuckers going at it. They shucked and plucked non-stop all evening;

no wonder the restaurant trucks in crateloads of Louisiana bivalves every night.

Don't skip dessert, especially if you've never experienced a real blackbottom pie, and when it's all said and done, sit a spell and mull over the house motto:

Saville dar deygo
a tousan busis in arow
Nojo demsnot busis dems trucks
summit cousin summit duks.

Give up? Ask your waitress for a translation.

HOURS   Tue.–Thurs. 11 am–11 pm; Fri. & Sat. 11 am–midnight; Sun. 3 pm–10 pm.

SPECS   1501 E. Marshall Ave.; (214) 753-7691; all credit cards; beer and wine served in the dining room; private club with full bar (memberships available $4.00).

DIRECTIONS   Take Exit 596 to Eastman Rd. and turn left if eastbound, right if westbound. Drive 3½ miles to TX Hwy. 80/Marshall Ave., and turn left. Restaurant is on the right about a block down.

ABOUT MARSHALL

We arrived in Marshall on Sunday, a day when many of the city's restaurants slumber. But by driving around and asking a lot of questions, we were able to make note of several interesting spots you might wish to try for lunch, dinner, or even high tea.

While downtown Marshall is four miles off the interstate, a drive to the North Washington Historic District is worth the time. At the foot of the avenue, past the grandly restored Victorian homes, and alongside the railroad tracks, is the 1896 **Ginnochio Hotel,** now open as a restaurant. **Sam's Cheesecakes,** which used to be next door, has, alas, moved to Red River Village on Hwy. 59 and is also worth seeking out if you're a cheesecake connoisseur.

On the other side of the interstate, **Marshall Pottery,** the largest maker of red clay pots in the U.S., has opened a lunch and tea room about which we hear excellent reports from no less an authority than Ruthmary Jordan, a well-known East Texas restaurateur. The pottery also sells glassware, dried flowers, candles, linens, cookware, and more in a shopping area so extensive you'll need to stop for a cup of tea and some ribbon sandwiches while you study the pottery's map.

DIRECTIONS To get to the **Ginnochio,** take Exit 617 onto TX Hwy. 59 and go left 4 miles to Hwy. 80 (Grand). Turn left on 80 and continue 1 mile to North Washington, turn right, and drive one block. You'll pass **Sam's** on the way in, on the right side of Hwy. 59.

For the **Pottery,** use the Farm Road 31. It's 2 miles down.

New Mexico

TANDOOR, *Exit 3, Las Cruces*

When friends in Las Cruces suggested we go to an authentic Indian restaurant for brunch one Sunday we thought we'd be in for blue corn pancakes, sopapillas, and other dishes which highlight the mix of Native American and Mexican cooking. Imagine our surprise when we found Indians not from New Mexico pueblos, but rather from the Eurasian subcontinent.

Tandoori food, we quickly learned, finds its greatest popularity in India's north and in Muslim lands through the Middle East to Morocco—and in Las Cruces. Our fixed price buffet ($6.95) consisted of lentil soup, vegetable pakoras (subtly spiced vegetables in small fritterlike balls), and a refillable choice of rice, kofta pasand (curried meatball in herb sauce), curried chicken, and a vegetable curry with potato, bell pepper, sweet potato, carrots, and cauliflower. Two breads—naan (soft yogurt bread) and papad (lentil-based, hand-rolled, sun-dried, and matzohlike) —added greatly to the meal. Gulab da man was our dessert—a soft, almost spongelike ball made from milk that has been boiled hard, spiced with cardamom, fried in vegetable oil, and soaked in honeyed rosewater.

The meal tasted wonderful from start to finish, and its authenticity was underscored when we learned that owner Geeth Pai's cook prepares meals with white hot charcoals in a traditional tandoori clay oven. Most lunch dishes are under $5; most dinners cost less than $10. Indian music plays in the background and on weekend nights there is Middle Eastern belly-dancing.

HOURS   Lunch: Mon. & Wed.–Fri. 11 am–2 pm. Dinner: Mon. & Wed.–Sat. 5–10 pm. Closed Tuesdays and on July 4, Thanksgiving, and Christmas.

SPECS   100 Wyatt Drive; (505) 523-8833; V/MC/DC; beer and wine.

DIRECTIONS   Northbound: Turn left at Exit 3, and stay on Lohman Ave., which becomes one-way after 1.2 miles and changes its name to Amador. Shortly thereafter, turn left onto Main St., and follow it past the Alameda Blvd. light. ■ Shortly after crossing Alameda, you'll see Tandoor's sign high in the air on the other side of the median strip. Make a U-turn between the center islands at the next opening, and Tandoor will be at the first corner (Wyatt Dr.) on the right. Return to I-25 North by turning right onto Main Street for 3.7 miles.

Southbound: Take Exit 6-B into Las Cruces on Routes 70/82 West, which become Main St. after a mile. Stay with Main one-way around the downtown mall (at this point it's called Water St., but it becomes Main once more when it's two-way again). It'll be 3.7 miles to the light at Alameda Blvd. Go straight at this light, and then follow directions above, from ■. Return to I-25 South by turning right on Main and right again at the second light, which is Lohman; pick up the freeway in 1.8 miles.

LA POSTA, *Exit 6-B, Mesilla (Las Cruces)*

See page 43 for description of this comfortable restaurant serving food in the authentic New Mexico style.

DIRECTIONS   Southbound: Take Exit 6-B, Route 70, into Las Cruces, where it becomes Main St., and stay on it until Avenida de Mesilla (Route 28), where you turn right. Follow this road under I-10 (p. 44), and pick up Route 28 directions, above.

THE COTTON PATCH, *Exit 41, Hatch*

Know how you can step into a restaurant and just *know* that it's good? That's the way it is at The Cotton Patch, a swell little restaurant whose existence is a well-guarded secret among the locals. The décor is standard steak house, with those thick red vinyl tablecloths that feel like car seats, and yet we knew, one foot in the door, that the food was going to be freshly prepared and well presented.

And boy, was it ever. Breakfast, lunch, and dinner are simple but generous country fare: eggs, steaks, chops, chicken, fish, and burgers. But beyond that, it's carefully cooked to order. Entrees are served with salad bar and choice of potato, or family-style servings of ranch beans, coleslaw, and fries. For two bucks each extra plate, you can split an entree and the all-you-can-eat fixings. We could tell from listening to the regulars that the steaks are some of the best for miles, so we decided to push our luck and order the fish dinner and a burger.

The $2.95 Patch Jr. burger was so lean, we'd swear it was chopped sirloin. The fixings were the traditional lettuce, onion, tomato, and pickle, but the lightly grilled oval-shaped bun and medium rare pattie were far above ordinary. Even after a day of sampling burgers, we found this one to be superb. The lightly breaded and sautéed whitefish tasted as though it had never been frozen. The Cotton Patch is performing miracles out there, light-years from the ocean. There's even a Thursday night crab legs dinner.

Salad bar choices were equally extraordinary: pasta salad, cauliflower, radishes, Chinese noodles and (we couldn't believe it) two kinds of sprouts. For dessert there's hot apple strudel.

The Cotton Patch is a local favorite, the kind of place where the waitresses know everybody by name, so expect that your meal will be peppered with overheard details on wrecked cars, marriages, and a breezy exchange of insults. And don't be surprised if you get involved in some inter-table chatting: the Hatchlings are friendly, despite the posted rates for answering questions (one buck for dumb questions, four for a correct answer: dumb looks are still free).

On the way out pick up a copy of the Hatch Chile Festival cookbook of award-winning recipes.

HOURS   Tues.–Sun. 6 am–8:30 pm. Closed Mon.

SPECS   W. Hall; (505) 267-4847; MC/V; no bar.

DIRECTIONS   Take Exit 41 and turn right if southbound, left if northbound into town. It's about a mile to the stop sign where you should turn right onto W. Hall. The Cotton Patch is a couple of blocks down, on the right.

ABOUT TRUTH OR CONSEQUENCES

We guess you can't expect much from a town named for a game show (T or C used to be called Hot Springs). We thought we might find at least one worthy meal here, but it didn't work out that way. From our sampling, we'd say you're best advised to carry on to Hatch, where we found one of the best restaurants in the state, or stop in for an Owl Burger in San Antonio (see below), before you shell out any cash for mediocre fixin's in T or C. For those who can't wait, we'll say that **Los Arcos** is the "nicest" restaurant in town though we weren't impressed by its steaks or seafood (overcooked and overpriced). And the **Turtle-back Inn,** a fifties vintage coffee shop, serves up a good bowl of menudo and a filling platter of chile fries (a mess of french fries topped with chile con carne and a glob of cheese—the kind of meal that fuels nightmares). The view alone justifies Turtleback's existence. As we pushed around our chile fries and listened to the waitress complain about the grumpy cook, the moon rose over the Caballo Mountains and we forgot for one moment that there were miles to go before we slept.

THE OWL, *Exit 13, San Antonio*

This wide spot in the desert is the home of hotelier Conrad Hilton (we crossed paths with his first hotel in Cisco, Texas), as well as being the gateway to the Bosque del Apache Wildlife Refuge, the winter home of thousands of sandhill cranes and a couple of whoopers. So while there is some legitimate reason for San Antonio to continue to exist, we like to think it's best known for the hamburgers served at The Owl, a traditional stopping place for those fond of free-form, squishy burgers and homecut french fries. Nothing fancy (we don't think they serve much else, though we never bothered to ask), and it's all rather dark and dusty. But if you love your burgers big, fat, and just greasy enough (there's nothing like a well-seasoned grill), you should join The Owl's fan club. The price of "admission" is just $1.70; fries are extra.

HOURS   Mon.–Sat. 8 am–9 or 10 pm; closed Sun.

SPECS   Hwy. 380; (505) 835-9946; no credit cards; full bar.

DIRECTIONS   **Southbound:** Take Exit 13 as it veers left and crosses under I-25 a couple of miles to the Owl, on San Antonio's main drag.

Northbound: Take Exit 13 right into San Antonio. In a couple of miles you'll find it on San Antonio's main drag, Hwy. 380, the only road in and out.

LA CASITA, *Exits 150 and 147, Socorro*

Tucked and rolled black naugahyde booths, golden tile and mock adobe brick walls make this cool, dark restaurant an unexpectedly plush oasis in a cement and formica wasteland. Enlarged and remodeled numerous times over the course of 40 years, La Casita built its all-new home in 1982. Fortunately, the restaurant boasts one holdover from its humble beginnings— cook Juanita Martínez. Hired by the restaurant's original owner in 1948, Juanita created La Casita's menu and continues to oversee its preparation. Rolling out over a million sopapillas has done nothing to dampen her enthusiasm: her kitchen continues to garner accolades from the likes of *Newsweek* and *People* magazines.

Not really hungry but anxious to confirm the legendary abilities of Juanita, we ordered an à la carte cross-section of the menu: a red chile tamale (50 cents), chile relleno ($1.50), Mexican-style barbecued pork rib ($2.95), and a sopapilla. As it was late in the day, we had the place to ourselves, so we wandered around looking at the framed sets of then-and-now photos of Socorro, then settled into a serious evaluation of the table hot sauce, which was tamed by tomatoes but good.

Then the real food arrived. The pork rib was a turkey-leg-sized club of meat, smacking of chile but without the heat, moist and delicious. The chile relleno was absolutely the best stuffed pepper we'd eaten anywhere in the state (although slightly greasy, a fact we attribute to our dead-of-the-afternoon visit: the fryer had probably been turned off after lunch and wasn't sufficiently reheated when our chile was lowered in). The problem was quickly overcome when our sopapilla arrived minutes later, perfect, lightly fried, and not a bit greasy. The only weak spot in our little spread was the tamale: a high dough-to-meat ratio and rather bland. All the food seemed to have been cooled to accommodate gringo palates, but even chile aficionados won't mind, given the care that goes into each dish. From our sampling, we can highly recommend the dinner plate of barbecued ribs (number 8) served with refried beans and rice ($6.25) or a relleno platter ($5.25).

The menu gives equal space to steaks and seafood, but as long as Juanita Martínez reigns in La Casita's kitchen, you shouldn't waste your time with such standard fare.

HOURS   Open 7 days, 11 am–9 pm.

SPECS   California St./Business 25; (505) 835-2801; MC/V; full bar.

DIRECTIONS Southbound: Take Exit 150 as it veers right into town, 1½ miles to the railroad tracks. La Casita is on the left, just past the tracks. To return to I-25, continue south along California/Business 25 for ½ mile to the interstate.

Northbound: Take Exit 147 into town (Business 25). La Casita is on the right, just over ½ mile from the exit (before the railroad tracks). To return to I-25, continue north through town on Business 25/California.

GIL'S BAKERY AND DINING ROOM, *Exit 195, Belen*

On our way into Gil's we ran into the proprietor of the Belen Sugar Bowl Bowling Lanes, who assured us that Gil's is and always was *the* place to eat in Belen, especially if you've got a sweet tooth. We believed him. We wanted to crawl into the bakery cases and embrace the chocolate doughnuts, cream puffs, eclairs, cherry danish, banana bread, coffee cake, cinnamon buns, and cheese turnovers, but settled for a seat within arm's reach of the bear claws (filled with blueberries and pecans). Watching the old boys gobble matchstick fries and burgers, served straight or with chile, cheese, and bacon, we knew Gil's was our kind of place.

Since it was our first meal of the day, we stuck to the breakfast selections (served all day) and decided on Gil's Breakfast Sandwich, an English muffin stacked with sausage, cheese, and an egg, and served with hashbrowns ($2.35) that puts the chain restaurant's McVersion to shame. Another breakfast order brought huevos rancheros: a house tortilla topped with eggs that peeped through the smoking hot green chile like double suns. Served with a side of toast, skillet-fried hashbrowns, and beans, it's an overwhelming platterful of food for $3.

Gil's menu includes everything from steaks and chops to broiled halibut and fried shrimp ($7.95–$9.95), but you shouldn't leave without at least one sticky bun in your pocket; on second thought, it's wise to cough up the extra 15 cents for a box to put it in.

Gil Sanchez himself (that's him wearing glasses and center-parted hair) presides over the pale-green, clean, but spare dining room. Only three decorative touches—an immense calendar, a portrait of JFK, and a painting of yucca in flower—compete with the glories of the bakery cases. There is a second dining room, but the best view in the house is of the sweets and the cigar boxes filled with plastic brides and grooms, football players, happy faces, and hunters.

HOURS Tues.–Sun. 6:30 am–5:30 pm. Closed Mon.

SPECS 239 No. Main; (505) 864-3636; no credit cards; no bar.

DIRECTIONS **Southbound:** Take Exit 195 as it becomes Business 25 and curves south into town as Main St. Main St. parallels I-25 for 4½

113

miles to Gil's, on the the right. To return to I-25 south, continue along Business 25/Main south 2 miles.

Northbound: Take the first exit for Belen (if you miss it, you'll have to backtrack in from north of town, as above). Drive into town on Business 25/Main 2 miles to Gil's, on the left. Return to I-25 by continuing north along Main until it reconnects with the interstate in 4½ miles. You will be parallel to I-25.

THE FRONTIER RESTAURANT,
Exits 224A & 224B, Albuquerque

"Oh, they've got the best hot-buttered cinnamon rolls in captivity," a friend gushed when we mentioned the possibility of visiting the Frontier. Well, we don't know of any wild cinnamon rolls, but her endorsement sent us to this University of New Mexico hangout across the street from the Johnson Gymnasium.

Over the years this expansive short-order diner has won a place in the history of the UNM community. It is justifiably famous for its hot cinnamon rolls coated with a topping of melted margarine and sugar (72 cents). Sweet and soft, the roll practically spills over the side of its plate; accompanied by fresh-squeezed orange juice (75 cents to $1.50), it serves as a daily meal for hundreds from UNM and hangers-on who keep the Frontier hoppin' all day and half the night. We were mesmerized by the Rube Goldberg machinery that automatically slices and squeezes whole oranges in one sweeping motion.

The rest of the fare is standard counter food: eggs, pancakes, huevos rancheros, and omelette breakfasts ($1.95 to $3.25 with coffee or tea); a variety of hamburgers and sandwiches from grilled cheese (95 cents) to Bonanza (a double cheeseburger with all the trimmings, $2.45); and Mexican dishes highlighted by the green chile stew (three sizes, 65 cents to $1.50).

Much of the Frontier's popularity comes from an atmosphere that at first glance appears to be sterile, with its place-your-order-pay-and-pick-up production line. But after watching the crowd for a while, a pattern emerges: artsy types and families congregate in the no-smoking dining room or the quiet back room with its Indian rugs, talky students sip coffee in a middle room, and most of the noisy in-and-out traffic is contained in a single room up front. "I call it a bar without booze," says co-owner Larry Rainosek, who opened the Frontier with his wife Dorothy in 1971. "In fact," he added with evident pride, "a sociology student from the University of Southern California is doing a paper on the makeup of our customers."

The Frontier's walls show the local artistic community's loyalty: paintings and impressionistic sketches of the Frontier, including one of the Frontier in the 1800s with horse-drawn wagons out front, which hang proudly next to more conventional Indian paintings.

HOURS   6:30 am–midnight, daily. Closed Thanksgiving, Christmas, and New Year's Day, and early the previous afternoons.

SPECS   2400 Central, N.E.; (505) 266-0550; no credit cards; no bar.

DIRECTIONS   **Northbound:** Take Exit 224A (Lead Ave./Coal Ave./ Central Ave.), turn right at third light onto Central Ave. (Presbyterian Hospital is at the corner). The Frontier is at 2400 Central N.E., on the far right-hand corner at the Cornell Rd. light (1.1 miles from the freeway).

Southbound: At exit 224B (Central Ave./Grand Ave.), turn left at the second traffic light onto Central. The Frontier is in 1.2 miles.

M&J SANITARY TORTILLA FACTORY,
Exit 224A, Albuquerque

While traveling through South America a couple of years ago Tom met an overeducated couple from New Mexico who had decided to chuck it all and buy a working hacienda way back in the Andes. Running a working farm and ranch in an underdeveloped country had proven difficult, but with abundant tenacity, they seemed to be surviving. When asked if they'd ever consider returning to the States, the two blurted out opposite replies, then slowly looked at each other. "Why would you possibly want to go back?" the wife asked her husband. "Oh, I don't know," he answered. "I guess I miss the M&J."

The M&J has earned so much praise, first by word of mouth, then from a four-page paean in *The New Yorker*, that we thought it in danger of suffering from overpopularity. But our most recent visit convinced us that the terrific food, chatty service, reasonable prices, and fluorescent lights are as firmly in place as ever. The customers in this roomy cafe come from glassed-in downtown high-rises, run-down low-rent flophouses, and everything in between. Over the years, Beatrice and Jake Montoya have maintained their high standards by buying quality ingredients for their authentic New Mexico food—chile peppers, blue corn, and beans, for example—and taking the time to prepare them right. Such is customer loyalty to the M&J, Bea said, that "I have people who come in here six days a week. It's a wonder they don't look like fat burritos."

The most popular dish, carne adovada, fills you up with diced roast pork marinated in red chile sauce, wrapped in a flour tortilla, and soaked in chile sauce ($5.75 with refried beans, rice, salad, and sopapillas with honey). M&J's sopapillas, which come with some dishes, may also be ordered as a side dish ($1). A variation is to have them stuffed with red and green chile and refried beans or beef chunks ($2.90). Tim's Special, a dish named for a regular patron, includes carne adovada, blue corn enchiladas, a side of sour cream, and iced tea. (A staple in the Indian pueblos, blue corn gets ground into the tortillas that wrap M&J's enchiladas.)

If you frequent Mexican restaurants enough, you should know by now that menudo does not refer to clean-scrubbed Puertorriqueños, but rather a soup whose main ingredient is the lining of cows' stomachs. The Montoyas use honeycomb menudo, which comes from young cows, as opposed to the smoother but more rubbery kind from older cattle.

The M&J's corn tortillas come fresh from a huge tortilla-making machine in the back, and are so good that the other restaurants around town buy from them daily. In fact, the M&J sells well over *one million* corn tortillas a year.

HOURS Mon.–Sat. 9 am–5:30 pm. Closed Sun., Memorial Day, Labor Day, Thanksgiving, Christmas, and New Year's Day.

SPECS 403 2nd St. S.W.; (505) 242-4890; no credit cards; no booze.

DIRECTIONS   **Northbound:** From Exit 224A (Lead Ave./Coal Ave./ Central Ave.), turn left at the second traffic light onto Lead Ave., a one-way street. ■ After 1.2 miles, Lead Ave. rises over the railroad tracks; turn left when you get to Third St. on the far side of the bridge, left again at the corner onto Coal Ave., and left once more onto 2nd St. M&J is under a Seven-Up sign about three-quarters of the way down the block on the left.

Southbound: Take Exit 224A (Lead Ave./Coal Ave.), turn right at the light onto Lead Ave., and follow northbound directions from ■. Return to I-25: Turn left on Lead Ave, left on Third St., and left on Coal Ave. straight out to the freeway.

SWEETWATER'S CAFE, *Exit 225, Albuquerque*

Remember the health-food scare a few years ago? Well, this place is a survivor, and deservedly so. It has caught on for its well-conceived menu, quality baked goods, and agreeable prices. We dropped in for a Sunday brunch, with offerings including French toast with strawberry sauce, poppyseed pancakes, eggs Benedict, and huevos rancheros (all slightly under $3), in addition to the regular menu. The sandwich selections looked terrific, especially the tuna salad with walnuts and apple on homemade bread; the beef brisket, green chile, and a blend of three cheeses wrapped in a flour tortilla; and the house special of grilled ham, fresh-baked turkey, and cheese (also around $3). The green chile stew, a daily offering, is augmented by a rotating choice of mulligatawny, minestroni, and other foreign soups.

On impulse we tried the coconut chess pie from Sweetwater's bakery, with its firm custard interior and a coconut-shell exterior. The consistent flavor and contrast of textures made for one of the finest desserts we'd had in a long while.

Sweetwater's serves only Colombian coffee, a classy nerve-jangler for only 48 cents (refills half price). Perhaps the weekday regulars—students from nearby medical and law schools—sip it while discussing malpractice suits.

HOURS   Mon.–Fri. 7 am–4 pm; Sat. & Sun. 9 am–3 pm. Closed Thanksgiving, Christmas, and New Year's Day.

SPECS   1844 Lomas, N.E.; (505) 243-3330; MC/V; no bar.

DIRECTIONS Northbound: From Exit 225 turn right if northbound, left if southbound, onto Lomas Blvd. past lots of new car dealerships. After 0.7 mile, Sweetwater's is on your right.

SADIE'S, *I-40 West Interchange, Albuquerque*

See page 190 for description of this place—we found it in the back of a bowling alley!

DIRECTIONS At the Grants Exit, enter I-40 West to Exit 159. Stay in the middle lane past the bottom of the off-ramp, then get over to the right to turn right onto North 4th St. Sadie's is inside BG's Valley Bowl, on the right, in about 3 miles.

ABOUT SANTA FE

Surrounded by miles of barren interstate along which fine dining comes to mean coffee that isn't oily and food that won't kill you, Santa Fe can offer blessed relief from abusive waitresses and formless globs of melted cheese. While it isn't a city that's easily conquered (many streets closely resemble mule trails), it would certainly be painless to stop over a day or two to fully explore the town's culinary offerings, history, and personality. Although most of the restaurants listed here are within five minutes of the interstate, it's just possible you'll spend more time being lost or searching for a parking place than actually eating. We suggest ferreting them out at your leisure. It isn't difficult finding them once you've oriented yourself to town.

Jimmie's Tiny's is a low-rent favorite of our friend Jack Parsons, a local photographer, who shows up there when he feels the urge to gorge on chicken flautas (tortillas filled with chicken, rolled into "flutes" and deep fried). You can dance here, too, on Friday and Saturday nights.

For classic Mexican cuisine and a strong dose of Santa Fe à la carte, we suggest **La Choza**, a casual restaurant serving that classical regional mainstay, the blue corn tortilla. **The Ore House,** a tony, sometimes tourist-infested restaurant overlooking the Plaza, serves the best of the city's fresh seafood and above-average steaks and lamb. For prime ribs, head for the brick and timber **Steaksmith,** a slickly rustic, efficient, well-organized restaurant—something to be grateful for in a town where service can range from eccentric to indifferent.

The classiest all-around lunch spot, open for dinner only on Friday nights, is **Rincon del Oso,** which serves blue corn and chicken enchiladas for less than $5. The same dish, ill prepared, can cost almost twice as much elsewhere.

The Santa Fe phone book has a fairly dependable street map, but it's probably just as easy to ask someone. All these restaurants are local favorites.

VICTOR'S, *Exit 282, Santa Fe*

Since we didn't have any expectations when we were led into Victor's by two friends who had said little by way of introduction, we couldn't have been disappointed. We weren't exactly overwhelmed at the door: Victor's is like clotted cream—it looks like nothing special but one taste and you're addicted. Thick, time-worn adobe walls feature nothing more demanding of your attention than light switches. The color scheme never strays from the ivory and navy of a moonlit night. The service is superb, yet somehow invisible. Everything is orchestrated to allow for undivided attention to the food.

We began with a carafe of house wine, and a heavy, crusty loaf of Italian bread that we promptly devoured. A second loaf soon replaced the first and it too became the subject of a cross-table tug of war. Anxious to try as many dishes as possible, we decided to order four entrees and a set of long-handled forks (we had to settle for stretching). Becky ordered the antipasto platter since reserving room for dessert was her primary consideration ($7.95). On a basil binge, Jack ordered fettucine al pesto ($11.95) to follow a bowl of the day's pasta-basil soup. We quickly decided on each of the night's specials: a swordfish steak ($12.95), and lasagne stuffed with chicken, veal, pork, mozzarella and ricotta.

First things first. The antipasto platter was composed of four tidy wedges of cheese, a dish of marinated vegetables, Italian peppers, sausage, meatballs, and grapes. The real flurry of forks began when the swordfish arrived, shrink-wrapped in moist, flaky lettuce and smacking oh-so-lightly of olive oil and fennel. This masterful dish was graced with a side of baby artichokes and a salad of homemade pasta, artichoke hearts, and black olives. If there hadn't been four forks working over it, it might have been too much of a good thing. As things were, to reach for the butter was to risk a hand in the crossfire of tines.

As for the lasagne, never has a peasant dish been elevated to such heights. In a word: rich. In another: delicious. The forks flew once more.

Then Jack's fettucine arrived. Any other time and place, such a butter-and-pine-nut-rich pesto would have been the hit of the evening, but this night the competition was just too great. Even the pesto soup was equal to the entree.

We ate ourselves silly. A round of espresso was expected to bring us to our senses, but instead inspired true decadence. We ordered dessert: lush red strawberries, sprinkled with lemon peel, wallowing in heavy cream and blushing with Grand Marnier, and an equally disarming lemon cheesecake with a thin layer of cinnamon and chocolate wedged between the sour cream topping and the slightly tart cheese filling.

We had come in search of mussels, steamed with white wine and herbed butter; but we never even missed them.

HOURS Lunch: Mon.–Fri. 11:30 am–2:30 pm. Dinner: 7 days 6 pm–10 pm.

SPECS 423 W. San Francisco; (505) 982-1552; AE/MC/V; full bar.

DIRECTIONS **Southbound:** Take Exit 282 and turn right onto St. Francis Dr. ■ Continue 3 miles to Alameda and turn right. Drive ½ mile to Guadalupe and turn left. Victor's is one block down, on the left.

Northbound: Take Exit 282, turn left onto St. Francis Dr. and cross under I-25. Then as above from ■.

A little complicated but worth every missed turn.

BOBCAT BITE
EL GANCHO, *Exits 290 and 284, Santa Fe*

Both El Gancho and the Bobcat Bite offer interstate accessibility, avoid Santa Fe proper, and serve admirable food. Predictably, the Bobcat Bite serves meat—burgers and steaks ($5.95–$9.95)—in a roadhouse atmosphere. Servings are huge and customers are as likely to be construction workers and traveling salesmen as Santa Feans seeking to escape the tourist hordes. Seating is limited (seven tables and a counter), but the no-frills atmosphere accounts for a quick turnover.

Down the road a bit, the more elegant El Gancho serves fresh seafood, steaks, and veal, as well as more surprising specialties such as salmon en croute and live Maine lobster.

HOURS   Bobcat Bite: Tues.–Sat. 11 am–7:50 pm. Closed Sun. and Mon.
El Gancho: Open for dinner only, Wed.–Sun. at 6 pm, and for Sun. brunch.

SPECS   Bobcat Bite: Old Las Vegas Hwy.; no credit cards; no bar.
El Gancho: Old Las Vegas Hwy.; (505) 988-5000; AE/DC/V/MC; full bar.

DIRECTIONS   **Southbound:** Take Exit 290 to yield and turn right. At stop sign turn left onto the old Las Vegas Hwy., which parallels I-25. The Bobcat Bite is two miles south, on the right. El Gancho is another mile south. To return to I-25, continue south along the old highway another 3½ miles.

Northbound: Take Exit 284 left to cross over I-25. Turn right onto the old Las Vegas Hwy., which parallels the interstate. El Gancho is 2½ miles north, on the left, and Bobcat Bite is another mile beyond it. To return to I-25 heading north, continue along the old highway 2½ miles to its intersection with the interstate.

ABOUT LAS VEGAS

Las Vegas officially dates to 1835, but records show that the Coronado expedition found signs of civilization here as early as 1541. By the time the railroad huffed into town in 1879, Las Vegas was a well-established stop on the old Santa Fe Trail and a favorite hunkering-down place for gamblers and lost women. More respectable and prosperous citizens established an opera house, literary club, and theater, but as befits a frontier town, even the most flush circles boasted a rowdy edge. Almost done in by a series of economic disasters at the turn of the century, the former boomtown has held on, many of its grand façades sagging with age and crumbling from neglect. Recently, however, a surge of historical self-consciousness has inspired the onset of renovation and revitalization that is saving the lives of the city's architectural grande dames.

The architecture alone makes Las Vegas worthy of a visit, and the town still boasts the hot springs that once made it a favorite retreat of *ciboleros* (buffalo hunters), starlets, and other monied moths. Ask for directions to the old Montezuma resort, a sprawling chateau that is now the United World College. The building is open for tours by appointment, and the public baths are adjacent to the college grounds. Brochures for walking tours around the fine two-story territorial adobe homes and Victorian commercial buildings are available from the Plaza Hotel, a recently restored Renaissance Revival palace surrounded by the tarnished splendor of downtown. Although not quite competent at the preparation of more ambitious continental dishes (the veal marsala was a disaster), the Plaza's dining room has a deft touch with steaks and native New Mexican specialties. Fresh fruit, vegetables, homemade soups (a creamy shrimp chowder when we visited), and properly heavy sourdough rolls make the lace-curtained parlor a worthwhile escape from the chuckwagon trail. Be warned, however; service can be dreadfully slow.

Across the plaza from the hotel, **La Cocina** prepares regional dishes for crowds of tourists and locals. A bit off the beaten path is **Spic and Span,** a tidy little cafe noted for its baked goods.

If you plan to spend some time exploring Las Vegas, check into one of the Plaza's splendid rooms (ask for one of the octagonal ones overlooking the plaza) and ask directions to the hot springs. The hotel will provide towels and even a boxed lunch or picnic on request. Enjoy the eccentric pleasures of the old town and the surrounding mountain meadows that inspired its name.

STOCKMAN CAFE, *Exits 414 and 412, Springer*

Good food doesn't necessarily mean a palatable environment or pleasant service. It was a delight to find all three at the Stockman, the quintessential no-frills cafe, clean and cheerful, staffed with helpful waitresses, and overflowing with local families enjoying Sunday dinner.

The daily special of roast beef, brown gravy, green beans, mashed potato, rolls, and dessert ($4.20) looked as good as it sounded, and watching the cowboy in his Sunday best—orange shirt and bolo tie—enjoy his plateful, we decided that his expression told us all we needed to know about its quality.

Determined to test the Mexican specialties, we ordered a jumbo burrito and small bowl of menudo. The burrito was monstrous, a mountainous ridge of pinto beans wrapped in a fresh soft tortilla and topped with meaty green chile (guaranteed to make your nose run, $2.65). The small bowl of menudo—served only on weekends, when the demand for the traditional hangover cure is greatest—turned out to be a deep soupbowl full of more tripe and red chile stew than the average weekend *borracho* could ever eat. Those who find the smooth and chewy texture of tripe unappealing will discover this deep-red, hominy-rich version to be excellent (elegantly served with lemon, minced onion, and a buttered, folded tortilla, $2.30).

Lots of table pushing and pulling went on as the dining room was adjusted to fit the needs of bigger and smaller families, but the demands of the crowds never affected the steady shuffle of steaming hot dishes from the kitchen.

A few wonderfully curious things about the Stockman: The homemade pies are cut in the kitchen, where each slice is individually wrapped in cellophane, then carried out by the armload and lined up along the counter; homemade pizza is a house specialty (served after five); the men's room in this female-run establishment dispenses French ticklers in a choice of three colors, 50 cents each; and among the posters featuring lambs, calves, and longhorns, there is an enormous portrait of a skunk emerging from his hole. From the chile powder sold by the pound to the 30-cent sopapillas (huge kite-shaped puffs of dough served with a cinnamony desert honey), the Stockman is one of the most endearing cafes in New Mexico.

HOURS Open 7 days 6 am–9 pm.

SPECS 400 Colbert (Maxwell); (505) 483-2301; no credit cards; no bar.

DIRECTIONS **Southbound:** Take Exit 414, cross over I-25 left, and wind south into town 2 miles to the cafe on the right, past the Cactus Cafe and next to the Chevron. To return to I-25, continue south along Hwy. 58/Colbert (Maxwell).

Northbound: Take Exit 412 and follow Hwy. 58 into town. The Stockman is on the left, at the corner of 4th and Colbert (Maxwell). Return to I-25 by continuing north on Hwy. 58 for 2 miles.

ABOUT RATON

Other than a dozen Mexican cafes, a hotel strip, and plenty of fast food, Raton is short of fine dining establishments. If too many New Mexican chile dishes have turned your palate to asbestos, relief is just a swordfish steak away. Prefer a baby pink filet mignon, or shrimp in garlic sauce? Take a drive into Raton's downtown district to the old Palace Hotel, now the **Palace Res-**

taurant. Across from the restored railroad station, the 1896 hotel is a fine china and crystal refuge from macramé plant hangers and velvet paintings. Massive chandeliers cascade from the ceiling and Victorian wallpapers surround the dining rooms. The Palace was closed the Sunday afternoon we stopped by, but we know its cousin restaurant in Lamy (the **Legal Tender**) and if good taste runs in families, we can recommend the **Palace** as the ideal place to practice a little self-indulgence. Don't miss the old Haven Hotel next door with its lions-in-chains architectural detailing. The Haven shares a wall with the 1880 Coors building, now a museum.

UNCLE LOUIE'S, *Exit 452, Raton*

We had to drive practically to Colorado to find it, but in Raton we found New Mexico green chile at its incendiary best. Uncle Louie's ten-table restaurant may be a Siamese twin to a dance-hall–lounge, it may not be pretty (plastic placemats), and it will force you to compete with the juke box if you want to be heard, but we challenge chileheads to find the state vegetable put to better use anywhere along the interstate.

There are rules for eating chile this hot: (1) let it fall to the sides of your tongue and chew. *Chew.* Let your mouth absorb the heat and then savor the flavor. Swallowing quickly to wash the fire out of your mouth will land you in big trouble. It will, as Barbara's mother says, get your goozle. Which is a way of saying your epiglottis will leap from the fire and you'll either choke to death or come down with terminal hiccups. (2) Have a beer at arm's reach before you even think about taking that first bite. A cold brew is more efficient at quenching a chile fire than water. (3) If it's just too hot for you, salt it down (akin to putting ashes on a campfire). However you cope, try to absorb the color, the smell, the experience. This is emerald green chile at its searing, flavorful best.

The timid or virginal of palate may wish to abstain from this experience: simply order your entree sans chile. We especially like Uncle Louie's beef and potato burrito; without the chile topping, it is something like a tortilla full of skillet goulash (ground beef, onions, and fried potatoes, $2.95). Luncheon specials, served from 11 am to 4 pm, cost right around two bucks and feature burritos, tacos, enchiladas, and a green chile cheese omelette served with beans and sopapillas. We spotted Uncle Louie, a mountainous man, happily noshing on a sopapilla like a teething baby.

On weekend nights you can eat to your heart's content, then work it all off with a swing around the dance floor to the music of the Diamonds or Buenas Neuvas. At any time you can crank up that juke box classic, "Jose Cuervo, You Are a Friend of Mine."

HOURS Mon.–Sat. 11 am–9 pm; Sun. noon–9 pm.

SPECS 255 Sugarite; (505) 445-3457; no credit cards; full bar.

DIRECTIONS **Northbound:** Take Exit 452 to Hwy. 72 and cross over the interstate left. Wind into town 0.8 mile to Uncle Louie's on the left. Enter at the arrow beneath the yellow sign.

Southbound: Take Exit 452/Hwy. 72 and turn right, then as above.

Texas

ABOUT TEXARKANA

Texarkana is a typical mid-sized city which just happens to straddle a state line. People queue up to get their picture taken, one foot in Texas, the other in Arkansas. The restaurant we'd heard the most about during our visit to Texarkana was the **Acadian Seafood House.** We went for lunch and found it closed. But we were able to sniff the Acadian stewpot—crawfish étouffée, softshell crab, and lobster. "We used to be open for lunch," the manager told us from beneath an umbrella of a black hat, "but the parking was too scarce." It broke our hearts to be that close to Cajun cooking and come away hungry. After 5, you'll have no trouble finding a spot for your car; let us know if the food tastes as good as it smells. From Exit 223A head downtown on E. Broad St. It's between State Line and Olive, in Arkansas.

High rollers might wish to dine at **Park Place,** a gourmet Cajun restaurant (they take off their hats here) that is equally famous for its steak and shrimp Acapulco. It too is open only for dinner. Take Hwy. 245 exit south to Arkansas Blvd. and turn right. It's on the right of Sanderson Lane.

If you're feeling really adventuresome, drive five miles north on Hwy. 71 to a *real* country restaurant, **The Hush Puppy**—a catfish and steak house locals rave about. For Texarkana-style Hunan, read on.

HUNAN PALACE, *Exit 223-A, Texarkana*

We didn't really know what to do about reporting restaurants in two-faced Texarkana—it seems like the lion's share of restaurants are on the side of town in Arkansas, a state that isn't supposed to be included here. After scouring the possibilities on the Texas side of the State Line, we decided that almost was close enough. When you turn left off State Line, you'll be in Arkansas for lunch. It's worth the trip.

The Hunan Palace may look like your typical quick-wok restaurant, but the resemblance ends with the lacquered red and black decor. If you've plenty of time and money, ask about the House Special Dinner—for $11.50 per person you get the chef's multi-course specialty of the day (sizzled beef with scallops and prawns the day we visited). If you've less time, try one of the lunch specials ($2.50–$3.50). We liked the Fragrant Pork—shredded pork, crisp strips of bamboo shoots, ear mushrooms, and water chestnuts in a tangy, sweet, delicately hot garlic sauce. Lunch specials are served with a well-stuffed and lightly fried eggroll, egg drop soup, steamed rice, and hot tea. Not to be missed is the rumaki, an appetizer of chicken livers and water chestnuts wrapped in bacon and fried. Dip them in hot mustard or plum sauce. Incredible.

In fact the only complaint we had concerned a 25-cent lunchtime surcharge for fortune cookies, free with dinner. All was forgiven when we discovered these cookies were homemade—a far cry from the cardboard prepackaged version most Chinese restaurants serve.

HOURS   Lunch: Mon.–Sat. 11 am–2:30 pm. Dinner: 5 pm–10 pm (Fri. & Sat. until 11 pm in summer only). Sun. open all day until 9 pm. Sunday all-you-can-eat buffet 11 am–2:30 pm.

SPECS   110 E. 36th St.; (501) 773-3838; DC/CB/MC/V/AE; full bar.

DIRECTIONS   Westbound: Take Exit 223-A to State Line Ave., cross over the interstate and continue on State Line for 1 mile to E. 36th. Turn left on E. 36th (across from Wendy's). Hunan's is ½ block on the right.

Eastbound: Exit 223-A (State Line Ave.) and turn right onto State Line, then as above.

MARKET FARE DINING ROOM, *Mount Vernon Exit,*
Mount Vernon

We were really anxious to eat here, having read about it in *The Best Country Cafes in Texas* (written by our friends Scuzzy Forsyth and Meg Tynan). But as we pulled up one dull gray winter afternoon, the Market Fare Dining Room was shut tighter than the county jail. We did visit with the owner of the adjacent flower shop, and he told us that the restaurant had changed hands since the days our friends enjoyed Russian chicken and rice here and that the Methodist minister's wife was now running the place. But, he opined, the Dining Room was as good as ever. He suggested we go down the block, across the tracks, and . . . we lost him, but he was trying to direct us to the minister's house, so that we might interview the Mrs. We decided to let her enjoy her afternoon off, and we can only tell you that Scuzzy and Meg loved the Market's fare before, and the florist loves it now.

HOURS　Mon.–Sat. 9:30 am–2 pm; Fri.–Sat. 6 pm–10 pm.

SPECS　Corner of Scott and Kaufman, ½ block down from the southwest corner of the square, entrance on the side; (214) 537-2176; no credit cards; no bar.

DIRECTIONS　Take the Mount Vernon Exit and had downtown to the square. The Market Fare Dining Room is ½ block off the square, at the back of the building which sits on the corner of Scott and Kaufman.

ABOUT DALLAS

See our overview of Dallas restaurants on pages 158–159.

LA BOTICA, *Exit 47B, Dallas*

It's hard to imagine what you might find behind the façade of this seasoned storefront in the heart of a traditional Mexican neighborhood east of downtown Dallas. But don't be shy. You'll find the former pharmacy (that's what La Botica means) stuffed full of briefcases, blond bobs, and the young up-and-coming folks who own them.

Having driven in on the crest of a blue norther, we decided to begin with the caldo tlapeño (a chicken, avocado, and chick pea soup flavored with smoky hot chipotle chiles). Served with fresh, hot, flour tortillas and butter, the soup became a meal in itself. But we didn't stop there. We felt it our sacred duty to try the Enchiladas Mexicanas, two beef enchiladas topped with salsa roja (a red chile sauce), jack cheese, and potatoes, served with beans and rice for $4.95. Pretty standard Tex-Mex, but that's what we were hungry for. The $5.75 lunch specials of fajitas, carne asada (broiled sirloin in a thick chile hot sauce), and filete tampiqueña—all served with refried beans, guacamole, and pico de gallo—smelled and looked wonderful. And you can get an old-fashioned Mexican breakfast here any time of the day. We recommend the chorizo con huevos, eggs scrambled with spicy Mexican sausage and served with refried beans ($4.25).

For dessert, order one of the old Dallas Drug Co.'s specials—ice cream sodas and banana splits.

HOURS Lunch: Tues.–Fri. 10:30 am–2 pm. Dinner: Tues.–Fri. 5 pm–10 pm; Sat. 5 pm–10 pm; Closed Sun. and Mon.

SPECS   1900 N. Haskell; (214) 824-2005; MC/V; full bar and Mexican beer.

DIRECTIONS   Eastbound: Take Exit 47B and turn right onto Haskell, which is one way south. At the first light, turn left (Parry) and then left again at the next light onto Peak. Peak, which is one way north, parallels Haskell. Continue on Peak 1½ miles north to Munger ■ and turn left. La Botica is on the right at the end of the block, on the corner of Munger and Haskell. To return to I-30, simply follow Haskell south back to the interstate. Pass under the interstate and turn left at the first light (Parry) and left again onto Peak, just as you did before. Peak has access to the interstate.

Westbound: Take Exit 47B and turn right onto Peak and continue 1½ miles to Munger, then as above from ■.

THE BRASSERIE*, *Exit 45, Dallas*

*Ideal for late night stops—<u>not</u> to be attempted during rush hour.

Shade your eyes against the glare of the doorman's gold braid and step into the darkly elegant lobby of the Fairmont Hotel. To the left of the registration desk and beneath cascading chandeliers is the entrance to the Brasserie, a 24-hour restaurant the likes of which you've never imagined. Eggs Benedict under Glass at 3 am? No problem. Hot biscuits with honey? Be right out. They'll even wake up one of the tanked lobsters for an intimate late dinner.

Though hardly inexpensive, the Brasserie is quite reasonable considering the abilities and the imagination of the kitchen. We were smitten with the Eggs Sardou (poached eggs and creamed spinach served on artichoke hearts and smothered in hollandaise, $7.25). And, we thought the famous Brasserie Brunch of fresh fruit, eggs Benedict, pancakes Oscar (buckwheat pancakes layered with marshmallow meringue and hot strawberry sauce), and a bottomless pot of coffee to be a real bargain at $10.50. Less pricey but equally filling, and equally well presented, is the spiced baked apple in heavy cream ($2.75) and a bowl of natural whole grain oatmeal that Goldilocks would have died for (served with brown sugar, cinnamon, and raisins). The Danish are baked right here and an order brings two big hot ones, dripping with butter.

Lunch and dinner menus also are served in the wee hours. The daily special when we dropped in was a saffron-rich paella, generously studded with shrimp, scallops, sausage, clams, and chicken ($8.50).

Located in downtown Dallas, only a block away from the new art museum, the Fairmont can be inaccessible around 8 am and quitting time, but if you're passing through town late at night, an hour spent here can be a dream.

HOURS   7 days, 24 hours.

SPECS   Fairmont Hotel, Ross and Akard; (214) 748-5454; AE/MC/V.

DIRECTIONS   Take Exit 45/Ervay from left lane and head toward downtown. Ervay becomes Akard after ¾ mile. The Fairmont is on the left, at the corner of Akard and Ross. Valet parking available in the hotel or catty-corner from the Fairmont in the Baptist Parking Garage ($1.75 after 6 pm).

LA CAVE, *Exit 428C, Dallas*

See page 161 for our description of a fine and affordable Dallas-style French restaurant where you can get it all to go.

DIRECTIONS   **Westbound:** As you pass through downtown Dallas, merge right at the 428C/I-35 Exit and continue about ¾ mile to Exit 429B Continental. ■ Exit and turn right at the light onto Continental, which becomes Lamar as you pass under the bridge. La Cave is in the red brick warehouse on your right. Parking is available on all sides of the building. To get back to I-30, retrace your route to the interstate (I-35) and cross under to second light. Turn left and enter I-35 heading south. Continue to the I-30 Exit, about a mile.

Eastbound: At downtown Dallas, merge with I-35 at Exit 428C and continue to Exit 429B/Continental, then as above from ■.

MERCADO JUAREZ, *TX Hwy. 360 Exit, Arlington*

You won't believe this place. Hidden away in a high-tech warehouse district, directly across from the Friendly Village mobile-home park, is an authentic Mexican market. No doubt about it, Mercado Juarez is pure bordertown chic. The white stucco walls surrounding the market are crowned with broken bottles—the traditional Mexican security system. Pass through the iron gates and into the Mercado and you'll swear you've just crossed an international bridge. The first room of the restaurant is a jumble of piñatas, ceramic frogs, embroidered dresses, and thingamajigs. Along one wall are shelves full of everything you'd ever need to stuff a Mexican picnic basket. But don't drop all your pesos right away, because the real attractions are in the dining room.

The restaurant portion of Mercado Juarez is vast (it used to be a helicopter warehouse) but festive. Dozens of papier-mâché parrots hang from the exposed ceiling pipes, and piñatas, sombreros, and paper flowers surround the handcrafted tables and chairs. The walls of the dining room are peach, the ceiling is black, and the furnishings are red, green, purple, yellow, and pink. A mounted bull's head oversees the proceedings.

First, shovel a tortilla chip into the picante sauce on your table —gravy thick, hot, and salty, like a mini-cauldron of stew. Now, consider the house specialties: parrilladas (grilled shrimp), cabrito (kid goat), steaks, and chicken. *Muy sabroso, delicioso, y precioso.* We loved all these dishes except the rubbery shrimp. The meats were superb and the presentation marvelous. Do as we did and try them all with a parrillada combinada ($10.95)—your choice of any two meats served with charbroiled onion, peppers, Spanish rice, bean soup, pico de gallo (a hot cha-cha-salsa of onions, chiles, and cilantro), and guacamole salad. Parrilladas are served after five only, so if you're too early, try the pork fajitas—tenderloin of pork marinated and mesquite broiled until it's fork tender, easily the best fajitas we've had anywhere.

HOURS Sun.–Thurs. 11 am–10 pm; Fri.–Sat. 11 am–11 pm.

SPECS 2220 Miller Rd.; (817) 649-3324); MC/AE/V; full bar—*cuervoitas* (margaritas) recommended.

DIRECTIONS **Westbound:** Take the exit for TX Hwy. 360 and loop around to the first light. Stay in the right-hand lane and cross over the interstate. ■ Continue on Hwy. 360 ½ mile to Avenue J. Exit onto Avenue J and turn left at the light. Continue on Avenue J until it runs into Miller Rd., a couple of blocks down, and turn right. Mercado Juarez is just around a curve, on the left.

Eastbound: Take the exit for TX Hwy. 360 and cross over I-30, then as above from ■.

Note: There was a lot of road construction surrounding the Mercado, including a more direct route back to I-30. Ask your waiter for directions.

ABOUT FORT WORTH

See page 99 for an overview of Fort Worth restaurants. Directions from I-30 to **Hunan** and a thorough description of **Tours**, also quite accessible from I-30, follow.

HUNAN, *Hulen Drive Exit, Fort Worth*

See page 99 for an understated, elegant Chinese restaurant.

DIRECTIONS   **Eastbound:** Take the Hulen Exit to the light. Turn right onto Hulen Dr. and ■ continue 2 miles (over the river and rail yard) to Hunan, in the shopping center on the left.

Westbound: Take the Hulen Exit and cross over I-30 left on Hulen Dr., then as above from ■.

TOURS, *Exit 12, Fort Worth*

We should have known that our high school friend, the studious, serious, and somehow exotic (for Fort Worth) Julie Shaw, would grow up to be a chef. Not a cook, mind you, but an honest-to-gawd, Paris-trained, toqued and aproned master-chef. Surrounded by the gray walls and vaulted ceiling of her classy little restaurant, we grew nostalgic. We laughed at the years between pep rallies and the university, the miles between Paris and dear old Cow Town. We watched Julie greet the graying parents of our old chums and smiled to see them line up for her tables.

Already we wanted to rave, but we assumed the mantle of objectivity and listened to the blue-haired matron order her vodka martini with two olives, whiffed the exotic orchids, approved of the art gallery lighting, took a deep breath, and turned to the menu.

The handwritten slate of dishes changes about every 2½ months, or at Julie's whim, and it always incorporates the freshest and most interesting regional game, fruit, and produce available. This is not the menu of an anonymous generic French cafe; it is Julie's menu, a mirror of her and husband Craig's tastes, experiments, and desire to improvise on classical presentations of American, Southwestern, Mexican, and even Texan dishes.

We began our meal with Roquefort flan. The dainty, molded custard blushing with a wine butter sauce was pleasantly tart and had a slightly salty aftertaste. Impressed, we moved on to salads. The house green salad is primarily a nest of leaf lettuce, but a liberal sprinkling of sesame and pumpkin seeds, almonds, and freshly grated parmesan saves it from being ordinary. The seasonal salad of hearts of palm and fresh pineapple proved that the house philosophy of pairing the unusual can have remarkable results.

Now we were primed for the main course. The shrimp in garlic butter sounded good, but predictable. Red Snapper Veracruzana was tempting, but we finally decided on the Duck Breast Saint-Germain, if for no other reason than to see the dish one good ol' boy had dared to send back to the kitchen claiming it was "beef." We saw no resemblance, but then we'd only had one champagne cocktail. The well-grained, generous serving of breast meat was enhanced but not overwhelmed by a topping of fresh peas, bacon, pearl onions, and potatoes in a peppery brown gravy. Equally pleasing was a second entree of sweetbreads Virginia, served with pepper-cured Virginia ham in a mushroom sauce ($14.95).

Our old chum can cook. Everything she serves is made fresh; everything we sampled was several notches above average, and everything told us we'd eaten entirely too much to consider dessert. We weren't ready to face the rain outside or end the evening, however, so what could we do? We had to try the Boule de Neige (snowball). This chocolate mousse brownie blanketed in whipped cream is so dense and so rich, and served in such an enormous portion ($3.75), that we nearly fell ill to hear about the regular customer who eats two per sitting.

At last, long after the waiters had disappeared and the rain had stopped, we said our goodnights, patted our doggy bag, and drove out of Barbara's hometown, satisfied that Tours was everything we'd hoped it would be.

HOURS   Tues.–Sat. 11:30 am–2 pm, 6 pm–10 pm. Closed Sun. and Mon.

SPECS   3429 B West 7th; (817) 870-1672; AE/MC/V (5 percent service charge); full bar.

DIRECTIONS   **Westbound:** Take Exit 12 as it curves around right to the light and turn left onto University Dr. ■ Continue along University 1.3 miles to the 7th St. light (3rd light from the exit). Make a hard left turn so that you cross in front of the 7th St. Theater and continue 3 blocks to Chicotsky's Center, on the left. Tours is tucked between the Chicotsky's Center Package Store and a grocery store.

Eastbound: Take Exit 12 left and go under I-30 on University, then as above from ■.

Texas
Oklahoma

Texas

ABOUT NUEVO LAREDO, MEXICO

If you're too early for lunch at the Tack Room (page 138), you can shore up your appetite by parking at the hotel and taking the short walk across the old bridge (one block east) into the heart of Nuevo Laredo's shopping district.

Just after you cross, in the first block, on the right is **Jugos Californias,** one of the town's best stops for fresh fruit drinks (called *licuados*). Simply select the fruits of your choice (papaya, mango, strawberries, bananas, watermelons, guayaba, pineapple, even carrots), a mixer of water (don't worry, it's *purificado*) or milk, and any extras (pecans, soy beans, granola) you might want thrown in. Pointing will work, and most of the girls speak a little English. Everything is heaped in a blender and whirled till frothy. We swear by these liquid lunches. If you need an energy boost (and you will, to deal with persistent shopkeeps), try the Samson Bomb: orange juice, fresh coconut, papaya, honey, and spirulina (sea kelp). Another favorite of ours is the Fruit Salad Shake: milk, eggnog, and cherry liqueur.

Just down the street, you'll pass **Nuevo Leon,** the best spot in town for authentic barbecued cabrito (roasted kid). You'll recognize the restaurant by the spitted goat in the window; don't hesitate to try it. Ordering is a cinch since cabrito is the only thing on the menu.

If it happens that you decided to drive over the bridge, you'll find **La Palapa,** a favorite stop for fajitas (skirt steak) and alambres (shish kebab) sold by the kilo. Frijoles borracho (beans cooked in beer) and guacamole accompany the meals.

And of course to toast your day in Mexico, there's the obligatory stop at the original **Cadillac Bar** (we wrote about its Houston clone on page 69). Not quite the elegant dining spot it was when we were taken here as children, it's still a sentimental favorite. Stop in for the Ramos Gin Fizz, said to have been invented on the spot.

THE TACK ROOM, *Zaragoza Exit, Laredo*

Across from the manicured San Augustin Plaza, Tom Herring, local entrepreneur and hotel magnate, has breathed new life into a historic row of riverside structures. A convent lives again as a mini-mall, an abandoned import lot sees action as a disco, and at the center, a former high school has graduated into La Posada, as fine a hotel as you'll find anywhere, and certainly the loveliest in Laredo. A cool white, arched, and airy resort entwined by bougainvillea and encrusted with Mexican tile, La Posada has recently absorbed a two-story, verandah-swaddled turn-of-the-century home and restored it as an elegant bar and restaurant.

It would be hard not to like The Tack Room, even if it weren't serving some of the best food in the city. For one thing, the

138

pewter and forest green of it all contrasts marvelously with the dusty frontier town image Laredo has long sought to escape. Second, the staff is everything a fine restaurant demands—informed, helpful, attentive. And then there's the magnificent grill, copper-clad and faithfully attended by a be-toqued master of the medium rare.

Most patrons will tell you they adore the house specialty, a backstrap of baby Canadian spare ribs ($9). They are wonderfully juicy, as are freshly cut T-bones and tenderloins. And the Carpetbagger, a 12-ounce sirloin stuffed with oysters and herbs ($16.50), laid to rest all our preconceptions about Mexican food being the only thing to eat in Laredo.

The less carnivorous are not overlooked: they adore the tasteful chicken breast and fajita brochette ($11.50), and the artichoke hearts served with hot sourdough bread is delightful. The salad bar features a satisfying selection of fresh vegetables.

Putting talk of real food aside for a moment, let us say that one of the things that most impressed us was the much-touted rosin-baked potato. After a highly detailed explanation of this unique contraption that melts the pine rosin into which the potato sinks, we, of course, had to try it. Yes, believe it or not, it does produce a better potato: moist but not gummy, slightly flavored by the rosin. You'll like it, except that you can no longer nosh on the skins, because they have been transformed into an unchewable shellac.

As for the rest of our meal, a filet mignon cooked to order and topped with pimentos, mushrooms, onions, and fennel was delicious. A dinner special of a crabmeat omelette served with a broiled tomato and cream of broccoli soup couldn't have been more *sabrosa*.

HOURS Sun.–Thurs. 4 pm–midnight; Fri. & Sat. till 1 am.

SPECS 1000 Zaragoza; (512) 722-1701; V/MC/AE/D; full bar.

DIRECTIONS **Southbound:** Take the last exit before the new International Bridge (Zaragoza) and drive along the frontage road south for 3 blocks to Zaragoza, the last street before the river. ■ Turn right onto Zaragoza and drive 2 blocks to the plaza. La Posada is on your left (parking available in the hotel garage), and The Tack Room is on the east end of the complex.

Northbound: Turn left at Farragut (first U.S. light after crossing the bridge), cross I-35, and turn left on the east frontage road. Continue to Zaragoza, then as above from ■.

COTULLA STYLE PIT BAR-B-QUE, *Exit 3A, Laredo*

In 1968, Manuel Sanchez moved his restaurant (and his father's before him) from the family's chaparral hometown of Cotulla to the Gateway City of Laredo. Once there, he set up his barbecue pit in back of a tiny cottage. That rickety structure is now lost within the heart of a block-wide complex of dining rooms, prep room, freezers, and kitchens. If the higglety-pigglety expansion of Cotulla Pit doesn't clue you in to the popularity of the restaurant, consider the fact that *the* pit is now *two* pits, two *forty-foot* pits! When you see pits like these you know that the house specialty is barbecue. And indeed no one prepares barbecued beef and brisket like the Sanchez family.

Barbecue this tender requires a pit-stoking ritual that is begun as early as 2 am on weekends. When the mesquite has burned to just the right temperature, the meat is loaded into a position that allows it to cook overnight in indirect heat. The result is legendary—ask anyone in Laredo.

Where there's barbecue and handmade flour tortillas, you'll find that South Texas staple, the mariachi (soft tortilla tacos). Throw in the variables of potato, egg, onion, beans, cheese, chiles, sausage, avocado, and tomatoes, and you get 22 varieties of fillings for the more than 3,000 tortillas rolled each day by the good ladies of the kitchen (they're paid by the tortilla).

During the week, as many as nine cooks and four tortilla ladies assure everything from meat to guacamole is made up fresh daily. On weekends, the Sanchez brothers serve barbacoa, barbecuing hundreds of cow heads for patrons, who line up around the parking lot. We can only assume that a penchant for eyes and tongues is an acquired taste, but we were comforted to learn that the more familiar forms of barbecue are available for the squeamish.

HOURS Tues.–Sat. 8 am–5:45 pm; Sun. 8 am–2:45 pm.

SPECS   4502 McPherson; (512) 724-5747; no credit cards; no bar.

DIRECTIONS   Take Exit 3A (Calton) to the light and turn right if northbound, left if southbound, onto Calton. In 1.4 miles, turn right on McPherson. Cotulla Pit is on the left, less than a half mile down.

REYES' CAFE, *Exit 39, Encinal*

Dusty Encinal, population 704, supports three cafes and a snack bar. Maybe all that food for those few people is the reason that the town is full of barrel-chested cowboys settling into barrel-bellied old men heavily dependent upon their suspenders. But then Encinal has always been a popular place to eat: its recorded history began in 1777 when travelers found the area grazed bare by a herd of some 3,000 mavericks.

It was a hard choice between a nameless but air-conditioned cafe and Reyes', but we liked the *El Macho* emblazoned on Reyes' roof, and the faded shamrocks and green crepe paper taped to the windows. Inside the cool, dark cafe/general store, turquoise and red booths skirt a central dining room. The broad path between booths and counter leads to a rust-red back room with priscilla curtains and the original black-and-white tile floor.

For breakfast we ordered mariachis, soft tortilla breakfast tacos offered with a variety of fillings. We tried the carne guisada, a specialty of the house, along with Mexican sausage and eggs, and refried beans. All the fillings were delicious, well-seasoned (but not too hot), and piled into fresh, thick, hot flour tortillas. The tariff—75 cents each. Beware the yellow plastic coffee cup in the center of your table; it's filled with the most picante salsa in Texas, crunchy with serranos and guaranteed to make your ears sweat. If you indulge in the hot sauce (and you should), note that beer is $1.35 a quart. You may need a gallon!

The day's special included fried chicken with cream gravy, baked potato, pork and beans, and salad for $3.25 (an extra piece of chicken is 50 cents), and our carne guisada plate (beef stewed with bell pepper, onion, and potato in a thin chile gravy) was served with Spanish rice, refried beans, and salad for the same price. The handwritten menu is crowded with Mexican specialties, but it also brags about the house burgers and steaks.

141

Popular with young mothers and little girls in their First Communion dresses, gas station attendants, and farm workers just passing through, Reyes' is a colorful, marvelous stop along a long and empty road.

HOURS   Open 7 days, 7 am–10:30 pm.

SPECS   Main St. (no number); (512) 948-7374; no credit cards; beer only.

DIRECTIONS   From Exit 39, turn right if southbound, left if northbound, until you reach the stop sign. Turn left here onto Encinal's main drag; Reyes' is on the left.

CHUCK WAGON CAFE, *Exit 68, Cotulla*

A family of five, a flock of snowbirds, two grande dames, a chain-smoking old lady in a leopard print blouse, and three stout highway patrolmen were already seated when we squeezed into the Chuck Wagon at high noon one blistering hot day in early March. They weren't there for the decor (standard steakhouse issue in the back, bright but plain cafe-style up front). They were there for the food: good and cheap. The $3.95 daily special brought lightly breaded strips of buttery chicken breast, canned corn, and a mess of fresh spinach plus a couple of boxy dinner rolls, sweet butter, and a cube of dry chocolate cake held together with canned icing.

Dessert aside—and our waitress was quick to lament the fact that it wasn't homemade, telling us that when a local lady shows up with home-baked goods, Chuck Wagon patrons stomp all over each other getting in the door—the meal was perfectly acceptable, while nothing to write books about. Homemade vegetable soup and a well-kept salad bar make this a dependable stop, but it was the leopard lady (in the end she crashed the grande dames' party) who made it memorable.

HOURS   Sun.–Thurs. 6 am–10 pm; Fri. & Sat. 6 am–midnight.

SPECS   Main St. (no number); (512) 879-2860; V/MC; full bar.

DIRECTIONS   From Exit 68 turn left if southbound, right if north-bound, onto U.S. 81. In 0.8 mile you'll reach the Chuck Wagon, on the left.

ABOUT PEARSALL

The seat of Frio County is a desert oasis in a sea of farm and ranch land—50,000 acres of watermelons, peaches, grain sorghum, cotton, cattle, pigs, and let us not forget the goobers (pay homage at the downtown Peanut Monument). Crops and farmers' markets everywhere, but not a place to eat. At least not when we visited.

Family-owned **Mi Tierra,** four blocks south of downtown on Frio, was recommended to us by everyone in town, but the doors were barred the Monday afternoon we tried them. Our second choice, the rickety Campbell House mansion on the north side of town, has closed forever. If you arrive in town between Tuesday and Saturday, our informants would steer you to Mi Tierra's cheese enchiladas or chicken-fried steaks. Otherwise, **Porter House Inn** on the interstate served us a decent steak the last time we dodged tumbleweeds here, and these days it's rumored to bake its own cinnamon rolls, making it worthy of further investigation.

TRIPLE C STEAKHOUSE, *Exit 122, Devine*

The waitresses wear pink jumpers and ties, the walls are veneered with pseudo-plank paneling, the art is mostly big-eyed Indian children and sultry, bare-shouldered squaws, and the furnishings are so new they squeak. All that said, Triple C just might serve the best steaks in Texas, simply and perfectly prepared. There's nothing better after a day of driving though South Texas brush country.

One of the only completely integrated meat operations in the country, Cox Cattle Company (Triple C, get it?) raises, grains, butchers, and sells its own cattle by the pound or platter. You can have the cut of your choice in just about any increment you fancy. Even a plain old top-butt sirloin is served in 4-, 6-, 8-, and 12-ounce portions ($4.95–$7.95 with salad bar and potato), and it arrived just about as close to fork-tender as a top butt can be, gorgeously grained and cooked to a medium-rare turn. It's basically meat and potatoes here, but if that's what your teeth are aching for, this is the place.

Oh yes, the pies ain't shabby either—mounds of coconut, peach, and Dutch apple. And breakfast (with grits) is served till 11 o'clock.

A word to greenhorns: Texans don't insult a premier cut of beef by slathering it with steaksauce; if you ask for the stuff, Triple C will serve it, but as the menu says they'll charge you 25 cents for the chef's hankies.

HOURS   Open 7 days, 6 am–10 pm.

SPECS   I-35 at TX Route 173; (512) 663-5290; V/MC/AE; full bar.

DIRECTIONS   Northbound: Take Exit 122 and continue north along access road to stop sign. Turn left and cross under I-35 to restaurant on the left.

Southbound: Take Exit 122 and continue on access road to Triple C, on the right at I-35 and TX Route 173.

ABOUT SAN ANTONIO

We are so fond of San Antonio that it is difficult to limit ourselves to recommending a simple two or three favorite restaurants from among the dozens we frequent. We have featured **Ras Tzemru,** an excellent Ethiopian restaurant, and the less colorful but equally superb **Viet-Nam Restaurant** under I-37 (pages 177–179). Under I-10 we give special attention to **La Fogata,** one of our favorite Mexican places in the Western (or any other) Hemisphere (see below and page 60). But here we offer a round-up of several other San Antonio standouts for your consideration should you be lucky enough to be spending some time in this splendid city.

410 Diner is just what its name suggests, a diner serving road-food classics like chicken livers and meat loaf, accompanied by mounds of fresh vegetables. In addition to the old standbys, there are a few upscale surprises (broiled redfish, spinach soufflé). A popular, crowded place, but there are two of them, both reachable from I-10 (8315 Broadway at Loop I-10, and Wurzbach at I-10).

When we have a little extra cash, which isn't often enough, we visit **Crumpets,** where the chef never disappoints us with his beautiful presentations of dishes such as scallops on green pasta, tortilla soup, and Sicilian Chicken (5800 Broadway).

Downtown, you shouldn't miss the institutional **Mi Tierra** (in the Mercado). Although we find it more interesting for its pan dulce (Mexican sticky buns and cakes) than for its Mexican dinners, we do love those year-round Christmas lights and the 24-hour service. And you can't beat the huevos rancheros.

Not to be missed on a Sunday is the champagne brunch ($14.95) laid out by **Las Canarias,** the restaurant of La Mansion, a grande dame among the Riverwalk hotels. This brunch is nothing short of spectacular, offering an endless variety of fresh baked breads, smoked salmon, oysters on the half-shell, boiled shrimp, delicacies such as salmon en croute and beef Wellington, made-to-order omelettes, and dozens of salads; we pray for the courage to pass over the dessert table. Las Canarias serves excellent dinners too, complete with a floor show of flamenco dancers.

Finally, a stop as pleasant for a walk as for lunch is **Los Patios,** a shopping center that looks like a nature center. There are three restaurants—the **Gazebo, La Hacienda,** and the **Brazier**—tucked away among the art galleries and design studios, all pleasant, but we really come here to watch the Mandarin ducks swimming in the creek that runs through extensive grounds. Kids and adults alike love the swinging bridge (Exit 22 off Loop 410 westbound).

VIET-NAM RESTAURANT,
Hildebrand Exit, San Antonio

See page 178 for a fine Vietnamese restaurant.

DIRECTIONS Follow directions on page 179. I-35 and I-37 are one and the same at this point.

LA FOGATA, *I-10 Interchange, San Antonio*

For Mexican food in a town that prides itself on Mexican food, you can't do much better than La Fogata. At least we never have. See page 60 for a description.

DIRECTIONS At the interchange, take I-10 West (toward El Paso) about a mile to Exit 565. From I-10 Exit 565, turn right onto Vance Jackson. La Fogata is about a mile down, on the left.

KRAUSE'S CAFE, *Exit 46, New Braunfels*

We've always liked Krause's Cafe, but we liked it a lot more before everybody else discovered it. Even as recently as 10 years ago, all the cakes and pies were baked on the premises; these days, close to 30 varieties are brought in from the local bakery, Naegelin's (an institution in its own right). Oh, they're good all right, but we think the fact that the kitchen no longer bakes is symptomatic of how tourist hordes can overload a small-town operation.

But we won't stop eating here. There's no place else we'd rather jawbone over pork hocks and sauerkraut ($4.25), stewed spare ribs (with sauerkraut and dumplings, $4.50), or bratwurst ($4.25). Just the same, we think the addition of barbecue and Mexican food to the menu has pushed Krause's cooks to their limits.

Though it looks purebred, Krause's is actually a German deli-come-lately; when Gene Krause opened the cafe in 1938, he was strictly a burger and stew man. The deli line was added by Krause's son and daughter-in-law. We like the German plates best, especially during slow times, when we don't have to compete with the river rats for the kitchen's attention (New Braunfels is famous for its Comal River tube chute and Guadalupe canoeing).

But even in winter, you're likely to find Krause's full; locals fond of the daily specials pack the four dining rooms every day. When we visited, they were stuffing themselves on grain-fed catfish, hash browns, baked eggplant, macaroni and cheese, and green beans (with choice of two vegetables, $5.75). All that chow —and it was good—comes with homemade cornbread (and, alas, margarine).

German dinners are served with black bread, corn pones, kraut, and fried potatoes. We suggest you avoid the Mexican food, chef salad, and barbecue. Chili, stew, and vegetable soup are as good as they were when Mr. Krause was in the kitchen. And breakfast still brings light biscuits, home-smoked bacon and ham, and plate-sized hotcakes.

Do try the goodies from **Naegelin's Bakery** (Black Forest cake, chocolate mint Bavarian pie, German chocolate, and on and on). Even better, stop in at Naegelin's yourself; it's just a couple of blocks away.

HOURS   Mon.–Sat. 6:30 am–8:30 pm. Closed Sun.

SPECS   148 S. Castell; (512) 625-7581; no credit cards; imported beer and wine.

DIRECTIONS   Take Exit 46 to bottom of ramp and immediately turn right if southbound, left if northbound, onto South Seguin Ave. Continue 1 mile to Coll (4th light) and turn left, then immediately right onto Castell. Krause's is a block down, on the left. For **Naegelin's Bakery,** instead of turning onto Coll from S. Seguin, continue two more blocks along Seguin and you'll see it on your right.

ABOUT AUSTIN

We'd be doing you a disservice if we were to write a word about Austin and not mention East Sixth Street (west of I-35), a five-block stretch of historic buildings that have been restored as art galleries, bars, and oh-so-many restaurants. We'd be doing you a greater disservice if we didn't tell you that parking anywhere near Sixth can be a pain (try the Littlefield Parking Garage on Brazos). But if you have a few hours to spend and feel like shopping, nibbling, dining, or just plain people-watching, this is the hottest street in town.

Among our favorite spots for lunch, dinner, or drinks are **Santi's Pasta** (love those artichokes and dream about that pizza); **Dan McKlusky's** (great steaks); **Maggie May's** (an Irish pub); and **Wylie's** (a Texafied wine bar, if you can imagine such a thing). Tucked around the corner, on Neches, is **Chez Nous,** a totally unpretentious but thoroughly French cafe.

Leaving Sixth Street behind, some of the best restaurants in town are off the beaten track. **Jeffrey's** is quite possibly the best restaurant in the city, though a little tricky to find (1204 West Lynn; ask anyone for directions).

Back on the interstate, we are quite fond of **La Talavera** (at La Mansion), an expensive, exquisite, dinner-only restaurant. Though quite convenient to the highway, its elegance doesn't favor it as a typical highway stop, but if you're an atypical highway driver you might like to pause for what may be an unforgettable meal (when's the last time you ate an orchid?). And you can even spend the night at La Mansion, as gracious as the haciendas south of the border.

Finally, we must mention our favorite place for Mexican cuisine, **Abuelita's.** It's hidden away in the university area, so you may have to battle your way through regiments of the prep and punksters, but once you get a table, you'll know why we sent you (hint: best fajitas in town). Recently opened is the more accessible uptown Abuelita's (310 Colorado Street), several blocks west of I-35.

In the meantime, most I-35 passers-by will probably be very happy availing themselves of the two easily accessible restaurants that we feature below.

THE HEARTH, *Exit 234C, Austin*

We figured we'd just better admit it straight out that the real reason we keep coming back here is to eat the popovers. Huge, light, hot popovers. We don't care what's on the menu after the basket of these monsters arrives. But for those who don't share our popover fanaticism, we have to say that the Hearth does some pretty nice things with fish, beef, and vegetables, too.

Special entrees change weekly, but last time we visited this pink and gray Victorian parlor we found ourselves intrigued by an offering of leg of lamb in a chocolate coffee marinade (interesting but not totally successful, $12.50). For our second entree we had a hard time deciding between the "Egyptian" game hen (a Cornish game hen made Egyptian with a stuffing of bulgur, red and green peppers, and walnuts) and the more traditional sweetbreads with pears (and rice pilaf, $12). The sweetbreads edged the hen and won our hearts. An appetizer of tomato gin soup (thick with onion, celery, and mushrooms, but with little flavor of gin) and a mixed green salad (butter lettuce, avocado slices) in a honey-lemon dill dressing were just fine, too.

We resisted the evening's pastries, but chocolate truffles arrived with the check.

HOURS Lunch: Mon.–Fri. 11:30–2. Dinner: Mon.–Sat. 6–10. Closed Sun.

SPECS Symphony Square, 11th and Red River; (512) 477-6647; V/MC/AE; full bar.

DIRECTIONS **Northbound:** Take Exit 234C (6th–12th sts.) and continue along the frontage road north to 12th. Left on 12th to cross over I-35, and drive two blocks to Red River. ■ Turn left; the Hearth is in the middle of the block in Symphony Square.

Southbound: Take Exit 234C and immediately get into the far right-hand lane for a right turn at the light (12th). Drive 2 blocks to Red River, then as above from ■.

CARLA'S, *Exit 235B, Austin*

Carla's is all Austin. The little cottage with hardwood floors. The cats on the porch. The mix of the vested and high-heeled with the sneakered and backpacked. What brings them together is freshly prepared, healthful food. Yuppies like Carla's, but so does the university crowd, and even some of the lunatic fringe. We eat at Carla's frequently, but while we were driving around the Southwest being unfaithful to our hometown favorites, Carla's closed, remodeled, and reopened. We'd heard about the larger serving area (a brick patio under the trees), but we were anxious to see whether these ambitious changes had affected the kitchen.

What we found were the same basic lunch and dinner menus, with an even wider variety of daily specials—the key to Carla's success. Still featured is our favorite stir-fry dinner (seasonal veggies, ginger, and garlic, all wok-fried in peanut oil with or without a chicken breast ($4.75/$5.95). The day's blackboard specials included Thai beef salad (marinated tenderloin, oranges, red onion, and tomato in a chile, lime, and cilantro dressing, $6.95); Acadian peppered shrimp (shrimp sautéed in pepper, herbs, and butter and served over rice, $7.95), and another Carla's classic, black bean soup. All seemed well at Carla's, and we heaved a sigh of relief.

In addition to the blackboard specials, soups and salads make up the light lunch menu, along with hot brisket and melted cheese sandwiches (Swiss, blue, and jack). Some of our past feasts have centered on dishes such as rainbow trout Provençale, rack of lamb, and baby salmon with raspberry butter (marvelous viewing as well as eating). At lunch and dinner, everything is served with fresh bread from the Dutch Royal Bakery.

Satisfied that all the changes at Carla's were for the better, we relished the anticipation of a Saturday or Sunday brunch on the patio listening to the birds, reading the paper, lolling in the sun, and addressing our gustatory attention to biscuits, home fries, pancakes, and exotic coffees. Carla's made us glad to be home.

HOURS   Mon.–Thurs. 11 am–10 pm; Fri. 11 am–midnight; Sat. 9 am–midnight; Sun. 9 am–10 pm. Brunch: Sat. & Sun. 9 am–2 pm.

SPECS   2113 Manor Rd; (512) 476-5858; V/MC/AE; beer & wine.

DIRECTIONS   Northbound: Stay on the lower level of I-35 as it passes through town (the two left lanes). Just after the interstate divides into upper and lower decks, take Exit 235B (Manor Rd.) and immediately get into the far right lane for a right turn at the first light (Manor). ■ Carla's is ½ mile down, on the right in a beige house. The sign is small, so keep a sharp lookout.

Southbound: Take Exit 235B to light and cross over I-35. Turn left on Manor, then as above from ■.

ABOUT ROUND ROCK

One of the best restaurants along I-35 is found in Round Rock, just off the interstate. Unfortunately, **The Inn at Brushy Creek** is open only Thursday, Friday, and Saturday nights, and is so popular that it usually requires advance reservations. Still, we can't write about Round Rock, Texas, without telling you about this tin-roofed, frontier inn (a restaurant only) and its elegant country menu: coulibiac of salmon, beef braised with claret and cream, trout Verdi, a memorable Portuguese soup, and more. If you're passing through on a weekend or spending some time in Austin, you should try your luck.

THE ALPINE COTTAGE, *Exit 253, Round Rock*

The Alpine Cottage is actually a cement-floored, pre-fab garage. We tell you that because we defy you to remember it ten minutes into the restaurant, surrounded by singing, dancing crowds, bustling waitresses, and steaming platters of hot apple streudel.

Being in the Alpine Cottage reminded us of being kids and turning the linen closet into a treehouse. Here, with a little imagination, anything is believable. As we ate our Leberknödel soup (the knödel is a mound of pâté rising out of a rich, oniony beef broth like a desert island) and gulped our dark beer, we began to believe we were in a German beer drinking hall rather than a few yards off the Missouri Pacific line in Round Rock, Texas.

Such is the power of good food, charming waitresses, and German bock beer. After filling ourselves on soup, fresh-baked rye bread, and hunks of sweet butter, we went ahead and ordered a bratwurst plate. The pale and tasty beef and pork sausage links arrived with a full escort of sauerkraut, red cabbage, and real German potato salad—not too sweet, not too vinegary ($6.95 for the plate, which included the aforementioned soup). Equally delicious was a plate of liver and bacon, done to a turn, and covered in a smooth pan gravy. And while we stuck to the peasant dishes, you shouldn't hesitate to order Spiessbraten (Chateaubriand).

If the food here doesn't make you want to join the singalong (Thursday through Saturday nights), Johanna Maddox wants to know about it. After all, she didn't bring her recipes from Munich to disappoint her customers. You won't have to look for Johanna, she'll be around to make sure you're happy. And if you plan on going anywhere after topping off your meal with her hot cheese streudel and ice cream, you'd better ask her to show you the steps of the Chicken Dance. It's guaranteed to return your mobility.

HOURS Lunch: Mon.–Fri. 11 am–2 pm. Dinner: Mon.–Sat. 5:30–9 pm.

SPECS 1103 Wonder Drive; (512) 255-0517; V/MC; wine and beer.

DIRECTIONS Take Exit 273 to light and turn left if northbound, right if southbound. Continue along this road as it curves past Safeway. Less than ½ mile from that point, just before the railroad tracks, turn right onto Wonder. The Alpine is on the right.

SMITTY'S, *Exit 300, Temple*

There's something Early College Student about Smitty's, a natty little burger-basket restaurant just off Temple's main drag. Maybe it was the juke box just inside the front door (you play, Smitty pays), maybe it was the video games. Whatever it was, we certainly never expected to find several local grandmothers staking out booths here. Yet they were all around us, devouring their burgers with great gusto. No wonder: Smitty turns out ten varieties of monstrous half-pound "Famous Burgers" that even *your* grandmother would approve of (average $2.50). And it's not only the burgers that are 100 percent fresh, 100 percent real: nothing here is frozen or pre-fab. Be sure to try the house spuds, called "Kurly Q's," sliced thin and fried into curls ($1.35).

Burgers and fries, homemade chili, potato skins heaped with beans and cheese—if you're hungry for some basic chow, you can't go wrong here. We were especially taken with the Fanciful Fruit Basket (everything is served in baskets): a mound of miniature fried pies. These crusty little crescents are stuffed with apple and pineapple bits, deep fried, sprinkled with cinnamon, and served with a strawberry yogurt dip ($3.95). One order would serve the whole neighborhood (and probably does).

Grandmothers and country cottage décor aside, Smitty's reminded us of late night pig-outs the night before finals. Indulge your sophomoric streak here, and slurp down one of the house drinks: frozen margaritas, piña coladas, and strawberry daiquiris on tap.

HOURS   Mon.–Sat. 11 am–10 pm. Closed Sun.

SPECS   1615 West Ave. L; (817) 773-0869; MC/V; beer, margaritas, piña coladas, and strawberry daiquiris.

DIRECTIONS   Southbound: Take Exit 300 and cross under the interstate to Avenue H. ■ Continue along Avenue H less than 1 mile to South 31st and turn right. Smitty's is ½ block down, on the left.

Northbound: Take Exit 300 and continue along access road to Ave. H. Turn right on Ave. H, then as above from ■.

BLUEBONNET CAFE, *Exit 300, Temple*

This cafe is as fifties-modern as it was the day it opened. Neat as a pin, all chrome and vinyl and no frivolity, the Bluebonnet is a cafe devoted to good food and friendly service. From baby T-bones to the anything-but-standard chicken-fried steak (recommended as a statewide best in *Texas Highways* magazine), the food is cooked to order from the freshest local ingredients. We'd been eating all day by the time we pulled up here, but we couldn't resist ordering up a bowl of black-eyed peas and a side of cornbread muffins ($1.50). We weren't disappointed: the peas were well-seasoned and laced with green beans, and the warm muffins tasted as if they'd just been plucked from the oven. Stuffed, we still managed to dig into a huge wedge of egg custard pie: a creamy blend of nutmeg and eggs, it was everything we expect of a first-class dessert (85 cents).

The Bluebonnet has always been run by the J. C. Pitts family, and when Mrs. Pitts wants to know if you've enjoyed your meal, she really means it. We can't imagine that you'd ever have to say no.

HOURS   Fri.–Wed. 5 am–9 pm. Closed Thurs.

SPECS   705 South 25th; (817) 773-6654; no credit cards; no bar.

DIRECTIONS   **Southbound:** From Exit 300, turn left to cross under the interstate on Ave. H. Continue on Ave. H for 1 mile to 25th. The Bluebonnet is on the corner, on the left.

Northbound: From Exit 300, continue along the access road to Avenue H. Turn right onto Ave. H, and go 1 mile to 25th. It's on the corner, on the left.

THE HEALTH CAMP, *Exit 333-A, Waco*

We assure you there's absolutely nothing healthy about this joint. In fact, we think it's only one cut above the local Dairy Queen, but so many people and publications have raved about the place (the *Washington Post* reported Health Burgers to be among the best hamburgers in the U.S.) that we feel obliged to tell you about it anyway.

Yes, we ate one of the famous, greasy Health Burgers ($1.10); no, we didn't try one of the 10 different flavors of malts and shakes which include cherry, butterscotch, coffee, and root beer. Our opinion? We liked the orange-haired, extremely unhealthy-looking waitress best. We have to think that the prices (cheap) and the camp are the draw, not the burgers. Then again, you might love 'em.

HOURS   Open 7 days, 11 am–10 pm.

SPECS   2601 Circle; (817) 752-2081; no credit cards; no bar.

DIRECTIONS   Southbound: Take Exit 333-A to the second light and turn left to cross over I-35 on La Salle. ■ Continue 1 block to traffic circle and circle ¾ of the way around to the Health Camp.

Northbound: Take Exit 333-A to first light and turn right, then as above from ■.

THE WATER WORKS, *Exit 335-C, Waco*

Mobil Oil's flying red horse, an MKT boxcar, "In Memoriam" stained glass windows, brass beds turned into booths, the hum of neon—get the picture? We long ago tired of restaurants done up in nostalgic hodgepodge, but we thought the 1914 Waco Water Works building was somehow suited to all its eccentric miscellany. And we'll forgive chef and owner Geoffrey Michael his indoor streetlights as long as his kitchen continues to turn out such bountiful, well-prepared, and well-presented plates.

We began with an omelette Grand Mere, which turned out to be at least three eggs overflowing with sautéed mushrooms, potatoes, and bacon, topped off with a ladling of a rich Mornay sauce ($4.25). Another order brought the mignonettes of beef Oscar, a tenderloin of beef surrounded by king crab, asparagus, mushrooms and topped with béarnaise sauce ($10.50). Geoffrey Michael, who began his career at New York's Plaza Hotel, knows a thing or two about perfect sauces. Next time we're going to try his unadulterated pepper steak, encrusted with cracked peppercorns and broiled, and served with sautéed onions and mushrooms ($8.50).

Side dishes were equally pleasing. The clam chowder had plenty of clams and the baked zucchini was rich in Swiss and Romano cheese.

The only flaw was the table crock of herbed butter. We suspect the kitchen used garlic salt in an already salted butter—it was salty enough to require a warning label from the Surgeon General.

HOURS   Lunch: Tues.–Sat. 11 am–2 pm; Dinner: Tues.–Sat. 5 pm–10:30 pm; Sunday brunch 11 am–2 pm. Closed Mon.

SPECS   101 Mill at Lake Brazos; (817) 756-2181; AE/DC/MC/V; full bar.

DIRECTIONS   **Northbound:** Take Exit 335-C to lights and cross under I-35. Turn left and drive 1 mile to the Water Works, on the right.

Southbound: Take Exit 335 to Lake Brazos Dr. and turn right. Go 1 mile to the Water Works, on the right.

LAKE BRAZOS DINER, *Exit 335-C, Waco*

Even though we were unable to try it out, we heard such good things about the Lake Brazos Diner that we had to pass along the information. It may not look like much more than a shoe box, but we hear that inside you'll find LaVerne Gore cooking up some of the best soul food in Texas (open for lunch and early dinner). It's on the right on the way to the Water Works, above.

ABOUT I-35E AND I-35W

As I-35 approaches the dual metropolis of Dallas/Fort Worth, it splits into I-35E and I-35W, which rejoin on the far side of the Metroplex. I-35E goes through Dallas, while I-35W cuts its swath through Fort Worth. Through travelers can take their pick.

Here we present restaurants accessible from I-35E in Dallas and Waxahachie. On page 163 we give directions to an excellent Fort Worth restaurant accessible from I-35W. You may also want to read "About Fort Worth," page 99.

THE 1879 TOWNHOUSE, *Exit 397, Waxahachie*

Waxahachie may look familiar: *Places in the Heart* is only one of many movies filmed here. Almost always there is a production crew in town. It's easy to see what draws visual artists to this gently rolling, gingerbreaded, and tornado-threatened prairie. Even if you couldn't get a hot dog in Waxahachie, it would be worth a drive-through. The good news is that you can get cooking to make you homesick here, free of tinny flavors and freezer burn. At the same time, you can pick up news on the Annual Gingerbread Trail Home Show and local flea markets.

It was too late to make reservations at the world-famous (thanks to those movie crews) Durham House, so we knew we wouldn't be dining on rack of lamb the evening of our visit. But with no complaints, we made our way to The 1879 Townhouse. This century-old building (a restaurant and bar since the thirties) may not be as exquisite as the Durham House, but its simple fare more than satisfies. Stake out a view of Waxahachie's awesome courthouse and you'll never miss the Durham House's mahogany mantels.

From the Good Things First column, we ordered a bowl of chili, followed by a vegetable plate chosen from the Better Things Second lineup (three veggies for $2.75). Our fresh-cooked black-eyed peas, fried okra, and green beans were served with a basket of steaming hot corn muffins, and the chili (we sinned and ordered ours with beans) fired us up against the day's chill.

Observing the Sunday diners around us, we determined that the pot roast ($4.75) and T-bone ($9.95) were as well prepared as our little sampling. But we did wonder about the old gent seated in the back who kept raising his hand. The waitress would skitter over and as soon as she got there, he'd lower his hand and return to eating his ice cream. Finally, he caught her perplexed expression and explained that ice cream made him cough and that raising his hand when he felt a whooping fit coming on cut the hacking short. Obviously, giving up ice cream was out of the question. It was homemade peach!

HOURS   Open 7 days 6:30 am–9 pm (until 10:30 on weekends).

SPECS   South College and Franklin; (214) 937-7261; AE/MC/V; full bar upstairs.

DIRECTIONS **Northbound:** Take Exit 397 and wind 2 miles into town. ■ As you cross the bridge into downtown Waxahachie, note the old wooden bridge to the right. You'll see the courthouse ahead on the horizon. Continue to the traffic light and turn right on Main to drive to the town square. Circle left around the courthouse to the southwest corner of the square. To return to I-35 heading north, return to U.S. Hwy. 77 and follow it north out of town to I-35E.

Southbound: Take Exit 397 and cross over I-35 left and go 2 miles into town. Then as above from ■.

ABOUT DALLAS

Dallas is home to some of the finest restaurants in the state, many of which, unfortunately, are not accessible to the traveler owing to hours, location, dress codes, or prices. If you plan to be in town overnight or longer, however, do yourself a favor and visit one or more of the following:

Callaud's (2619 McKinney). A classic French restaurant that bears no resemblance to its delicatessen forebears. Now it's a spot for chicken pâté in champagne aspic, grilled salmon with wild mushrooms, or rack of lamb. Jacket required.

Jean-Claude (2404 Cedar Springs). As French as they come, but with a floor show—the chef operates in full view of the dining room. Though the menu changes frequently, you can usually count on frogs' legs mousse. Coat and tie.

Routh Street Cafe. If you haven't yet discovered the New American Cuisine, this is the place to experience the delightful and innovative pairing of the old and new, the classical and the regional: quail and tomatillos, hickory-smoked pheasant, and wild strawberries in red banana ice cream. This is one of our favorite restaurants anywhere. Dinner only. Reservations required. *Prix fixe* ($42). Less pricey appetizer-sized nibbles of the evening's fare available a la carte in the lounge.

Uncle Tai's Hunan Yuan. Szechuan at its most elegant. Jacket at dinner (Galleria).

If you've only one night for indulgence, we must say that of all the restaurants in Big D, the **French Room** (the Adolphus Hotel) wears the star-studded crown. In fact, the truly self-indulgent will wish to check into the Adolphus (built in 1912 by beer baron Adolphus Busch as a baroque token of his esteem for the Texas city he regarded as his second home). Enjoy afternoon tea as well as a late dinner in the French Room. Then just take an elevator ride to one of the splendid rooms—ask about a skylight or terrace suite.

Tea is served weekdays (3–5) in the walnut-paneled main lobby amidst Louis XV and XVI furnishings. As you make your selections of finger sandwiches and pastries, the likes of which can seldom be found this side of heaven (or maybe they're too sinful), a 6-foot portrait of Napoleon Bonaparte, resplendent in ermine robes, greedily eyes the clotted cream.

Dinner in the French Room means choosing from 50 various dishes (appetizers, soups, salads, entrees). Never fear, waiters who seem to be as highly trained as the chefs are ready to discuss every selection. Not that their full and mouthwatering descriptions make it any easier to choose from among the delicacies such as snowpea soup with red caviar (almost too beautiful to eat), frogs' legs salad (boneless flesh tossed with watercress, bacon, and a warm vinaigrette), and entrees that include some of the best game dishes served anywhere. And we can scarcely think about the morel mushrooms or truffle raviolis without our mouths watering. As for dessert, well, we want to leave something for you to discover, but we will say that the chocolate truffles that arrived while we were making up our minds did nothing to still our appetites for the Spanish strawberries. In a word: unforgettable. (Reservations a must; coat and tie; very expensive.)

For more accessible, more affordable eateries, read on.

GENNIE'S BISHOP GRILL, *Exit 426B, Dallas*

Blink and you'll miss this blip of a neighborhood grill, but the smells of home cooking will keep you from going too far astray. A onetime sleeper, Gennie's has been discovered by Dallasites hungry for big eats and little prices. During its limited hours, Gennie's is packed to the rafters with hardhats and downtown refugees. Never mind—just like Grandma's table, there's always room for one more.

One step into this homespun cafeteria, and we were overwhelmed by the yeasty smells of homemade rolls the size of softballs, and the crackle and pop of grills and fryers turning out hamburger steaks and chicken-frieds. Grab a tray and line up for the meat of your choice and three heaping servings of side dishes ($3.55). This is a macaroni and cheese, fresh green beans, liver and onions, mashed taters and okra kind of place. As the sign says: WE COOK TEXAS FOOD TO FEED TEXANS, NOT FRENCH FOOD TO FEED FRENCHMEN. Don't overlook those mountainous slices of meringue pies, or the house specialty: peanut butter pie. Might as well stick some of that to your ribs while you're at it.

HOURS Mon.–Fri. 11 am–2 pm. Closed Sat. and Sun. We can't help but think that with its increased popularity, Gennie's will expand these hours.

SPECS 308 Bishop; (214) 946-1752; no credit cards; no bar.

DIRECTIONS **Southbound:** Take Exit 426B/8th St. and turn right onto 8th (which becomes Davis in a few blocks). Follow 8th/Davis to Bishop (about 8 blocks) and turn left. Gennie's is on your left.

Northbound: Take Exit 426B and cross over the interstate left on 8th. Stay on 8th, which becomes Davis, to Bishop (about 8 blocks) and turn left. Gennie's is on the left.

LA BOTICA, *I-30 Interchange, Dallas*

See page 129 for a review of this Tex-Mex restaurant in a genuine Tex-Mex neighborhood.

DIRECTIONS At I-30 Interchange, take I-30 east to Exit 47B, then follow directions given on page 130.

THE BRASSERIE, *I-30 Interchange, Dallas*

This restaurant is an ideal late night stop. See page 131 for a description.

DIRECTIONS   From the I-30 Interchange, take I-30 east to Exit 45, then follow directions given on page 132.

LA CAVE, *Exit 429B, Dallas*

Take a superlative wine cellar in a richly renovated ware-house, add peachy silk flowers, forest green table linens, some amiable kitchen arguments (in French and Spanish), and a menu that includes lamb chops and artichaud froid farci (a steamed artichoke stuffed with shrimp), and you've got La Cave, a Texan-Parisian cafe close to the heart of downtown Dallas.

We chose a seat overlooking the construction of a nearby by-pass but scarcely looked up after the arrival of a fresh loaf of French bread and a rose-topped crock of sweet butter—a simple, rich, peasant's delight as satisfying as the meal that followed. After breaking bread, we ordered ratatouille Provençal—a slightly spicy salad of eggplant, zucchini, green pepper, tomato, onion, and garlic gently sautéed in olive oil ($4.75), and the house sandwich, an elegant smear of chicken liver pâté seasoned with shallots and brandy with melted brie on French bread ($5.25). Both dishes arrived looking too pretty to eat and proved to taste as good as they looked. As we noshed, the smell of the house blend of Arabica coffee-beans wafted irresistibly toward us. We ordered a pot and were delighted with the smooth, rich flavor ($1.75 for several demitasses).

From the parquet floors and rose-colored stemware to the cases filled with freshly baked fruit tarts, La Cave is an oasis of affordable luxury. In a hurry? This is Texas-style French cooking. For a mere 50 cents extra, you can have it to go.

HOURS Lunch: Mon.–Fri. 11:30 am–2 pm. Cheeseboards and a limited menu from 2 pm–6:30. Dinner: Mon.–Sat. 6 pm–midnight. Sun. brunch 11 am–3 pm.

SPECS 2019 N. Lamar; (214) 871-2072; CB/DC/MC/V/AE; extensive wine list by the glass or bottle; retail prices in the wine cellar with $2 corkage).

DIRECTIONS **Northbound:** Take Exit 429B and turn right at light onto Continental. ■ Continental becomes Lamar as you pass under the old bridge. La Cave is in the red brick warehouse with green awnings immediately on your right. Meter parking on all sides of the building. To return to I-35, retrace your path and turn right at the first light.

Southbound: Take Exit 429B (Continental Ave.) and turn left at the light onto Continental. Then as above from ■. To return to I-35, retrace your path down Continental to second light and turn left onto access road.

KELLER'S DRIVE IN
THE MECCA, *Exit 435, Dallas*

Sometimes you're hungry for a burger. Not a fast-food burger, but a burger you can get your hands on *fast*. Keller's is the old-fashioned answer to that problem—a drive-in. You remember, the kind of drive-in that pre-dates the drive-through. We no sooner pulled up beneath the awning than we were greeted by an order-pad-in-hand carhop. About the only decision to be made is whether or not you want cheese with your burger. And you can order your greasy-good hamburger, with mustard, loaded with lettuce and tomatoes, along with french fries or tater tots—all for less than two bucks. That's the way it's always been at Keller's, although the same burger used to cost two bits. Don't forget to tap your horn before you take off: you'd look pretty silly driving around town with a tray sticking out from your window.

If you're in the Harry Hines neighborhood (north of downtown Dallas), but burgers don't fit the bill, drop in at the **Mecca,** a roadhouse diner famous for its crack of dawn Southern-style breakfasts (grits, biscuits, ham) and field hand lunches (they tell us the fresh vegetables disappear fast). The Mecca is one block south of Keller's, in that two-story house surrounded by cars.

HOURS   Keller's: Mon.–Fri. 10 am–midnight; Sat. 10 am–1 am; Closed Sun.
The Mecca: Mon.–Fri. 5:30 am–3 pm; Sat. 5:30 am–2 pm.

SPECS   Keller's: 10554 Harry Hines; (214) 357-3572; no credit cards; no bar.
The Mecca: 10422 Harry Hines; (214) 352-0051; AE/DC/MC/V; no bar.

DIRECTIONS   Northbound: Take Exit 435 onto Harry Hines and drive 1½ miles to the Mecca, on your right. Keller's is one block north. Don't backtrack to get back on I-35E. Harry Hines parallels the interstate for a couple of miles and then merges with it. You can turn left at the first light north of Keller's to get back on, or continue along Harry Hines until the two roads merge.

Southbound: Take Exit 435, cross under the highway on Harry Hines and drive 1½ miles to the Mecca on the right.

ABOUT FORT WORTH

See page 99 for an overview of Fort Worth restaurants. Our number one favorite, Tours, is quite accessible from I-35W (directions below).

TOURS, I-30 *Interchange, Fort Worth*

Even if you didn't know chef Julie Shaw in high school as we did, you'd want to know her after eating in Tours. See page 134 to find out why.

DIRECTIONS   From I-30 interchange, take I-30 West to Exit 12, then follow westbound directions given on page 136.

ABOUT DENTON

There are some famous hash-slingers in this part of Texas, almost all of them dishing up copious country cooking. If it's rabbit food and home-canned relishes you're hungry for, head over to the **Clay Pot Eatery** in Krum. The more than two dozen selections overflowing the house salad bar include baby corn, watermelon rind pickles, green tomatoes, barbecued rice, and on Saturdays, homemade potato chips. Daily specials include all-you-can-eat catfish, barbecue or fried chicken dinners, but it's hard to pass up the deep-fried Cornish game hens. (Four miles west of I-35, take the Krum Exit and follow the signs. Closed Mon. and Tues.)

Southwest of Denton, in Ponder, the **Ranchman's Cafe** is famous with movie stars and other celebrities (Jimmy Carter's mama even bought the cafe's outhouse) in attendance for hand-cut steaks and daily lunch specials your mother would be proud to serve. Real chocolate (not pudding) pie inspires those in the know to reserve a slice before they even take a seat. (On Main St., 6 worthwhile miles west of I-35. Open all day, every day.)

In Denton proper, **Tom and Jo's Cafe** serves an honest burger and home fries. Nothing to overwhelm you but decent food at a decent price. Individual juke boxes, plus a great neon sign. (702 South Elm, downtown.)

GOURMET II GAINESVILLE, *Exits 498 A and 499,* *Gainesville*

"Y'all ready to eat?" The blue-eyed woman at the door greeted us as if we were her personal dinner guests. "I knew you were coming, so I've got a table already set for you," she continued. As we settled into the modified French provincial chairs she described the buffet with the fervor of a car salesman itemizing the extras. "Sound like a good deal?" she finished. It did. Five bucks bought an honest Swiss steak (more meat than tomatoes), macaroni and cheese with hefty hunks of ham, a tasty, sweet cold roast beef salad (the meat is marinated in a secret sauce that smacks of french dressing), pea salad, carrot and raisin salad, fried zucchini wheels, cucumber and tomato salad, pickled beets, and hot rolls with sweet butter.

Soon after we loaded up, the green-eyed waitress (who turned out to be the cat-eyed sister of the maître d') encouraged us to "go through the line as many times as you like." As much as we would have liked to indulge in seconds, we were just too full. Especially since we had our hearts set on a slice of buttermilk pie—served warm, oozing with butter, with a slightly lemony taste to cut the sweetness. We were still licking our lips miles down the road.

Gourmet II owner and chef Donald McKerson lays out a mean buffet, but then he learned his trade at his mother's apron strings (Mazola McKerson owns the well-established original Gourmet in Ardmore, Oklahoma; see page 166). McKerson is justifiably proud of his lunchtime buffet, but even prouder of his Friday night seafood suppers and Sunday smorgasbords (always turkey and dressing plus pork or chicken, fresh vegetables, and desserts for $7.50). The less than ravenous may order from the menu: chicken, crab, and chef salad plates, sandwiches, and homemade vegetable soup at lunch. For dinner there's shrimp creole, steaks, and chicken in mushroom gravy.

There's nothing too fancy about the Gourmet II. It's just a snug little restaurant with plenty of tables and chairs, some local artwork, and serious soul in the cooking.

HOURS Lunch: Tues.–Fri. 11 am–2 pm; Sun. 11 am–2:30 pm. Dinner: Tues.–Sat. 5:30 pm–9 pm. Closed on Mon.

SPECS North I-35, Service Street; (817) 668-8464; MC/V; no bar.

DIRECTIONS **Northbound:** Take Exit 499 and turn left to cross over the interstate. Then turn immediately right to continue north on the westside access road. Gourmet II is on the left.

Southbound: Take Exit 498A right to the door.

Oklahoma

KWAME'S BARBECUE AND SEAFOOD ROW, *Exit 31A, Ardmore*

In the beginning there was the Gourmet restaurant, founded in Ardmore a generation ago by Mazola McKerson. Then came Gainesville's Gourmet II, a baby restaurant born of Don McKerson's internship at his mother's stove. And now, brother Alfred, a.k.a. Kwame (rhymes with swami), has decided to throw his hat into the family restaurant ring, straying slightly from the family's tried and true smorgasbord formula to serve barbecued ribs, brisket, chicken, and sausage, by the plate or pound. Still, Kwame's is more than a meat and potatoes pit stop; fresh vegetables, beans, potato salad, and a well-stocked salad bar carry on the family tradition of four-square cooking.

Counter service was the order of the day when we visited, but there was some talk of hiring waitresses in the near future. Meantime we were happy to fetch our own ribs (two meaty, juicy, smoking hot specimens, $2.50). Properly messy (allow two to three napkins per rib), Kwame's ribs nevertheless inspired us to do something we could never get away with in Texas (where real men take their barbecue straight); holding our breath, we dunked a rib into sauce the color of an Oklahoma sunset. When the earth failed to shudder, we did everything but bathe in the peppery hot sauce. Two freshly grilled slices of what we always called "Texas" toast cushioned our ribs' basket and proved more interesting than many a doughy relative to the south.

Past the antique gate-leg tables, wood veneer booths, ceiling fans and country collectibles, the line for barbecue starts on the right, while seafood fans (trout, catfish, shrimp) queue up to the left. More exotic but untried offerings include lobster and frogs' legs. The only mystery on an otherwise straightforward menu was the offering called Mr. and Mrs. Potato: baked potatoes and salad bar for two ($2.50). And just to stoke some family rivalry, let us be the first to say Kwame's blueberry cobbler and sweet potato pie are equal to brother Don's blue ribbon buttermilk pie.

Not hungry for barbecue? Cross the street to Mazola's Gourmet, home of the original McKerson smorgasbord, and exclusive domain of the matriarch of this good-cooking clan.

HOURS   Mon.–Sat. 11 am–9 pm. Closed Sun.

SPECS   1717 W. Broadway; (405) 223-7916; DC/V/MC; no bar.

DIRECTIONS   Northbound: Take Exit 31A and veer right onto Hwy. 77/Broadway ■ and continue east one mile to Kwame's, on the left, just past the stadium.

Southbound: Take Exit 31A and turn left to cross under the interstate on Hwy. 77/Broadway. Then as above from ■.

FIELD'S RESTAURANT, *Exit 72, Paul's Valley*

Don't be fooled by the abominable A-frame façade. Field's has been around in one incarnation or another even longer than the art deco tire station next door. A 1923 tavern that later mellowed into a drive-in (the first between Dallas and Oklahoma City), Field's is as much a part of Oklahoma as the OU-UT football rivalry. In fact, Field's used to be the traditional stopping place for students fueling up for the annual bash in Dallas or Norman. Creators of a world famous pecan pie, the Field family had long since sold out of the restaurant business, although they continue to supply current owners with the pecan, German chocolate, and lemon chess pies baked at the family plant outside town.

A far cry from the nickel it cost in 1925 (the original menu is posted on the wall), a slice of the pecan-rich caramel custard is still a bargain at 90 cents. But while it's tempting to stick to desserts at Field's—aside from pies there's Field's Little Red Devil, a red velvet cake with chocolate icing (95 cents)—the house steaks and burgers easily rival the sweets. Try an onion burger, a quarter pound of beef fried up with onions and served with pickles for $1.85. Or one of the Field's Family of Famous Filets—tiny tot, mighty mite, or Oklahoma king-sized, fork-tender filet mignon. Chicken-fried steaks are hand-battered, crisp fried, and meaty. Entrees are served with soup (homemade unless the cook is busy—then she's forced to open a can of tomato or chicken noodle), salad bar, vegetable or potato, and homebaked bread. Omelettes are served all day. Whatever you order, the restaurant is anxious to please. If your steak isn't cooked just the way you like it, send it back and they'll try again. And if you're hungry for something not on the menu, you're encouraged to make a special request.

The food is fine, but the real joy in a stop at Field's is listening to the waitresses greet their customers by name and inquire about the particulars of family, health, and business. On a busy day skilled eavesdroppers will get the inside skinny on the citizens of Paul's Valley in less than an hour.

Still a drive-in at heart, Field's is furnished in vinyl banquette seating that lines up patrons as if they were seated on one long car seat. The white banquettes in the rear are for Cadillac-style dining.

HOURS   Tues.–Thurs. 7 am–9 pm; Fri. 7 am–10 pm; Sat. 8 am–10 pm; Sun. 8 am–8 pm.

SPECS   320 W. Paul; (405) 238-7558; AE/V/MC; no bar.

DIRECTIONS   Northbound: Take Exit 72 and turn right on Hwy. 19. ■ Continue 2 miles to first light and turn right on Ash. Turn left at stop sign onto Paul. Field's is on the right.

Southbound: Take Exit 72 to Hwy. 19 and turn left to cross under I-35, then as above from ■.

LEGENDS, *Exit 108B, Norman*

We were so amazed by this jumble of mirrors, glassware, and happy contradictions (plank flooring and oriental rugs, upholstered church pew banquettes, waiters in black tie and a cotton-candy-haired waitress in a sequin cummerbund) we could hardly concentrate on a menu so sophisticated (swordfish, blackened redfish, poached salmon) that were it not for the red dirt on our shoes we might have believed we were in the Big Apple, or Dallas at least. In the middle of the room a splendid grand piano competes with the hissing of a hammered copper espresso machine. Subtle arrangements of red and yellow tulips, pink hyacinths, and exotic boughs of yellow blooms are overwhelmed in this oddly attractive restaurant where platforms and corner niches overlook an entire wall of lock boxes. It seems that Legends has been around 15 years or so, long enough for some of the regulars to want to stock a locker with their favorite vintage, coffee cups, current reading, little black books, or whatever strikes their fancy. Once you've been issued a key, you can stash anything it takes to make your dining complete.

We looked around at the wire-haired professors (OU is headquartered in Norman), the penny-loafered bankers, the preppies fretting about grades over their frozen margaritas, the mad-eyed sockless poets, and wondered what treasures they all might have under lock and key.

Our speculations were cut short by the arrival of our late-night snack of salmon (Scotch cured Nova Scotia smoked, $3.95) and Quiche Lorraine (served with an elegant spinach, sprout, mushroom, and cucumber salad bar, and a cream-cheese-stuffed baked apple, $4.55). The three slices of salmon make a generous appetizer, but we layered ours with capers, minced onion, and horseradish and then piled it on oven-warm rolls to make a light supper. The quiche was a nicely textured, even blend of Gruyère cheese, ham, and onions; and the baked apple gets our vote as the most unusual and satisfying side dish in the Southwest. We'd even like it for breakfast. Speaking of which, Legends caters everything from breakfast in bed (with some advance notice) to hot-air balloon rides (they arrange the transportation). Tired as we were, we couldn't think of anything nicer than a sweet dreams snack of champagne and fresh-baked pastries. Next time we're in Norman, we're going to ask Legends to cater a midnight supper at the nearby Econolodge.

HOURS   Open 7 days, 11 am–4 pm and 5:30 pm to midnight.

SPECS   1313 W. Lindsey; (405) 329-8888; AE/MC/V; full bar.

DIRECTIONS　Northbound: Take Exit 108B and turn right into town on Lindsey. Continue 1 mile to Legends, on the left.

Southbound: Take Exit 108B left and over into town on Lindsey. Go 1 mile to Legends, on the left.

Texas

ABOUT CORPUS CHRISTI

Amazingly enough, it isn't all that easy to find good seafood in Corpus Christi proper, but one of the best seafood restaurants along the Texas Riviera can be found a short 30-minute drive (or ferry hop) up the beach, in Port Aransas. For 100 years, the **Tarpon Inn Restaurant** has been serving the fruits of the sea to fishermen, flappers, old salts, and college students in a slightly tilted, pleasantly spartan cottage behind the equally seasoned Tarpon Inn. The redfish sautéed with bananas is alone worth the ferry ride, and a bright, spicy snapper Vera Cruz can be downright sensational. After dessert, ask to see the tarpon scales papering the inn's lobby—one of the largest is proudly autographed by Franklin D. Roosevelt.

In Corpus, we like the **Yardarm,** a cheerful blue and yellow cottage on the bay. Open only for dinner and Sunday brunch, the Yardarm is slightly elegant (in a seaside sort of way), never pretentious, and always kitchen-conscious. The only problem can be the crowds (our name was overlooked on the waiting list, and we were left sitting on the deck for three hours). If it's a busy night, expect a 20- to 60-minute wait, not at all unpleasant when the weather is warm and breezy. But keep your eye on that list.

The sandy-feet crowd crack their claws at casual **JB's Crabpot,** a checkered tablecloth and jelly glass restaurant just this side of Padre Island (right before the causeway). When the food is good, JB's is the perfect spot to spend an evening wrestling blue crabs and listening to the would-be surfers dream about the Big One. Even when the food isn't up to snuff, we're happy to spend an evening popping hushpuppies and posing as beach bums. JB's isn't close enough to the open sea to hear the crashing waves, but sit here long enough on a balmy summer night and you'll begin to hear them all the same.

BLACK DIAMOND, *Ocean Drive Exit, Corpus Christi*

The Black Diamond restaurant isn't particularly close to the interstate, but if you've followed I-37 as far as Corpus, you probably intend to beach it here for a couple of days. There's nothing like a day spent gurgling saltwater for whetting one's appetite for bivalves, and the best place for oyster slurping is the original Black Diamond. It's located in something of a black hole, but the surrounding traffic jam will be your clue that you're close. There wasn't a slot in the lot when we pulled up late one spring night. Luckily, the store next door had plenty of spaces.

It's hard to believe the number of customers sardined inside this two-room restaurant, but don't let the logistics of finding a table turn you away; the crowd, the noise, the limited entrees (all fried) are the attractions at the Black Diamond, a restaurant that's legendary among locals. They continue to pack the old gal, while its spin-off, the tricked-up Black Diamond, seduces the tourists with promises of *broiled* dishes. But when it comes to shuck and jive, there's just no question that the original Black Diamond is the location of choice—it's justly famous for fresh, delicate, mouth-sized morsels like no others in town (plenty of places serve oysters from a jar).

Fried entrees can be risky, but we drew an ace with an order of paprika-encrusted redfish (not blackened)—a delicious, generous hunk of fish for just $7.95. The side of gumbo was a little bland, but rich with shrimp. Equally worthy of stomach space was an order of jalapeños stuffed with crabmeat (four for $3.20); unbelievably, the crab held its own in an intense flavor battle. Nibblers should go for the Diamond Deluxe Smorg for two: two shrimp, clam strips, one fish fillet, two oysters, two deviled crabs, two scallops, four boiled shrimp, one quail, one frog's leg, french fries, cole slaw, and (ugh) Texas toast—in other words, a few bites of everything on the menu and well worth the $16.60 price.

While you eat, fish through the nets full of business cards. You might land a good contact. Ours are there, in the quiet dining room, but we actually preferred the bar dining room. It roared with deep fat fryers pitched to a noise level that seemed to inspire the outrageous in even the most polite company. Then again, it may just be the proximity to the brew meister.

HOURS   Mon.–Sat. 11 am–11 pm; closed Sun.

SPECS   5712 Gollihar; (512) 991-9912; no credit cards; beer.

DIRECTIONS   Follow I-37 to its conclusion at the T junction with Ocean Dr. Turn right. Follow Ocean Dr. as it winds along the bay for 3¾ miles to Airline. Turn right and drive ¼ mile to Gollihar, and turn right. The Black Diamond is the first building on the right, just past the Feudor parking lot.

ELMO'S, *Exit 11B, Corpus Christi*

There's really no reason to eat at Elmo's if you're spending a few days in Corpus; there are plenty of good restaurants downtown or near the beach that serve more interesting food, although it would be hard to beat Elmo's prices. So if you're on your way out of town, and have got a carload of kids who are already howling with hunger, Elmo's is a perfect last-minute filling station.

The kids will love the atmosphere—sort of early gas station clutter with weathered wood façades of boomtown buildings and just about every scrap of gasoline memorabilia imaginable. Does anyone remember Thrifty Browder or Deep Rock Purol?

173

The word on the food at Elmo's is that it's good. Plain old-fashioned good. The "Running Board" special included a choice of beef tips on rice or fried flounder, each served with a red-skinned potato, pinto beans, zucchini, hot rolls, and a cherry tart ($4.25). The beef tips were just fine, and the vegetables were cooked with care. A hamburger arrived medium rare, as requested, and the accompanying french fries came recently from a potato, not a freezer.

As we said, there's not much about Elmo's to quicken the pulse of the more demanding diner, but when you're looking for a reasonably fast, well-prepared, four-square meal, Elmo's capable kitchen fills the bill and keeps it low.

HOURS   Lunch: Tues.–Fri. 11:30 am–2 pm; Sun. 11 am–2 pm. Dinner: Tues.–Sun. 5–10 pm; Fri. & Sat. 5–10:30 pm. Closed Mon.

SPECS   I-37 at Violet; (512) 241-0621; V/MC/AE; full bar.

DIRECTIONS   Northbound: From Exit 11B, continue along access road to Elmo's, just over the rise.

Southbound: Take Exit 11B to bridge and turn left to cross over I-37. Elmo's is on your left.

CURLEE'S, *Exits 34 & 36, Mathis*

Okay, so Curlee's isn't pretty. The green bathroom tile and gold vinyl accents just don't do a thing for us. In fact, we thought about making a run for it the moment after we sat down. But then the waitress stopped by for a little chat about the daily lunch specials (chicken-fried steak or liver and onions, served with mashed potatoes, corn, green beans, and a salad for under $4). As she spoke, we saw delivered to the table next to ours a plate of the goods that looked A-Okay.

With full knowledge that I-37 is a culinary danger zone, we decided to risk it. After all, that's what we were there for, wasn't it? We ordered a half-order of fried oysters (five of them, with fries and slaw, $5) and a bowl of homemade stew with a side of hushpuppies ($2.95 for both). Then we sat back, closed our eyes, and said a brief prayer.

Thirty minutes later our very young waitress dropped back by. "I thought the cook had forgotten y'all," she giggled. So did we, we admitted. After assuring us that that wasn't the case, she told us of her beauty college aspirations, complimented our hair styles, and ran off to fetch a platter full of fresh-fried oysters, steaming hot hushpuppies, and a bowl of stew that must have had a pound of chuck if it had an ounce.

There were ten, not five, oysters in our half-order, and they tasted as if they had just been tossed from their shells, tumbled in cornmeal, and treated to a quick, hot fry. Excellent! The hushpuppies were also fried to order, pleasantly eccentric in size, oniony, and delicious. The stew would satisfy anyone's mother —loaded with vegetables as well as beef.

So, while we warn you that Curlee's ain't the best-looking place in town, its food is just fine. And the view of the Mathis Pirate Power watertower is a classic.

HOURS   Tues.–Sun. 5:30 am–5 pm; closed Mon.

SPECS   318 W. Hwy. 9; (512) 547-3297; no credit cards; no bar.

DIRECTIONS   Southbound: Take Exit 36 to stop sign and turn right on Hwy. 359 Business. Curlee's is one mile down, at the Y, on the left. To return to I-37 without backtracking, turn left leaving Curlee's and stay left at the Y, passing under the bridge. Turn left at the sign for I-37.

Northbound: Take Exit 34 and turn left to cross under the interstate. Drive 2 miles to Curlee's, on the the right just after you pass under the bridge. To return to I-37, turn right leaving Curlee's and follow Hwy. 359 one mile to the interstate.

TACO PATIO, *Exits 104 & 109, Pleasanton*

Pleasanton calls itself the Birthplace of the Cowboy, and that's reason enough to eat barbecue or steak here, rather than Mexican (unless you're a *vaquero*). But during breakfast hours the only restaurants open were Taco Patio and two cafes: the pink brick Town House (smoky and grim, but a great sign) and the Three Oaks (dimly lit with fluorescent lights but with great oaks). We weren't into either grim or dim, so that left Taco Patio with its $3.95 all-you-can-eat Mexican breakfast special, cowboy traditions notwithstanding. (McBee's BBQ looked tempting—a low-slung, well-aged, screen-porched roadhouse—but it was closed.)

Taco Patio isn't a chain restaurant; it's a family-owned establishment with fast-food aspirations. Counter service and plastic forks aside, a cheerful disorganization humanized the service. And the patio, complete with roll-up glass garage doors, plenty of geraniums, and a view of the anonymous art deco building across the highway is a sunny spot in which to read the morning paper.

Watching a new-fangled machine crank out a fresh batch of flour tortillas, we decided to order a couple of breakfast tacos, soft tortillas stuffed with just about anything from chorizo to potatoes. We ordered one filled with sausage and egg, another with carne guisada, plus a beef and cheese burrito just to push our luck. The burrito was deep-fried, making it something like a chimichanga, but it was nice and cheesy. As for the soft tacos, you just can't fault a fresh tortilla, and it's hard to go wrong with a filling of scrambled eggs and mild sausage. The carne guisada, slightly overwhelmed by the thick flour gravy, was tasty, if a bit on the salty side. We adjusted everything to our liking with a liberal dollop of the house pico de gallo—a wealth of serrano peppers give it a bit more bite than your average "rooster's beak" salsa.

Selected menu items are offered as all-you-can-eat lunch and dinner specials ($3.95) and a pound of fajitas served with beans, rice, guacamole, and tortillas is $8.99. No plates here, just tinfoil bundles, a serve-yourself relish bar, and paper cups. It's no frills, no thrills, but then again, no major complaints, either. After you eat, if you're curious about Pleasanton's heritage, you may want to visit the Longhorn Museum for the whole story of the cowboy from colonial times to the present.

HOURS   Open 7 days, 6 am–10 pm.

SPECS   815 2nd St. (Hwy. 281); (512) 569-6196; V/MC; no bar.

DIRECTIONS   Southbound: Take Exit 109 to stop sign and turn right on Hwy. 97; continue into town 3 miles. Jog left onto Hwy. 281 just past the Three Oaks. You'll see Taco Patio on the right. To return to I-37 without backtracking, turn right leaving the restaurant and continue out of town on Hwy. 281 South.

Northbound: Take Exit 104 as it merges with Hwy. 281 and continue 6 miles into Pleasanton. Taco Patio is on your left. To return to I-37 without backtracking, turn left out of Taco Patio and immediately right at the light (onto Hwy. 97). Follow 97 to I-37 (about 3 miles).

ABOUT SAN ANTONIO

See our overview of San Antonio dining on pages 144–146. Ras Tzemru and Viet-Nam Restaurant (both below) are the most accessible for the I-37 traveler.

RAS TZEMRU, *E. Commerce Exit, San Antonio*

We suspect that the fact that everyone calls this place simply the Ethiopian Restaurant finally persuaded the owner to paint that sobriquet on the sign out front. So the sign says one thing, the menu another, but whatever the official name of the restaurant, you'll be glad you found your way to this snug, colorful place on St. Paul's Square.

After the one waitress seats you, the restaurant's owner and cook arrives tableside to explain that her dishes are flavored with fire: chile peppers that make their Mexican cousins seem meek. She will look you in the eye and try to assess just how much heat you can take. If you're undecided about which of the beef and chicken dishes to order, she will suggest a sampler. We took the hint and delivered ourselves into her capable hands.

Dinner arrived on a single platter layered first with injera, a spongy bread about the thickness of a pancake. Our waitress (the entire restaurant is run by two people) showed us how to pinch off a piece of bread between the thumb and forefinger and use it to pick up the various bits of beef and chicken (forks are provided upon request).

Our first entree was beef alecha, meat cubes simmered in a

177

mild chile sauce with cabbage, carrots, and potatoes ($5.50). Next came kulwa, moist strips of lean beef sautéed with onion and tomato and some devilishly hot spices. The result was an intricately flavored sauce like nothing we'd ever tasted before ($8.50). Finally, we launched into doro watt, chicken in a moderately hot, slightly tart chile sauce ($5.50). After all the meat was eaten, we fell onto what was left of the injera, now heavy with the sauces of our meal to which it added its own yeasty flavor.

As we ate, the attentive waitress asked if we might wish to finish our meal with coffee, informing us that the kitchen needed 20 minutes to prepare it in the traditional manner. It arrived still brewing in a beautiful carved gourd. This was coffee so thick you could almost chew it, but milder and more flavorful than espresso.

As we pushed back from the table, we looked at the surrounding Ethiopian travel posters and folk art, and considered the sad irony of having discovered such a remarkable cuisine during such a tragically difficult time for its country of origin. Almost as if she sensed our sadness, the beautiful and gracious cook reappeared with a parting gift. Sprinkling pellets of incense on a grill of coals, she bade us farewell in a haze of fragrant smoke. "This is how we end our meals at home," she said.

HOURS　Mon.–Fri. 11 am–9 pm; Sat. 4–9 pm; closed Sun.

SPECS　1144–2 E. Commerce; (512) 224-6633; no credit cards; wine and beer.

DIRECTIONS　Take the E. Commerce Exit. At E. Commerce, turn left if you were southbound on the interstate; turn right if northbound. Restaurant is a block down on the right, in St. Paul's Square.

VIET-NAM RESTAURANT,
Hildebrand Exit, San Antonio

There's nothing fancy about this restaurant, just walls and a sea of tables. A recent bout of expansion and remodeling did little more than provide additional elbow room, which was about all they could have done to improve our favorite spot for Vietnamese eggrolls. These crispy, jam-packed bundles of pork, onions, mushrooms, and "egg-bean thread," are a hundred times more interesting than their standard Chinese counterparts.

Another favorite here is the crab soup with asparagus ($1.60), a marvelous marriage of rich flavors, slightly heavy on the crab side. Actually, crab dishes are the house specialty and all are good, but we can never pass up the lemon grass chicken, lightly grilled and crunchy on the outside, moist and lemony on the inside ($5.50). A truly unique dish is the spicy chicken, sprinkled with pork, emanating a sweet heat that reminds one of things Italian ($6.50).

Whatever you choose, accompany it with plum wine, sold by the glass or by the bottle.

HOURS   Open 7 days, 11 am–10 pm.

SPECS   3244 Broadway; (512) 822-7461; V/MC; beer and wine.

DIRECTIONS   Use the Hildebrand Exit; when you reach Hildebrand, turn right if you were northbound on the interstate, left if southbound. Continue 1 mile to Broadway. Right on Broadway, then drive approximately 1 mile to the Viet-Nam, on the left.

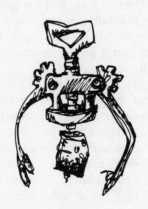

I-40

Arizona
New Mexico
Texas
Oklahoma

Arizona

HOUSE OF CHAN, *Exit 48, Kingman*

Why people are surprised to find Chinese restaurants in out-of-the-way towns beats us. Tommy and Mary Chan—he was born in Canton, her family emigrated six generations ago—are in Kingman because the railroad employed members of their families. Restauranting has also been a family trade, and now the one Mary and Tommy run is known as one of the best places to eat in this stretch of the state.

A clean and tidy place, the roomy House of Chan has both Chinese and American menus. The latter features the likes of veal cutlet ($6.25 with soup or salad) and roast turkey ($6.50). More interesting is the Polynesian chicken marinated in Oriental spices, broiled, and served with potato or soup and salad ($6.50); pan-fried frogs' legs ($8.25 with baked potato); and the typical Cantonese sweet and sours ($6.75). A relish tray comes before each meal and a glass of Chinese wine—Fu Jin or Wan Fu—can come after.

If the prices sound a touch dear and you've a starving brood in the back seat, you'll be happy to know that House of Chan also has a children's menu.

HOURS Mon.–Sat. 11 am–10 pm. Closed Sun., Christmas, and New Year's Day.

SPECS 960 W. Beale St.; (602) 753-3232; MC/V; full bar.

DIRECTIONS From Exit 48 (Beale St.), turn right if westbound, left if eastbound. The House of Chan is prominent, on the left after a couple of blocks.

DELGADILLO'S SNOW CAP, *Exits 123 & 121, Seligman*

John ("or Juan, you can call me either one") Delgadillo has a joy-buzzer sense of humor. The converted Dairy Queen building that functions as his restaurant is also his stage. Park next to his 1936 open-air Chevy Roadster with the Christmas tree in the back seat year 'round, walk inside through the door with handles on both right and left, and step up to the serving window below the charred No Smoking sign.

"Do you wanna look first before you order? Here." He pulls out a fake candy bar which says "Look" on it.

"Would you like today's coffee or yesterday's coffee? We got both. What do you want in your coffee, cream and sugar or sugar and cream?"

"Would you like a napkin?" He reaches under the counter and pulls out a handful of used napkins. "Here, choose."

"You want ketchup on your fries?" He squeezes a trick red plastic ketchup container at your face; a red string comes out.

"My card," he says, handing you his business card which says MY CARD.

Delgadillo's advertisement in the local *High Plains Trader* mentions "Dead Chicken" and "Male or Female Sundaes." "You know the difference?" he asks. "The male one has nuts."

If the Snow Cap had any chairs, Delgadillo would hide a whoopee cushion under each seat.

How John-or-Juan has managed to keep this up, day in and day out since the mid 1950s, is beyond us, but it certainly works. Taped to the window are fan letters and paper currency from customers living in countries such as Belize, Scotland, Czechoslovakia, Nigeria, and Vietnam. Delgadillo himself plays rhythm guitar in a family band, which includes his brothers, who run the grocery store–gas station and the barber shop on the same block.

Even if Delgadillo's food were inedible, this place would be the highlight of any trip across northern Arizona, but the cheeseburgers ($1.85), fried fish fillet sandwiches ($1.69), foot-long chili dogs ($1.69), and other standard-issue short-order dishes are perfectly decent. Of course, no one, least of all John-or-Juan Delgadillo himself, would dispute the fact that the cuisine is far less memorable than the entertainment.

HOURS Summer: 10 am–6 pm daily; Winter: 9 am–8 pm daily. Closed Thanksgiving, Christmas, and Easter.

SPECS 301 E. Chino Ave. (Old Hwy. 66); (602) 422-3291; no credit cards or booze.

DIRECTIONS **Westbound:** From Exit 123, turn right and head into town on Chino Ave. The Snow Cap is the Diary Queenish building on the left at the beginning of town.

Eastbound: Take Exit 121 into town; Snow Cap is on the right at the far end of town.

OLD SMOKY'S PANCAKE HOUSE & RESTAURANT,
Exit 161, Williams

In 1984, Williams, an hour south of the Grand Canyon, became the last town along the old Chicago-to-L.A. Route 66 to be bypassed by an interstate. To mark the occasion, the town staged a wake for itself. Bobby Troupe, who wrote the 1940s song "Route 66," was the guest. Afterward, business in the places that lived off the interstate plummeted.

Smoky's, established in 1947, is among the Williams businesses adapting to the change. At first glance it seems to offer your basic roadside fare—burgers, chili, chicken, bacon & eggs, sandwiches, and pies. But signs hung up here and there indicate an unorthodox overlay for a greasy spoon: homemade nutbread, herb tea, even tofu. The strawberry and blueberry hotcakes (each $3.25) and the pecan waffle ($3) were wonderful. Conventional daily specials like top sirloin roast, chicken, or fish run $2.95–$3.95.

Old Smoky's is just on the tidy side of cluttered: among the items lining the walls are, in random order, huge ponderosa pine cones, an old two-man saw, fake flowers, an 1892 grandfather clock, horseshoes, and a young child's artwork.

HOURS   Summer: Mon.–Sat. 6 am–3 pm; Sun. 7 am–12:30 pm. Winter: Mon.–Sat. 6:30 am–2 pm; Sun. 7 am–12:30 pm. Closed Christmas Day.

SPECS   624 W. Bill Williams Ave.; (602) 635-2091; no credit cards; no booze.

DIRECTIONS   Take Exit 161 onto Bill Williams Ave.; restaurant will be on the left after 1.4 miles.

SALSA BRAVA, *Exit 195B, Flagstaff*

Thirteen of us dined here together one evening, with 39 years separating the youngest from the eldest. In general, we try to avoid fast-food places, but this one, which serves Mexican food "Guadalajara style," came well recommended.

Fast definitely: as the twelfth and thirteenth at our table were placing their orders, the first and second were served theirs. As for the food, each person gave an opinion.

Colleen, age 12, taco carnita (soft corn tortilla filled with pork, and a charbroiled green onion): "It's, um, different. I haven't had anything like this before." Jim, almost 10, who had the same: "I *liked* it. That was good."

Julie, 4, quesadilla (flour tortilla with melted cheese on top, $1.90): gave it to an older sibling. Kevin, almost 7, quesadilla: "I liked it, but they gave me too much. I couldn't finish it." Dan, 11, also quesadilla: "I didn't like it that much."

Dave, 8, taco carnita: "It was kinda *good*." Mike, 17, taco carnita: "This is my second. Can I have another?"

Margaret, 19, chicken taco: "It's real good, but I couldn't taste the sauce."

Kate, 15, burrito carne asada al carbon (flour tortilla around charbroiled steak, melted cheese, salsa, and beans, the whole served with charbroiled green onion, $2.50): "It was real good. I'm used to corn tortillas. This was first thing like this I've had with a flour one."

Dad, 44, burrito carnita: "Excellent. And the green onion was very good, too." Mom, 44, chicken taco plate with rice and beans: "It was delicious." Why? "Someone else made it and someone else is going to clean up."

Valerina, 36, carnita taco: "It was good—tender, and laced with cilantro." Tom, 37, carnita burrito: "Real tasty. I've heard that the pork is cooked for hours in a sauce that has milk and Coca-Cola in it. Is that true?"

Owner, reluctantly: "Yes."

Salsa Brava serves two desserts, both good: flan (custard topped with caramel and whipped cream) and churros (a soft pretzel-like pastry dusted with cinnamon and sugar). All prices are quite reasonable.

In our Spanish-English dictionary, *brava* translates to manly or pungent. Either way, we'd come back for another fill-up.

HOURS   Mon.–Thurs. 11 am–7:30 pm; Fri. & Sat. 11 am–9:30 pm.

SPECS   Greentree Shopping Center; (602) 774-1083: no credit cards; beer.

DIRECTIONS   Take Exit 195B north onto State Route 89A North to the Greentree Village Shopping Center. Salsa Brava is on the near end of the main row of stores.

LA BELLAVIA, *Exit 195B, Flagstaff*

We confess a slight aversion to restaurants with plants hanging in macramé holders, butcher-block white oak veneer tables, cutesy menus, and waiters and waitresses who volunteer their names as they annouce that they will be serving you. At first we felt atmospheric indigestion coming on when we happened upon this place, but we discovered, much to our delight, that it stayed on the comfortable side of pretension.

Most important, of course, we found both of our breakfast selections—Swedish oat pancakes with hot cinnamon apple topping and fruit ($3.25), and pan-fried Idaho trout and eggs served with fruit and potato or buttermilk pancake ($4.95)—to be prepared with an experienced hand by a cook who cares about flavors and freshness. Eggs Bellavia (poached on a bagel, topped with hollandaise, sided with fruit and choice of potato or pancake) looked good enough alone ($3.50) and irresistible with ham or sausage ($4.75).

And that was just breakfast! Lunches run from the $2.50 veggie tortilla to the Swiss fondue for two (with soup or salad, $8.95). Most offerings—quiches, salads, and sandwiches—are in the $4–$5 range. At La Bellavia, even such mundane mug-fillers as hot chocolate are made with steamed milk, always a plus, and all baked goods except sandwich breads are prepared in the kitchen.

A good mix of downtowners and students from nearby Northern Arizona University eat here, soothed by cassettes of Ricki Lee Jones, Van Morrison, and Ry Cooder at breakfast, and Joni Mitchell, Gato Barbieri, and Steve Miller at lunchtime. A front-window seat affords a clear view of the Factory-2-U shop across the street.

HOURS Weekdays, 7 am–3 pm; weekends, 8 am–2 pm. Closed Thanksgiving and for ten days at Christmas.

SPECS 18 S. Beaver; (602) 774-8301; no credit cards; beer and wine.

DIRECTIONS Take Exit 195B north onto State Route 89A North. About ¾ mile after the Greentree Village Shopping Center, turn right at the light onto W. Clay Ave. In 3 blocks, turn left onto Beaver St. In 2½ blocks, La Bellavia is on the right, with picket fencing out front (just before a Laundromat).

THE BROWN MUG, *Exit 255, Winslow*

If it was good enough for The Eagles when they stood on a corner in Winslow, Arizona, it was good enough for us. So there we were, waiting for a girl in a flatbed Ford slowin' down to look at us. No such luck. For consolation, we dropped in to The Brown Mug, a good diner whose customers include trainmen from the Santa Fe station across the street, local businessmen and workers, and Indians passing through town to and from the nearby reservations.

Particularly appealing were the picarros (rhymes with "seek-a-rose"), mixed pork and beef in a deep-fried corn tortilla, served with rice and beans ($3.50 for three). The Navajo taco—a fried tortilla beneath refried beans, lettuce, cheese, and tomato—appealed to three fellows on the four-man rail yard crew during their afternoon break ($2.50), while the fourth got a Spanish hamburger steak dripping with red and green chile, with refried beans, rice, and a sopapilla ($4.95) on the side.

They were evidently satisfied with their meals, we were pleased with ours, and so everybody was happy—except the waitress who dropped a plate on the floor. At first she giggled nervously and squeaked out something about it being her first day on the job; relief became apparent when Josephine Perez, the cook, also laughed; finally, the waitress laughed openly when she saw Josephine's husband Joe, the manager, laughing as well. "I guess that's your initiation," Joe told her with a grin.

The flatbed girl never showed.

HOURS Mon.–Sat. 10 am–9 pm. Closed Sun. and all major holidays.

SPECS 308 E. 2nd St.; (602) 289-9973; no credit cards; beer and wine.

DIRECTIONS From Exit 255 (Business 40, Winslow/Payson) turn left if westbound, right if eastbound, at the stop sign. In 0.3 mile turn right onto East 3rd St., which becomes one-way. After 1½ miles turn left at the traffic light at Route 87 and left again onto E. 2nd St. The Brown Mug is on the left at the beginning of the next block. Return to I-40 by taking E. 2nd St. for 1.3 miles, and then bearing left onto the highway.

AGUILERA'S BAKERY & CAFE, *Exit 285, Holbrook*

This is the perfect quick stop. In the mornings, drop by for coffee and doughnuts with local workers; later in the day, fill up with red chile tamales ($1), flautas ($3.75), or a quesadilla (a warm corn tortilla folded in half with melted cheddar cheese inside, $1.30). Don't expect too much (other than local color) and you won't be too disappointed.

HOURS Mon.–Sat. 6 am–6 pm. Closed Sun. and during the Christmas holiday season.

SPECS 200 Navajo Blvd.; (602) 524-3806; no credit cards; no license.

DIRECTIONS **Westbound:** From Exit 285 (Holbrook/Business 40) turn right onto Hopi Dr. ■ Stay on Hopi Dr. for 1.7 miles to Route 77 (Navajo Blvd.), the first traffic light. Aguilera's is on the far corner, left side.

Eastbound: Turn left at Exit 285 (Business 40 to Route 77) onto Hopi Dr. and follow westbound directions, from ■.

New Mexico

IT'S ABOUT TIME

New Mexico, like almost all the rest of these United States, goes on Daylight Saving Time in the summer. Arizona does not. Therefore, from the last Sunday in April through the last Sunday in October, Arizona time is one hour earlier than New Mexico time. Take this into account when driving I-40 from Arizona into New Mexico (or vice versa), or you might be late for dinner (or early).

THE RANCH KITCHEN, *Exit 14, Gallup*

Although it opened during the Korean War, The Ranch Kitchen has been in its present comfortable building only since 1982. The Ranch is well known for its reliability and cleanliness, and meets its high standards with a crew that has been in place for years.

A since-retired Swiss cook left behind her simple recipes for many a day's special such as grilled German sausage with sauerkraut and Swiss cheese on rye ($3.95). Enchiladas, chimichangas, huevos rancheros, etc., have been slowly added to the menu over the years ($4–$6 range). "Our employees would come in with recipes from home," explained owner Earl Vance, "and we'd try them out with a little informal jury. The ones that rated best we put on the menu."

Clearly, there have been many successes. The chicken Mexican soup ($1.25–$1.75) tasted so good we asked if a list of ingredients might be available. It was: chicken, onion, tomato, crushed chile, cumin, salt and pepper, and whipped cream. The last ingredient makes this Ranch soup a couple of slurps better than soups elsewhere. New England clam chowder is another special that pops up occasionally, perhaps to remind Vance of his native stomping grounds. Saturday's special is almost always beef stew ($3.95), a favorite of the Indian families that come to Gallup from the reservations for their weekly trading.

The Ranch Kitchen is especially busy in mid-August during the annual Inter-Tribal Indian Ceremonial festivities, which include traditional dances and a parade with all the western tribes represented. Gallup is smack dab in the middle of Indian country, a presence apparent all over town. Gift shops, pawn shops, tony galleries, and side-street craft stores can confuse the novice looking for quality jewelry, pottery, and rugs. The Ranch Kitchen gift shop carries a line of regional Indian-crafted items that show obvious care in selection. Some of the prices may surprise you, but some knowledgeable explanation will convince you of their value. That aroma of smoking piñon and ponderosa pine comes from the fireplace that warms the back dining room.

HOURS Summer: 6:30 am–10 pm daily. Winter: 7 am–9 pm. Closed Easter, Thanksgiving, and Christmas.

SPECS   3001 W. Highway 66; (505) 863-4489; all major credit cards; beer, wine.

DIRECTIONS   Take Exit 14 onto Old Route 66 heading into town. You'll find the Ranch Kitchen is in 1.1 miles; it's between the Best Western and the Holiday Inn.

MONTE CARLO CAFE, *Exits 81 & 81B, Grants*

This town's economy rose and fell on uranium, discovered nearby in 1950. When the industry peaked around 1980, diners had their choice of more than a dozen prosperous restaurants on Santa Fe St., but with nuclear energy far less in demand than originally anticipated, Grants's economy is shot to hell. The only freeze movement you'll find here is the mercury dropping on cold winter nights.

With so many places gone out of business (even the Uranium Cafe has closed down. Is nothing sacred?), we were heartened to see the durable Monte Carlo still serving quality meals. Now in the second generation of the Mazon family—it opened in 1947— the Monte Carlo keeps its prices low and its food fresh. Out-of-town diners are noticed among the coterie of regulars, and are made to feel right at home right away in this wholesome family cafe. When you order a T-bone (with salad and potato, $7.50), the cook walks into a refrigerated room in the rear and cuts it straight from a carcass, a few of which are always hanging fresh on meat hooks. Likewise for a chicken-fried steak (smothered with green chile, with fries and refried beans, $5.25). Hamburger meat is ground on the premises. Most items, such as potatoes, gravy, vegetables, and even the pancake batter, are prepared fresh in the kitchen rather than thawed or taken from a dry mix or a can.

Ninety-nine cents breakfast specials include sausage and egg, hash browns, toast, and coffee, or a short stack of pancakes and a small omelette. The $3.25 lunch special was a large round sopapilla under taco meat in red or green chile, and refried beans, topped with melted cheese, lettuce, and tomato.

HOURS   Mon.–Sat. 7 am–9 pm; Sun. 10 am–3 pm. Closed Sun. in winter and all major holidays.

SPECS   721 W. Santa Fe; (505) 287-9250; MC/V; no license.

DIRECTIONS   **Westbound:** From Exit 81 (Grants/San Rafael), bear right and then turn right at the light. The Monte Carlo is on the right in 0.9 mile.

Eastbound: Directions are identical to westbound, above, but for eastbound travelers the exit is labeled 81B (Grants).

Return to freeway: retrace route on Santa Fe, bear left to veer back to interstate.

SADIE'S, *North 4th St. Exit, Albuquerque*

You know something's out of the ordinary when a highly recommended restaurant is located in the back of a bowling alley. When you walk in, an old iron grill stares at you, resting behind this sign: "Sadie's original grill for 28 years, with more than 1 million Sadieburgers plus your other favorites to its credit . . ."

Sadie's, it turns out, is another one of those secrets known to oldtime natives, but newcomers and travelers hardly ever hear of the place. And indeed Sadie's can take credit not only for its chile-doused Sadieburgers but also for its other favorites. Sadie's would be a find even if it weren't tucked beside 36 ten-pin lanes, or didn't afford a view through plate-glass windows of league play in progress, because Sadie's food is as good as its setting is unusual.

Papitas—cubed deep-fried potatoes smothered under cheese and red or green chile—come alongside frijoles with practically every dish, and make everything they garnish worthwhile. Most meals come in small and large sizes; the chile rellenos dinner (with papitas and frijoles under chile) costs $4.95 for one relleno, and a buck more for two; the same price spread is in effect for the chicken chalupas dinner. Spicy ground beef and frijoles smothered under chile sauce, cheese, and onions is called a Sloppy José ($4.50). But if you've got a real appetite, we would steer you to Sadie's Super (o-so-filling) Combination—chile relleno, taco, rolled meat enchiladas, and the inevitable papitas and frijoles under chile ($7/$8).

All dinners include sopapillas to eat with honey in the conventional manner or to dredge those last hard-to-get-at chunks of chile.

HOURS   Mon–Fri. 11 am–10 pm; Sat. noon–10 pm; Sun. noon–9 pm. Closed all major holidays.

SPECS   6132 4th St.; (505) 345-5339; MC/V; full bar.

DIRECTIONS   Westbound: Take Exit 159 and stay in the middle lane past the bottom of the off-ramp, then get over to the right to turn right onto North 4th St. ■ Sadie's is inside BG's Valley Bowl, on the right, in about 3 miles.

Eastbound: After leaving the freeway at Exit 158, get in the left lane and turn left at the light onto 4th St., then as above from ■.

THE FRONTIER RESTAURANT,
I-25 Interchange, Albuquerque

See page 114 for description of this University of New Mexico hangout known for its hot cinnamon rolls drenched under a melted margarine and sugar topping.

DIRECTIONS   From the I-25 interchange, enter I-25 South (toward Belen), then follow southbound directions given for the Frontier on page 115.

SWEETWATER'S CAFE, *I-25 Interchange, Albuquerque*

See page 117 for description of this moderately priced and elegant University of New Mexico neighbor.

DIRECTIONS   From the I-25 interchange, enter I-25 South (toward Belen), then follow southbound directions given for Sweetwater's on page 118.

M&J SANITARY TORTILLA FACTORY, *I-25 Interchange, Albuquerque*

See page 115 for description of this downtown classic, famous for its carne adovada and known from remote South America to the pages of *The New Yorker*.

DIRECTIONS   From the I-25 interchange, enter I- 25 South (toward Belen), then follow southbound directions given for the M&J on page 117.

MATEO'S, *Exit 273, Santa Rosa*

You know the apocryphal bus stop with great food? We found it in 100-year-old Santa Rosa. "Sneaky Pete" Baca took over this wayfarer's cafe adjacent to the Oasis "For the Rest of Your Life" Motel a year ago and has been hustling to get the charter crowds in his door ever since. Promising complete meals in 15 minutes, he feeds the busloads from a cafeteria line featuring hot lunch specials and homemade pastries. For the less harried there's a newly refurbished dining room away from the madding crowd. Ask for menu service if eating in an interstate refugee camp isn't your brand of entertainment.

The homespun menu looks like a 5th-grade class project with its scenic cover clipped from a magazine and plasticized pages: two devoted to breakfast (blueberry pancakes to huevos rancheros), a couple to lunch, another to native specialties. Amid all the numbered items, we couldn't resist the penciled-in Santa Rosa Special: Three flat enchiladas, rice, beans, sopapilla, and dessert for $2.99. It seemed impossible that so much food could be both good and cheap, but it was. We ordered our meaty open-faced enchiladas with green chile (slightly picante), but Pete later told us that he prides himself on his red sauce. The soup-style beans were a nice change from refritos, the thin, crisp sopapilla (a pillow of fried dough served with honey) was fresh from the fryer, and the dessert that we didn't have room for, but ate anyway, was a Mexican vanilla pudding—white, smooth, and sweet.

Another bargain, number 7 on the menu, is a pair of fresh, fat tamales made in Santa Rosa by hometown girl Angelina Martínez. Topped with melted longhorn cheese, these tamales are 90 percent meat to 10 percent dough, flecked with red chiles and delicious.

Making his rounds, Pete stopped by to assure us of the cook's willingness to bend the rules. If you want breakfast after the regular serving hours, you got it. And although Saturdays and Sundays are the set days for homemade Chinese food (lots of surprises here), if you drop in on a Wednesday with a hankering for egg foo yung, Pete Baca will make sure you get your wish. It'll take some extra time, but he assures us it's worth the wait.

So don't be put off by the rush and clatter of the cafeteria line when you first step in the door. Just ask the waitress to seat you in the more formal dining room, elegant only in comparison to the front room corral. Browse through the menu and ask if the eclairs are ready.

HOURS   Full service 7 days, 6 am–10 pm; pastries and sandwiches served 10 pm–6 am.

SPECS   516 Coronado W.; (505) 472-5232; no credit cards; no bar.

DIRECTIONS   Take Exit 273, which curves right into town. Mateo's is on the right, less than ½ mile from I-40.

LA CITA, *Exit 332, Tucumcari*

It's hard to miss La Cita, the only restaurant in Tucumcari wearing a giant sombrero. Inside, you'll have to forgive the garage sale surplus—macramé owls, hooked rug landscapes, and straw flowers—before you can appreciate the masterful salad bar that is the heart of the restaurant.

A full plate of potato salad, spiced apples, broccoli, beans, cauliflower, bell peppers, jalapeños, and more will cost you $2.25, well worth the price. As for the Mexican food, we sampled the cheesy chile relleno platter and found that the sweet heat of the fresh poblano pepper made up for the bland New Mexico–style Spanish rice ($4.25).

While we listened to our leather-vested neighbor describe the effects of a snake bite on a calf, we pondered one of life's greatest mysteries: why is it that the waitress's warning of a hot plate always inspires the customer to give it a touch?

HOURS　　Mon.–Sat. 11 am–8 pm; Sun. 11 am–3 pm.

SPECS　　812 S. 1st; (505) 461-9660; MC/V; no bar.

DIRECTIONS　　**Westbound:** Take Exit 332 to stop sign and turn right onto Hwy. 18/S. 1st. La Cita is a mile down the highway, on the right.

Eastbound: Take Exit 332 to Hwy. 18 and turn left into town. La Cita will be on your right in about a mile.

Texas

HICKORY INN, *Exit 35, Vega*

Okay, so the Hickory Inn does look like a gussied-up trailer house. But any place that serves breakfast day and night is OK with us. And not just any old breakfast, but homemade biscuits, grits, cinnamon rolls (saucer-sized, chewy, gooey, and chock full of spice, 75 cents), and buttermilk pancakes. If you never had real buttermilk pancakes, the sour flavor might take some getting used to. Just pour on the syrup and enjoy the contrast of flavors (one egg and a giant cake, $1.25).

We didn't try the lunch or dinner offerings, but we assume that if the Hickory can turn out a perfect over-easy egg, it can probably handle the frying of a pork chop or chicken-fried steak. Homemade bread, home fries, made to order fried pies, and a tidy salad bar guarantee you won't be sorry if you stop in.

Best of all we liked the poodle-haired woman in the corner who held forth with a wicked tongue on subjects as diverse as eye makeup ("Some of them gals can barely lift their eyelids"); Donahue ("He tells how the cow ate the cabbage"); and the proposed national seatbelt law ("It's no use getting maimed when you were meant to be killed").

HOURS   Open 7 days, 6 am–9 pm.

SPECS   Exit 35/U.S. Hwy. 385; (806) 267-2569; no credit cards; no bar.

DIRECTIONS   Take Exit 35 to U.S. Hwy. 385/Main St. Turn right if westbound, left if eastbound, and drive ½ mile to Vega. Turn left. The Hickory Inn is on the right beneath the giant diamond-shaped Cafe sign.

ABOUT AMARILLO

You've heard the myths about everything being bigger in Texas. Well, we have to tell you about the place to go for the biggest steak in the state—**Big Texan Steak Ranch.** There are plenty of wimpy little 8-ounce and single pounders here, but the real Texans (or would-be Texans) will want to wrestle the house 72-ounce monster—free if you can eat the *whole thing* in an hour. You'll find every Texas critter imaginable on the menu here, including rattlesnake, but this is the place to go when you're searching for the beef (on I-40 between Whitaker and Lakeside).

And just so you don't think Amarillo is all rough-edged frontier, we have to mention **Maison Blanche,** an elegant (and expensive) lunch and dinner spot serving a light and saucy menu of seafood and chicken dishes, salads, and crepes (2740 Westhaven Village).

For roadhouse food we recommend the **Blue Front Cafe**—you know the menu: burgers, liver, pork sandwiches (801 W. 6th). And finally, when you've got a hankering for Thai or Chinese cookery, there's only one place in Amarillo to get a hot and spicy fix: the **Blackstone Cafe,** also open for American breakfasts (202 W. 10th).

MEDITERRANEAN HOUSE, *Exit 68A, Amarillo*

We watched the cowboy and his date hesitate at the door, then sidestep to a table. They craned their necks after the costumed waitress and picked up the menus as if they were hot coals. About the time we were ordering our calamari (squid) we saw them scuttling toward the door. Our waitress shrugged. It isn't easy being a Greek restaurant in Amarillo.

That's not to say Mediterranean House is hurting for business. Tables all around us were filled with the booted, hatted, coiffed, and lacquered locals, all ordering up a storm from the menu that was . . . well, Greek to us. Oh sure, we know dolmades (stuffed grape leaves) and gyros (thin strips of beef and lamb layered into a single roast and cooked on a revolving spit), but *no comprendemos* taramosalata (potatoes and red caviar).

When we called on Tammy, the head waitress, to translate for us, she gave us such a thorough rundown that were it not for her Minnesota drawl, we'd have been convinced we'd just put in at Athens.

The hors d'oeuvre platter for two ($7.50) provides a taste of just about everything a novice would want to try: spinach pie, cheese pie, taramosalata, dolmades, calamata olives, feta cheese.

We could have made a meal out of these tidbits, but we couldn't resist the chance to try the fried squid, an appetizer so generous we could hardly finish it ($4.25). Although the texture was slightly disconcerting—extremely chewy—the buttery, crisp critters reminded us slightly of shrimp.

Full, but determined to keep going, we slurped down a bowl of Tim's Soup, a Grecian mother's answer to chicken soup. The lemony chicken broth, properly known as avgolemono, was filled with rice and barley. By the time our gyro plate ($7.50) arrived, we were wishing that that cowboy had stuck around so we could have shared it with him. Instead we let out our belts, grabbed a griddle-hot pocket of pita bread, and stuffed it full of the tender, spicy meat, tomatoes, and onions and topped it off with the dill-spiked Greek dressing. Simply splendid. The Mediterranean sports Tiffany lamps and gold lace curtains inherited from the previous tenants of the building, Victorian wallpaper hung with paintings of the Parthenon, and a plastic vineyard entwining an abandoned salad. The decor may be schizophrenic, but the kitchen is purebred Greek.

HOURS   Lunch: Mon.–Fri. 11 am–2:30 pm. Dinner: 5 pm–10 pm. Sat. 5 pm–11 pm.

SPECS   2100 Paramount; (806) 358-2716; AE/DC/MC/V; full bar.

DIRECTIONS   Take Exit 68A to Paramount and turn left if westbound, right if eastbound. Mediterranean House is two blocks down, on the right.

GOLDEN SPREAD GRILL, *Exits 114 & 112, Groom*

We were pretty sure the Golden Spread was the only restaurant in town, but we made a quick tour of Groom's main drag just to make sure we weren't overlooking anything. We caught the town librarian working after hours and although she filled us in on a couple of other local grills, we felt obligated to return to the Golden Spread and tell her sister-in-law, "the little bitty old lady zipping around" hello. We spotted a blur of sensible shoes and, sure enough, it turned out to be a rosy-faced, bright-eyed grandma. When she paused to catch her breath, we asked her if she was the librarian's sister-in-law. "No," she said, "she's *my* sister-in-law."

The librarian had shared our opinion that many cafe owners don't seem to care what they put in front of their customers these days, but she guaranteed that the good ladies in charge of the Golden Spread are different. They certainly have every right to be proud of their vegetable soup (a little potato dense, perhaps, but we like it that way) and corn muffins. We wanted to try the homemade hushpuppies, but they were all gone, and we just didn't have room for the chicken strips and "thin toast" everyone else was chowing down on ($3.25).

The Golden Spread is square and spare, a standard cafe with standard offerings: egg sandwiches ($1.45), fried catfish, enchiladas, and not so predictable lunch and dinner specials. Breakfasts are even more interesting, offering pecan waffles, homemade sweetrolls, and doughnuts.

Above average at any time is the apricot pie, a glossy, double-crusted, bottom-heavy fruitful delight (90 cents).

HOURS   Open 7 days, 6 am–10 pm.

SPECS   500 Front St.; (806) 248-2121; no credit cards; no bar.

DIRECTIONS   Westbound: Take Exit 114 and cross over the interstate. Turn left on Business 40. Turn right at the stop and drive 1 mile to the Golden Spread, on the right. To return to the interstate, continue west along Front/U.S. 66 for 5 blocks and then turn right to I-40.

Eastbound: Take Exit 112 and turn right. Drive to the stop and turn left on U.S. 66/Front and drive 5 blocks to the Golden Spread, on the left. To return to I-40, continue east along Front in the direction headed and follow signs to I-40.

WESTERN RESTAURANT, *Exit 163, Shamrock*

There's no obvious reason for eating in Shamrock, and unless you're famished, you're probably best advised to carry on to Amarillo or Oklahoma City before breaking bread. But if you need a break from driving, don't mind threadbare curtains, and find naive paintings of wild turkeys endearing, stake out a booth at the Western Motel coffee shop, order a cup of coffee, and ask for directions to the local Blarney stone.

The most memorable thing about the Western is the view of an art deco gas station and restaurant across the highway. A classy stone and green tile structure built in 1934, the building is now painted a vivid red, white, and blue at the gas station end and turquoise on the other—the restaurant is long gone. Our octogenarian waitress, formerly the cook across the street, laughed to tell us how many tourists stop to take pictures of the building's double clock towers (the clocks have vanished). Her opinion was that the "pretty thing" should have been restored rather than painted Day-glo colors, and she pointed out a section still showing its original colors. As much as we loved the audacity of the new paint job, we had to agree with her.

We were a little hesitant to try our luck with the food, but the grandmotherly manner of our waitress and the arrival of a pair of snowbirds announcing a return visit after three years inspired us to order a chicken salad sandwich—a pleasant blend of chicken, pimento, egg, celery, and onion on white toast ($2.00). The snowbirds brazenly ordered liver and onions, homemade vegetable soup, and a side of cabbage. While we watched to see if the food would have them twirling their handlebar mustaches, our booth took a tilt as three well-rounded matrons scooted and shoved in behind us. They dropped in strictly for pie, choice slices of chocolate, rhubarb, pecan, and egg custard, and moved on to a heated discussion of the attraction of polka dots.

So while we didn't find the Western's menu inspired, it isn't at all a bad place for a cup of coffee and a visit. But before you think about a drive into this dusty little burg in mid-March, consider the fact that some 40,000 Irish souls pour into town around Saint Paddie's Day.

HOURS   Open 7 days, 6 am–10 pm.

SPECS   104 E. 12th; (806) 256-2342; AE/MC/V; no bar.

DIRECTIONS   **Westbound:** Take Exit 163 to stop and turn left to cross over I-40 into town. Continue ½ mile to U.S. Hwy. 66 and turn left to the Western Motel, on the right.

Eastbound: Take Exit 163 and turn right on U.S. 83. Drive ½ mile into town until you see the Western Motel on the left.

Oklahoma

CAL'S COUNTRY COOKING, *Exit 7, Erick*

According to the newspaper clipping posted on Cal's brag wall, Erick is the hub of the nation and I-40 is its Main Street. Given that fact, it's no surprise that celebrities like Richard "John Boy" Thomas find their way to the one and only Cal's. It's an interstate institution featuring the same chef since 1946—Cal himself.

Inside the log cabin roadhouse we found a post-lunch fist of good ol' boys licking their chops and laying down a smoke screen. As the Marlboro men moved on, we spotted Cal doing what he has been doing virtually every day since he was old enough to hoist a fry pan—cooking up a storm. He's no longer the fresh-faced kid who sweated out World War II as a cook aboard the U.S.S. *Arthur Middleton,* but we recognized him just the same, thanks to a biographical photo essay that testified to his culinary heritage: a sepia-tone photo of stout-legged mother Marie shows her standing in front of her downtown Erick Cafe (long closed). Surrounding the photos of a rawboned 24-year-old Cal in front of his first cafe and a more portly Cal in his '50s joint are poems inspired by the kitchen skills of both mother and son, a restaurant review from *Road Rider* magazine, a letter from the Oklahoma lieutenant governor, and autographs and praise from hometown boy Roger "King of the Road" Miller. Miller's final word on Cal's cooking: "Lordy, Lordy, Lordy." As for Richard Thomas, he said Cal's had the best food this side of California. Cal liked the Walton boy, too, and says he's just as nice in person as on TV.

What we'd like to add to all this mutual admiration is that you're making a mistake if you don't stop in at Cal's to find out for yourself just how memorable a bowl of pinto beans and ham-hocks can be, served with Cal's homemade bread, $2.25. Or a baked ham sandwich on a homemade bun, or Cal's baked ham dinner (with potatoes, vegetable, dessert, and salad bar featuring hominy and black-eyed peas, $4.25).

The fellow staggering in at 3:30 in the afternoon was happy to discover that a country breakfast is served all day. He ordered three eggs, ham, and hash browns, and we were touched to see Cal himself deliver a second course of cornbread and gravy when the old boy announced from his chair—he seemed to be having trouble finding the counter—that he was still hungry. We hoped Cal's chow cured whatever was ailing him.

Sweet-roll connoisseurs should note that Cal's baseball-mitt-sized cinnamon rolls are worth twice the 90¢ toll, and the same number of pennies buys a slice of strawberry-rhubarb pie, or mince, or lemon crunch, or double crust lemon.

We left with two questions: Why does Cal insult his sour-dough loaves with margarine, and how could it have taken us so long to discover the delights of a rosy-red rhubarb pie?

HOURS   Open 7 days, 6 am–9 pm.

SPECS   I-40, Erick; (405) 526-3239; no credit cards; no bar.

DIRECTIONS   **Westbound:** Take Exit 7 to Cal's front door.

Eastbound: Take Exit 7 and immediately turn left to cross under I-40 to Cal's on the right.

BENTLEY'S, *Exits 82 and 80A, Weatherford*

This 1930s vintage pitched-roof, green brick cottage was a garage and car wash before the Bentley family bought the place in 1977 and turned it into a delicate little restaurant that reminded us of a baby nursery. All done up in pastel print wallpapers, quilted wall hangings, and samplers, it's hard to imagine Bentley's was ever a home for grease monkeys.

Bob Bentley is up front when he isn't spelling his mother or mother-in-law in the kitchen, and he says the food's better the days you find him behind the cash register. We can't tell you whether he's just being humble, but we can vouch for one mother or another's cooking: plain, sensible, good food. Lunch specials change daily, and ours offered a choice of chicken-fried steak, chicken, fillet of cod, or smothered round steak, served with green salad (unrelenting iceberg lettuce) or jello, whipped potatoes, navy beans or English peas, and hot rolls.

We opted for the pan-fried chicken, taters, and English peas, which arrived in a divided plastic plate, looking like a textbook example of home cooking. The chicken was crisp and non-greasy and the potatoes were indeed mashed spuds and not rehydrated flakes. Other lunch choices include a standard mix of hamburgers and sandwiches. A country breakfast is served until 11:00. If you get here too late for biscuits, try one of mother's excellent homemade cinnamon rolls (50 cents).

Well satisfied, we were about to call it quits when Bob Bentley insisted we try a slice of coconut cream pie. We're glad he did. It was a work of art, light, creamy, and not too sweet, with an admirable head of meringue.

HOURS   Mon.–Sat. 6 am–9 pm; Sun. 11 am–3 pm.

SPECS   221 W. Main; (405) 772-7331; V/MC; no bar.

DIRECTIONS   **Westbound:** Take Exit 82/Business 40 one mile to Bentley's, on the right at the corner of Main and 8th. To return to I-40 without backtracking, turn right out of Bentley's and continue west on Business 40 as it curves left and connects with the interstate.

Eastbound: Take Exit 80A/Business 40 as it veers into town and becomes Main. Bentley's is on the left at 8th. Carry on out of town east (left out of Bentley's) on Business 40 one mile to I-40.

A&T GARCIA'S, *Exits 150A & 150C, Oklahoma City*

Thought napalm was a chemical once used in Asia? Well, the locals refer to the salsa verde at this downtown restaurant as "Kermit's napalm." Spread a little on a hot buttered corn tortilla —a covered red dish holds a ready supply at your table—and roll the tortilla into a cylinder. Pinch the bottom shut, a friend warned us, so your pants don't catch on fire.

Garcia's tamales, Tex-Mex style, will make you think you'd died and gone to San Antonio. Other dishes (all in the $5–$7.50 range) include enchiladas, chalupas, guacamole, and other typical Okie-Mex standards. The bakery out front keeps its sweet Mexican bread hot and its prices low.

HOURS   Tues.–Sat. 1 am–9 pm; Sun. 10 am–3 pm. Closed Mon., Christmas, and Thanksgiving.

SPECS   409 W. Reno; (405) 236-1143; MC/V/AE; full bar.

DIRECTIONS   **Eastbound:** Take Exit 150A and turn left on Walker at the traffic light. In 0.1 mile turn right on Reno Ave. A&T Garcia's is a half block down on the left.

Westbound: Take Exit 150C, and stay in right lane all the way down the ramp. You're on SW 2nd; go straight at traffic light for .2 mile, then turn right on Walker. In one block turn right on Reno; restaurant is a half block down on the left.

CROCKETT'S SMOKE HOUSE,
Meridian Ave. Exit, Oklahoma City

Here's a quick Q-joint with cafeteria service. Most diners seem to like the Alamo Dinner—your choice of pork, pork ribs, sliced or chopped beef, Polish sausage, ham, hot links, or barbecued chicken, along with vegetables or salad, bread and butter ($6.95). The Alamo's meat weighs in at 16 ounces a serving (we put it on a scale to be sure!). But every aficionado knows that a Q-joint is only as good as its sauce, and Crockett's has a three-napkin sauce.

Sandwiches, the same variety, cost $2.25–$2.65. Stuffed spuds can test your creativity; for a stuff-it-yourself challenge, order a baked potato and a side of chopped beef, beans, or anything else that seems promisingly stuffable.

Have fun, eat hearty, but beware: signs on the walls warn thieves, fakers, thugs, and bunko-steerers that if you're found within the city limits after 10 pm, you'll be the guest of honor at a neck-tie party.

A final note—beer comes in old-fashioned Kerr jars, a nice touch to accompany your dripping good dinner.

HOURS   Sun.–Thurs. 11 am–9 pm; Fri. & Sat. 11 am–10 pm.

SPECS   4414 W. Reno; (405) 943-1333; no credit cards; beer.

DIRECTIONS   From Meridian Ave. Exit, turn left if eastbound, right if westbound, for 0.2 mile to Reno Ave. Right on Reno for 0.1 mile and Crockett's is on your right.

Oklahoma

TONY'S VIA ROMA, *Exit 125A, Oklahoma City*

You've just come into the city after a hard day driving cattle out on the range, or capping a well in the noonday sun, or closing a land deal speculating on suburbs and shopping centers—and what do you crave?

Salad. Olive salad. A big luscious olive salad that can be had on its own ($1.75) or, if you're planning on some serious eating, alongside an entree. The garlic bread is strong enough (and plentiful enough) to allow you solitude through the rest of the day.

Tony's Via Roma, in business since 1960, has built its reputation on salad, bread, and a delicious meat sauce that envelops the pasta imbotita, ravioli, and Italian dip sandwich. These items are all around $5 or $6, but elaborate dinners featuring creative veal dishes can get up into the $14.50 stratosphere.

Complaints and compliments always get to the management right away; Tony's family can usually be found at the first table in the cozy bar to the right of the entrance. They lend a nice family touch to what would otherwise be a seen-it-before Italian-American ambience.

HOURS   Lunch: Mon.–Fri. 11:30 am–2 pm. Dinner: Mon.–Thurs. 5–10 pm; Fri. & Sat. 5–11 pm. Closed Sun., Christmas, Thanksgiving.

SPECS   2743 Northwest Expressway (405) 842-2462; all major credit cards; full bar.

DIRECTIONS   Take Exit 125A and turn left at the light if eastbound, right if westbound. In 0.6 mile turn left on Northwest Expressway—also called Oklahoma Route 3. (The Penn Square Mall is on your right.) Go 0.8 mile to restaurant on right.

OKLAHOMA LINE RESTAURANT, *Kelley Ave. Exit, Oklahoma City*

After the grand tour at the nearby Cowboy Hall of Fame, mosey on over to this joint. (Remember—mariachis stroll, businessmen stride, drifters amble, and cowboys mosey.) At first glance you'd think it's too upscale for a barbecue house—real plates and all—but the ribs, as a local friend told us, "are as messy as a farmer's Back-40 after a spring monsoon." In fact, the view out the bar overlooks the city's more rural parts, with the skyline a comfortable distance away. The Mixed Plate ($5.95) combines ribs, sausage, and brisket, along with slaw, potato salad, beans, and fresh homemade bread.

The Oklahoma Line Restaurant's sauce has a slightly sweet taste to it, setting it apart from other barbecue houses in the area; the thick and meaty ribs are a favorite both for old hands and newcomers to the rib scene. We like the "wrappers" too—that's barbecue talk for wrapping a piece of brisket in a slice of bread, laying on some sauce and going at it ($4.50). A big bite of onion works well as a chaser (in more ways than one).

The lunchtime prices reportedly rise somewhat at night. Incidentally, the iced tea comes in the largest glasses in the state, or so management claims.

HOURS   Mon.–Thurs. 11 am–10 pm; Fri & Sat. 11 am–11 pm; Sun. 11:30 am–10 pm.

SPECS   1226 N.E. 63rd St.; (405) 478-4955; MC/V/AE; full bar.

DIRECTIONS   From the Kelley Ave. Exit, turn left if eastbound, right if westbound, onto Kelley Ave. for one block to 63rd St. Right on 63rd for 0.2 mile, then right again into the restaurant parking lot.

TRAIL'S END RESTAURANT, *Stroud Exit, Stroud*

With floor-to-ceiling windows and rough-cut cedar everywhere you look, the Trail's End wins our construction award. Here the ceiling beams are real stand-outs, quite literally, with the center cross beam a good 40 feet off the floor. We hope whoever changes the light bulbs here gets hazardous-duty pay —there are about two dozen hanging fixtures, with more than 88 light bulbs altogether.

The menu offers standard fare—fresh catfish, fried chicken, roast beef, chicken-fried steak, and Mexican plates in the $6 to $8 region; for the budget- or diet- minded, sandwiches are also available ($1.50–$4).

The best feature at the Trail's End is the stables, in case you're on horse power.

HOURS 5:30 am–10 pm daily.

SPECS Highway 99; (918) 968-9515; major credit cards; bar opens at 5 pm, serving beer (liquor-by-the-drink, passed in 1985, will soon be available).

DIRECTIONS Take Stroud Exit, and go left toward Drumright after exiting the toll booth. Cross over I-44, and the Trail's End Restaurant, which adjoins the Quarter Horse Inn, is on the right.

CASA BONITA, *Sheridan Road Exit, Tulsa*

The kids will love this one, and you'll probably get a kick out of it, too. It's like a theme park for people who've never been closer to Mexico than an old Dolores Del Río film on the late show. Designed in a Mexican hacienda motif, Casa Bonita has rooms, patios, pools, flowers, palm trees, fiesta lights, an exploding volcano, a waterfall—you get the picture. Kids seem to like playing with the flag at each table, constantly raising it to get the server's attention. It's so easy to get lost inside the casa that we considered leaving a trail of chips behind when we went to the restroom so we could find our way back!

The offerings—enchiladas, tacos, tamales, rice and beans— are simple and rewarding. Prices run $4–$5.45, and a Deluxe All-You-Can-Eat goes for $6.45.

HOURS Sun.–Thurs. 11 am–9:30 pm; Fri. & Sat. 11 am–10 pm.

SPECS 2120 S. Sheridan; (918) 836-6464; MC/V/AE; no bar.

DIRECTIONS Take Sheridan Rd. Exit (also 41st St.) to the light and turn right if eastbound, left if westbound, onto 41st St., staying in the left lane. A block later at the next traffic light turn left onto Sheridan for another 1.8 miles, then left into the Alameda Shopping Center Plaza, where Casa Bonita is the huge pink building.

THE HAMMETT HOUSE, *Claremore*

The Hammett House is *the* place to fill up after visiting the nearby Will Rogers Memorial museum and grave site. Don't let its fancy looks deceive you—you can waltz on in wearing jeans and a flannel work shirt if you like. Customers all have one thing in common: their affection for Will Rogers, whose optimistic folksiness permeates the atmosphere here.

Soup and salad cost $3.95, and we found it worth the price— portions were large, salad textures crisp, and pleasing flavors apparent. Specialty dishes, such as the chopped sirloin plate, run about $6.50. But the unquestioned climax of our meal was its finale. Our portion of coconut cream pie was so immense that we concluded they'd kept a slice of pie for themselves and given us the rest. And it was as delicious as it was sizable.

A final warning—don't practice your Will Rogers witticisms on the help here; they've heard them all before.

HOURS Tues.–Thurs. & Sun. 11 am–9 pm; Fri. & Sat. 11 am–10 pm. Closed Mon., Thanksgiving, and Christmas Eve through New Year's Eve.

SPECS   1616 W. Will Rogers Blvd.; (918) 341-5122; no credit cards; full bar.

DIRECTIONS   Take Claremore Exit, and turn left onto Oklahoma Route 20. After 1.3 miles, turn right for one block on U.S. 66 to Will Rogers Blvd. Left there, and the Hammett House in on the right after 0.9 mile.

CLANTON'S CAFE, *Vinita Exit, Vinita*

When dining out at a simple place, there are little favors you appreciate: chicken-fried steak made on the spot, not thawed and heated; a children's menu that isn't just the big folks' menu cut in half; seeing the owner in a white paper hat and apron; and a service that exudes genuine warmth of a small-town cafe the way it's supposed to be (as opposed to the way it often is).

Although Clanton's 16 booths keep a steady turnover, there's hardly any waiting for a place to sit down. What you'll get is pretty basic and basically good—fried chicken, roast pork with dressing, steak, or just a sandwich (all items in the $3–$6 range). A sign over the kitchen area reading CLANTON AND DAUGHTERS assured us what we'd already surmised—that we'd found a real family restaurant.

HOURS   Mon.–Fri. 5:30 am–8 pm. Closed weekends.

SPECS   319 E. Illinois; (918) 256-9053; no credit cards; no bar.

DIRECTIONS   Take Vinita Exit off of I-44. After the tollbooth, turn right on U.S. 60/66 for 0.7 mile toward Vinita. Clanton's is on the left.

Texas

ABOUT GALVESTON

Barbara spent her summers on Galveston's beaches, but in all her years of visiting the island as a kiddie-wink, she managed to overlook the Strand, the city's historical dock district. A string of turn-of-the-century buildings dating from the days when the avenue was known as the Wall Street of the Southwest, the Strand boasts the finest clutch of 19th-century iron-front commercial buildings still standing in the United States. Restored and reborn in the guise of trendy boutiques, galleries, grills, and bistros, the area is worthy of a day's sightseeing, shopping, and dining.

To reach the Strand Historical District, drive east along I-45 (which becomes Broadway/U.S. Hwy. 77) to 23rd St./Tremont and turn left. Continue 8 blocks to the Strand and turn right. For a listing of a dozen or more good restaurants within walking distance, begin your tour at the Strand Visitor's Center, 2014 Strand. Just across the street, our favorite for French cuisine and bakery goods is **Le Paysan,** serving everything from a truly continental breakfast (freshly baked croissant and stout café du jour) or peasant lunch of brie and fruit, to a multi-course besauced and bewitching dinner (2021 Strand).

For a black tie supper of Redfish Mousseline or uptown lunch of Artichoke Bolivar, stroll down the street to **The Wentletrap,** a venerable Victorian dining parlor associated with the exquisite Tremont House Hotel (2301 Strand). If you want to stock a gourmet *picnique* basket before hitting the beach, or simply down a pastrami on rye while perching on a pickle barrel, the **Old Strand Emporium** is a deli with a cache of tinned butter biscuits, smoked trout, fresh pâtés, and imported beers (2112 Strand). For fewer tourist trappings and what natives claim to be the best food on the island, abandon the Strand for **Clary's,** a coat and tie fish-house specializing in extraordinary oyster dishes innovatively prepared (8509 Teichman at I-46, across from the *Galveston Daily News*). But for the best-known, best-loved seafood restaurant on the Gulf Coast, you have to go to Gaido's (see below).

GAIDO'S, *Seawall, Galveston*

Gaido's is a family restaurant—both yours and theirs. When waiters wear fifty-year service pins, you know you're in a place where good service has become a tradition, and the Gaido family began establishing their high standards in 1911. Aspiring waiters must pass written tests, oral tests, and then apprentice for two weeks before they are allowed to join the ranks. Once in, they're liable to stay forever. Whether you show up windblown and sandswept or freshly coiffed and collared, the service at Gaido's is never anything short of gracious. Waiters easily recite and elaborate on an extensive and ever-changing menu of daily specials (based on the catch of the day) and remember every detail of your order without putting pen to paper.

All the fish served at Gaido's is as fresh from the sea as the bathers you spy through the windows, and three seafood platters offer the chance to sample the widest variety of the kitchen's offerings. Entrees never known to disappoint are the charcoal-broiled shrimp dishes, or lightly broiled and buttery oysters, scallops, and redfish. Our favorite light meal is a dozen Angels on Horseback: oysters wrapped in ham, skewered with fresh pineapple, and charcoal-broiled. Servings are generous, as is appropriate where the salt air whips your appetite into a frenzy. If you're not starving, go easy on the sesame rolls and apple jelly; it would be a shame to leave behind a single mouthful of the Gaido brothers' heavenly fish.

HOURS Open Tues.–Sun. 11:30 am–10 pm. Closed Mon.

SPECS 39th/Mike Gaido Blvd. and Seawall Blvd; (409) 762-0115; AE/MC/V; full bar and hundreds of domestic and imported beers, extensive wine list.

DIRECTIONS Drive east along I-45 to 39th/Mike Gaido Blvd., turn right and drive to the sea (Seawall Blvd.). Gaido's is beneath the giant crab.

TAJ MAHAL, *Exit 38B, Houston*

Tucked away in a down-at-the-heels shopping center, Taj Mahal is a bit on the seedy side, especially during the daylight hours when the tired carpeting is most obvious. At night, however, flickering candlelight and the elusive rhythms of sitars create the illusion of a palatial dining hall. But day or night, the food is as deliciously varied as India itself.

Lunch is served as an all-you-can-eat buffet of tandoori chicken, vegetable and rice curries, chicken curry, and spinach creamed with homemade cottage cheese ($5.95). At dinnertime you simply must try the tandoori specialties. These are marinated meats, charcoal broiled in a clay barrel-shaped pit called a *tandoor*. Chicken tandoori brings either a whole ($5.95) or half ($3.25) spring chicken marinated in a secret sauce—a lobster-red dish with a rich, smoky flavor. Most interesting is the mixed grill of tandoori chicken and lamb, served in a variety of cuts and flavors ranging from tangy to smoky, served sizzling hot, juicy, and topped with grilled onions ($6.95). In addition to broiling meats, the tandoor bakes breads, from the soft and fluffy naan (95 cents) to the more exotic keema naan, finely textured and stuffed with ground lamb and herbs—$1.50.

Curry fiends will love the subtle varieties of vegetable, chicken, lamb, and rice curries, all distinctively different but on the mild side; if you like it hot, tell the waiter. For a little bit of everything, the Taj Mahal combination dinner for two includes tandoori chicken, shrimp, fish, and lamb, along with curried fish, creamed spinach, a curried lamb dish ("a pristine recipe from the royal courts of India"), rice, green salad and naan—$19.95.

All the desserts sound strange and wonderful, but we opted for kulfee, a peak of frozen condensed milk studded with pistachio nuts and sprinkled with saffron—rich, rich, rich ($1.50). For a less-caloric treat, don't miss the bowl of fennel seeds and sugar crystals by the front door.

HOURS Lunch: Sun.–Sat. 11 am–2 pm. Dinner: Sun.–Sat. 6 pm–10 pm. Closed Mon.

SPECS 8328 Gulf Freeway at Bellfort; (713) 649-2818; AE/MC/V; full bar.

DIRECTIONS **Northbound:** Take Exit 38B to Bellfort. Turn left and cross under I-45, then turn right immediately past the north access road to enter the shopping center parking lot.

Southbound: Take Exit 38B and continue along access road 1 mile to Taj Mahal on the right, in the mirrored glass shopping center.

NINO'S, *Exit 47D, Houston*

See page 67 for a good, home-style Italian restaurant.

DIRECTIONS **Southbound:** Take Exit 47D/West Dallas and turn right on West Dallas. Continue 1.5 miles to Nino's, in the brick building on the left, at La Rue.

Northbound: Take Exit 47D and cross under I-45 on West Dallas, and continue 1.5 miles to Nino's, on the left, at La Rue.

CHARLEY'S 517, *Texas Ave. Exit, Houston*

Some of Houston's best restaurants can be difficult to find, especially for the uninitiated, and those in the heart of the beast are best avoided during rush hours. One downtown best-bet is Charley's 517, around the corner from the lovely Lancaster Hotel. We visited the cozy and elegant Charley's after the departure of Amy Ferguson, the chef who established the restaurant's reputation, but were pleased to find that the dishes inspired by Ferguson (named one of the top 25 U.S. chefs in 1984) are still central to the menu: mesquite-grilled fresh salmon with mint-marigold and pecan pesto butter, lamb in tarragon and madeira sauce, duck breast roasted with fresh ginger and garlic. Charley's is more than competent in the classical presentation of most any dish, but its true claim to fame is a liberal use of southwestern herbs, peppers, and wild game to prepare classical dishes with a regional twist.

We began our evening meal (reservations are recommended) with a creamy and tasteful shrimp bisque ($3.50) that stopped just short of being too rich, and without a moment's hesitation had it followed by the Shrimp Aromatic ($19.50)—shrimp flambéed in pernod and topped with a curried cream sauce, spiked with dill, paprika, and cayenne, and a hearts of palm and Texas vine-ripened tomato salad ($5.50). The shrimp were slightly oversalted, but otherwise the dish was as marvelous as its name. A second entree of red snapper buried in broccoli, cauliflower, snow peas, scallops, and shrimp was a simple masterpiece of varied flavors and textures ($19.50). Charley's has been one of Houston's favorite fine dining spots for 14 years, a tradition supported by consistently good food and service to match the abilities of the kitchen. The staff is first-rate, a fact that is no longer a given at fine restaurants. Not surprisingly, Charley's prices are high; don't come if you're on a budget.

Manager Clive Berkman knows a thing or two about what makes a restaurant tick (and he's no slouch in the kitchen either), but his true area of expertise is wine; the list includes some 700 vintages. Ask about special menu wine dinners.

Simply put, we're very fond of Charley's (coat and tie), and we're glad of its downtown address. It gives us an excuse to check into the Lancaster, with its English manor air, limo service to Neiman's, and accommodating staff. And the Lancaster Grill offers a lovely breakfast, lunch, and dinner menu itself. So if you're planning an overnight in Houston, you're well advised to find your way to this corner of elegance and good taste.

HOURS Lunch: Mon.–Fri. 11:30 am–2 pm. Dinner: Mon.–Sat. 6 pm–11 pm. Closed Sun. Reservations, coat and tie.

SPECS 517 Louisiana; (713) 224-4438; AE/DC/MC/V; full bar.

DIRECTIONS Downtown. Take the Texas Ave./Capitol Exit and follow Capitol east (right) to Louisiana. Turn right onto Louisiana. Charley's is a block down, on the right.

PAPPA'S SEAFOOD HOUSE, *Exit 60A, Houston*

A damn-them-with-faint-praise source recommended Pappa's as serving "better-than-average" seafood to huge crowds at affordable prices. Well, the crowd *was* huge (but we got right in), and the prices were low, but the food was a far cry above average. In fact, our meal at Pappa's turned out to be the best all-around dining experience in many a mile. Maybe we were just lucky, but the night of our visit, everything—from the day's special of blackened redfish (a 12-inch filet seared outside and juicy, sweet, and flaky inside), to pleasantly plump, delicately fried oysters—was nearly perfect, not an easy task with a full house.

While waiting for our entrees, we dove into an olympic-sized bowl of seafood gumbo, crowded with shrimp, crab, and oysters ($2.50), then worked over Pappa's Greek salad for two—olive rich, with just the right number of anchovies, it could easily serve four ($3.75).

Decorated in bare-bones, high-tech fashion—lots of neon, glass, and tile—Pappa's can be an acoustical nightmare, especially when the evening crowds are spawning. Never mind, it's a joyful noise. In fact, the only sour note of the evening's music was an off-pitch key lime pie.

HOURS Lunch: Mon.–Fri. 11 am–3 pm; Sat. 11:30 am–4 pm; Sun. noon–4 pm. Dinner: Mon.–Thurs. 5:30 pm–10 pm; Fri. 5:30 pm–11 pm; Sat. 5 pm–11 pm; Sun. 5 pm–10 pm.

SPECS 11301 North Freeway (I-45); (713) 999-9928; AE/MC/V; full bar.

DIRECTIONS **Northbound:** Take Exit 60A/Aldine and continue along access road to light. Turn left at light and cross under I-45 and immediately turn left onto southbound access road. Pappa's is on the right, just a wee bit up the road.

Southbound: Take Exit 60A/Aldine and drive to Pappa's just past the light, on the right.

THE GREAT WALL OF CHINA (AND HAPPY BUDDHA STEAK PALACE), *Exit 87, Conroe*

Don't be surprised when you are presented with a pair of menus at this two-in-one steak house and Chinese restaurant. Conroe wasn't ready for a restaurant that didn't serve plain old slab beef, so the anxious-to-please Great Wall simply added a second bill of fare to their traditional Chinese menu. So don't be fooled by the lacquer screen and Chinese lanterns; if you're the meat and potato kind, try Happy Buddha's steaks and Mongolian barbecue, served with soup (varies daily), homemade Chinese bread, a choice of Shanghai salad, Peking salad, or green salad, along with fried rice and vegetables or Chinese spaghetti. What is Chinese bread? The menu said it was a surprise, so we asked our waitress. She simply smiled. What could we do?—we had to try it. Don't tell them we told you, but the Great Wall's Chinese bread proved to be a dense and chewy white roll, with a thick golden-brown, fried crust—something like a very heavy cake doughnut. We topped ours with plum sauce and turned it into an Oriental jelly doughnut. And what is Chinese spaghetti? Round, yellow egg noodles. Shanghai salad? We had to draw the line somewhere. You try it and let us know.

From the Great Wall menu we sampled appetizers of teriyaki beef (four skewered slices, salty and delicious—$2.75) and egg rolls (overstuffed with bland cabbage). For dessert we opted for the sticky sweet fried bananas, tempura-battered, sprinkled with sesame seeds, and doused with honey—$2.50).

Chef K. J. Lee (yellowed newspaper clippings outside the front door attest to his fame) is best known for his specialty dish of Drunk Shrimps in Dancing Flame. We didn't try it, but we loved the poetry of its name. Servings of all entrees are more than generous, but for the absolutely famished, we can't imagine a better deal than the $3.93 all-you-can-eat Chinese buffet served at lunch!

HOURS   Open 7 days, 11 am–10 pm, Fri.–Sat. till 11 pm.

SPECS   519 W. Davis; (409) 539-9192; AE/MC/V; full bar.

DIRECTIONS   **Northbound:** Take Exit 87 to light and turn right on W. Davis/TX Hwy. 105. The Great Wall is about ½ mile ahead, on the right, on the corner of W. Davis and Frazier.

Southbound: Take Exit 87 to the light and turn left. Cross under I-45 on W. Davis/TX Hwy. 105. Go ½ mile to corner of W. Davis and Frazier, on the right.

THE JUNCTION, *Exit 116, Huntsville*

Fast food blinders in place, we blitzed past McDonald's, Tinsley's Fried Chicken, and Del Taco, and almost missed this colonial manor house dwarfed by a 200-foot expanse of lawn and centurion cedars. "Hey, wasn't that a restaurant?" Pulling an illegal U-turn into the exit lane of the Junction's driveway, we were met head-on by the fleet of Sunday diners just pulling out.

In the wake of such a crowd, we thought we might catch the Junction at its Sunday worst, but we were delighted with both food and service. Nothing fancy about this menu, but the food offerings are fresh, well prepared, and tasty.

Dinner entrees of fish and steak include a trip through the salad bar (a well-maintained iced garden of every vegetable known to man), and a choice of rice pilaf, French fries, or baked potato, served with an oven-warm loaf of wheat bread and sweet butter.

We decided to pass up the day's special of all-you-can-eat fried shrimp ($9.95) or catfish ($7.95) for the broiled red snapper. The waitress started to ask us how we'd like our fish cooked, caught herself, and admitted that she'd served nothing but steaks that day. So we weren't surprised when the snapper arrived a little on the watery side. It was salvaged by a generous ladling of melted butter (served bubbling hot) and lemon juice. An order of fried vegetables was unexpectedly tasty—fresh mushrooms and zucchini strips, a good six inches long, were hand-breaded and deftly fried so that they tasted more of fresh vegetable than batter. Delicious and not the least bit greasy.

Dependable food and pleasant parlor dining rooms are the reason this restaurant has been in business for ten years. Our only complaint was the radio station muzak, but the 12-foot windows and pleasant service made up for the squawk.

HOURS Open 7 days, 11 am–10 pm. Lunch specials served 11 am–3 pm.

SPECS 2641 11th St.; (409) 295-2183; AE/DC/MC/V; full bar.

DIRECTIONS **Northbound:** Take Exit 116 and continue north on access road to corner. Turn right onto 11th St. The Junction is one block from I-45, on the right, next door to Del Taco.

Southbound: Take Exit 116 to 11th St. and cross over I-45. Continue east on 11th one block to the Junction on the right.

THE WOODBINE, *Exit 142, Madisonville*

The Corral, a truck stop–cafe–curio shop just east of the I-45/TX Hwy. 20 intersection, rounds up the biggest lunchtime crowds hereabouts, and the food isn't bad. It's just that a mere two minutes into Madisonville proper you can sup in the turret dining room of the state's most beautiful historical inn.

Driving into town, nothing about the plain-Jane Main St. prepares you for your first glimpse of The Woodbine, a triple-decker gingerbread fantasy sprawling between humble clapboard neighbors. Built in 1904, with double three-story turrets, 12,000 fish scale shingles, galleries, porches, and nine shades of paint (primarily apricot and champagne), The Woodbine is delicious—inside and out.

Built by Russian emigrants eager to attract road-weary travelers hungry for home cooking, The Woodbine has continued to serve honest-sized helpings of simple rib-sticking food. For dinner (that's lunch to you city slickers) the sideboards groan with a chef's choice blue-plate special ranging from fajitas (served with tortillas and beans, salsa cruda, salad, and fries) to baked ham and garden vegetables. The supper menu (written in magic marker on paper sacks) includes T-bones, fillets, quail, catfish, shrimp, and fried oysters served with salad, homemade soup (a thick, beefy vegetable soup when we visited), and choice of potatoes. Homemade baking powder biscuits and sticky sweet cinnamon bread are a buck a basket. Lunch specials, including a killing dessert, run around $4, and a catfish dinner is $6.95. Steaks, perfectly prepared to your specifications, begin at $7.95. If you're too full for fudge nut pie or cherry nut cake, you'd better jog upstairs for a tour of the inn's Victorian bedrooms (don't those wallpapers remind you of grandpa's old flannel pjs?), then try again. Still too full? Better check in.

HOURS Lunch: Tues.–Sat. 11 am–3 pm. Dinner: Tues.–Sat. 5 pm–10 pm. Sunday brunch 11 am–3 pm. Closed Sun. evenings and Mon.

SPECS 209 N. Madison; (214) 348-3591; AE/MC/V; full bar.

DIRECTIONS **Northbound:** Take Exit 142 and turn left at the light at the end of the ramp. Cross over the interstate and continue west into town on TX Hwy. 21. ■ At the third light (2 miles from interstate) turn right onto Madison and continue a block and a half. You can't miss The Woodbine on the left.

Southbound: Take Exit 142 and turn right onto TX Hwy. 21 and continue into town as above from ■.

RAINBOW CAFE, *Exit 178, Buffalo*

The 50th Anniversary commemorative menu should give you a clue as to how long the Rainbow's been with us, and the morning shift waitress (5 am till 2 pm) looked as if she might have been working here since the front doors first opened. Beware— she's loyal and will tell you the biscuits are home-baked, but they ain't (well, they may *bake* them here, but they aren't made from scratch). Stick to the daily hot lunch specials—chicken and dumplings, barbecue sausage, and the like, served with two vegetables. If you must order off the menu, the safe bets are the genuine chicken-fried steaks, cut fresh daily ($4.30) and the fried local grain-fed catfish ($5.75).

A lukewarm endorsement, we know; the Rainbow can turn out a decent plate of vittles on a good day, but who knows what will be cooking when you hit town. If you just can't make it another 20 miles, try your luck. If you don't like the sound of the daily special, head on back toward I-45, but stop at **Buffalo's Farmers' Market,** a half mile or so from the Rainbow, on your right. The fresh fruit there is *always* recommendable.

HOURS   Mon.–Sat. 5:30 am–10 pm. Closed Mon.

SPECS   Main St./TX Hwy. 79; (214) 322-4901; no credit cards.

DIRECTIONS   Take Exit 178 and turn right if northbound, left if southbound onto TX Hwy. 79N. Drive 1½ miles into downtown Buffalo, just past a weatherbeaten strip of shotgun storefronts. The Buffalo Farmers' Market is on the left side of 79, about a mile from the interstate.

SAM'S ORIGINAL RESTAURANT, *Exit 197, Fairfield*

Sam's got the monopoly on restaurants here in Fairfield. The Drilling Rig and Ponce's Chicken are his places, too. But of the three, Sam's Original Restaurant is . . . well . . . the original, and it's open 24 hours. Sam's is in a new building now, but the place is still crammed with family photos and memorabilia (including some care-worn Teddy bears). Most importantly, however, Sam's is still serving the tried-and-true favorites that made him the restaurant magnate of Fairfield, Texas: pit barbecue and a homestyle buffet. The all-you-can-eat smorgasbord of fresh vegetables, salads, and hot meat entrees is kept heaping with kitchen-fresh refills. If your appetite can't do justice to such a lineup of chow, order a barbecue dinner ($5.95): beef, spare ribs, and ham are served with barbecued beans, potato salad, and hot homemade bread (luckily the Gold and Sweet Whipped Margarine man has made no inroads here; Sam's serves real butter).

Whatever four-square meal you eat, don't pass up a slice of homemade pie for dessert: apricot, Dutch apple, pineapple, or chocolate-pecan (an oven-warm gloppy cream pie studded with nuts).

HOURS   Open 7 days, 24 hours.

SPECS   I-45 and U.S. 84; (214) 389-4166; CB/DC/V/MC; no bar.

DIRECTIONS   Northbound: Take Exit 197 and continue straight across U.S. Hwy. 84 to Sam's, just a few hundred yards up the road.

Southbound: Take Exit 197, turn left on U.S. Hwy. 84 and cross over the interstate. Turn left to Sam's, just a few hundred yards away.

THE FAMILY TREE, *Exit 231, Corsicana*

Whether you're hungry or not, Corsicana is a town worth a leg-stretching stop. Navarro County has been producing oil since 1894, longer than any other county in the state, and brick-rich Corsicana (the buildings, the castle of a train depot, even the streets are brick) is a boom-and-bust-and-boom-again town whose fortune waxes and wanes with the black gold market.

Corsicana's contributions to the culinary history of the world include Wolf Brand Chili, created here in 1895 by a ranch cook, and the DeLuxe Fruitcake, baked by Collins Street Bakery since 1896 and shipped all over the world. (A Norwegian order addressed "Fruitcake, Texas" easily found its way here.) But chile and fruitcakes aside, you should know that the first restaurant north of Madisonville to serve something other than field-hand grub is tucked away in a downtown antique store—The Family Tree.

The shelves and alcoves of this twofer business are filled with Depression glass and Texas primitives, all for sale, except for the tangle of tea tables that make up the restaurant itself. Believe us, the food is equal to the collectibles—or better. The only drawback to The Family Tree is the limited serving hours: 11 am–2 pm. If you pull into Corsicana during lunchtime, indulge yourself in the Crab Gilbert (plentiful crab, slivered almonds, and a rich cream sauce); eggplant lasagne (a totally healthful version without salt, sugar, or fat); green chicken enchiladas (served with salad, zuc-chini, and home-baked cinnamon roll); or the chef's creation of the day—chicken breast in a wine mushroom sauce the day we visited. Homemade soups vary from day to day and are offered with a variety of sandwiches from chicken salad with apples and walnuts to homemade pimento cheese. Soup and a sandwich are $3.75.

In addition to the tearoom sandwiches, quiche, and salads, heartier entrees such as herbed pot roast and the famous King Ranch chicken casserole are served. All entrees come with home-made breads, the most memorable of which are the onion cream cheese loaf and the orange dinner rolls (or maybe the blueberry muffins or the cinnamon yeast rolls or . . .).

It's difficult to plan a day around being in Corsicana, Texas, between the hours of 11 and 2, but on this stretch of I-45, The Family Tree is a memorable dining experience.

HOURS   Mon.–Fri. 11 am–2 pm. Closed Sat. and Sun.

SPECS   129 W. Collins; (214) 874-3256; MC/V; no bar.

DIRECTIONS   **Northbound:** Take Exit 231 to 7th Ave., the first cross street. Turn right and ■ drive 1 mile to 7th *St.* Turn right onto 7th St. Collins is the second left off 7th St. The Family Tree is two blocks up, on your left.

Southbound: Take Exit 231 and turn right immediately, onto 7th Ave., then as above from ■.

OLD AVENUE BANK, *Exit 251, Ennis*

Without a doubt, the Old Avenue Bank is the finest interstate restaurant to be found between Houston and Dallas. Located on a revitalized downtown strip of Ennis Avenue, the restored 1883 National Bank building has been transformed into a cozy, richly decorated Victorian parlor. The bank's turn-of-the-century pressed tin ceiling, tile entry way, and Mosler vault (reborn as the safest bar in Texas) remain, and the brass fixtures, chandeliers, and etched glass are worthy of the most lavish bankers' lunch. But as lovely as the decor may be, it doesn't begin to compete with the riches of the kitchen.

A blend of American and continental cuisine, the restaurant's menu is a creation of proprietor Steve Fausett, who delights in his weekly specials—beef Oscar with crab imperial, red snapper bienville, salmon en croute with sorrel sauce—stuff one would expect to find at the French Room of the Adolphus, but never in the hometown of the National Polka Festival.

And be assured that the burgers, sandwiches, and steaks are prepared with the same attention to detail and served with equal panache. All entrees are served with soup (the mushroom soup du jour the day we visited was a dill spiked, butter-rich delight), freshly baked bread, and your choice of pan-browned potatoes or rice. Lunch prices range from $7.95 for chicken Kiev down to $3.50 for a hamburger, potatoes, and cole slaw. Dinner is pricier, but the cost isn't out of line with the quality, like Chateaubriand for two ($29.95), or shrimp tempura, $12.95.

The totally decadent won't wish to miss the chocolate mousse Amaretto pie, a dense, tongue-paralyzing mousse served in a pure chocolate shell: $3 for a lifetime of memories.

HOURS   Lunch: Tues.–Fri. 11 am–2 pm. Dinner: Mon.–Sat. 6 pm–10 pm. Closed Mon. for lunch and all day Sun.

SPECS   110 W. Ennis Ave.; (214) 875-8210; AE/MC/V; full bar in private club, temporary memberships $3.

DIRECTIONS   Northbound: Take Exit 251 to first left, Ennis Ave. ■ Drive one mile into town. Restaurant is a half block past the railroad tracks.

Southbound: Take Exit 251 to stop sign and turn right onto Ennis Ave. Then as above from ■.

ABOUT DALLAS

See below for directions from I-45 to La Botica and the Brasserie. You may also want to check our Dallas overview on page 158.

LA BOTICA, *I-30 Interchange, Dallas*

La Botica means "the pharmacy," but you won't find antacids or antibiotics here. It's a Tex-Mex restaurant in a genuine Tex-Mex neighborhood. See page 129.

DIRECTIONS   At the I-30 interchange, take I-30 east to Exit 47B, then follow eastbound directions given on page 130.

THE BRASSERIE, *Exit 284C, Dallas*

For 24-hour elegance, see page 131. But not at rush hours.

DIRECTIONS   **Northbound:** Just as I-45 becomes TX Hwy. 75 through Dallas, take Exit 284C/Live Oak and cross under the interstate left into town. Continue on Live Oak to Ervay. Turn right onto Ervay. ■ Just as Ervay becomes Akard, you will see the Fairmont Hotel on your left. The Brasserie is in the Fairmont at Ross and Akard.

Southbound: Take Exit 284C/Live Oak and turn right onto Live Oak. Continue to Ervay. Turn right onto Ervay, then as above from ■.

INDEX

ABOUT THE AUTHORS

Barbara Rodriguez is the former editor of Texas Monthly Press, instructor at the New York University Publishing Institute, and a full-time free-lance writer. She writes about food, restaurants, Mexico, travel, and all things Texan for *Texas Monthly, Texas Homes,* and other publications. She is a contributor to *The Best Country Cafes in Texas* and author of *52 Great Texas Getaway Weekends.*

Tom Miller is the author of *On the Border* and *The Panama Hat Trail,* and editor of *Arizona: The Land and the People.* His reports about conflict and culture in the American Southwest and Latin America have appeared in *The New York Times* and other publications, as well as on national television and radio programs. He has lectured often about the borderlands in both the United States and Mexico and has taught writing to students from grade-school level through college.

Our best source of leads to worthwhile restaurants is you, the traveler who cares. Please tell us of any you know that lie close to the road, and we'll check them out for future editions in THE INTERSTATE GOURMET series.

Send your suggestions to:

Summit Books
Code ISG
1230 Avenue of the Americas
New York, NY 10020

Restaurant name_____

Near Highway_____

Exit_____

City_____ State_____

Directions_____

_____

_____

_____

Comments_____

_____

_____

_____

_____

_____

_____